**The Arnold and Caroline Rose Monograph Series
of the American Sociological Association**

Ego defenses and the legitimation of behavior

Long before Freud, repression, projection, and other psychological defenses were seen as important in ordinary behavior and in psychopathology. In this book, Guy Swanson argues that the emphasis that modern psychology has placed on the roles that defenses play in neurosis has obscured their true nature and origins. Defenses, he maintains, are the justifications that people offer to themselves and to others for seeing themselves as acceptable despite having, as they invariably do, objectionable desires and interests. Defenses are, therefore, a routine, and, in most cases, effective part of ordinary social behavior. This book examines the way in which such defenses operate.

The analysis is based on a study undertaken by the author of the variation among the defenses that adolescents use to justify themselves. He shows that, as Anna Freud suggests, defenses differ in whether they justify a person's having undesirable wishes, or justify his or her expressing those wishes, and finds that the defenses used by adolescents are related to the kind of prohibitions their parents set in these matters. He also shows that the complexity of the defenses adolescents use depends at what level of complexity of social relations within the family there are strains. He further finds that adolescents' defenses are essentially unrelated to their, or their parents', intelligence scores, to their parents' defenses, or to the parents' levels of education or occupation, although particular defenses are shown to be related to the differential roles of mothers and fathers within the family.

This innovative study of the connection between psychological processes and social relations will appeal widely to scholars and students of social psychology and sociology, as well as to those interested in socialization, family studies, and the study of adolescence.

For other titles in the series turn to p. 231.

Ego defenses and the legitimation of behavior

Guy E. Swanson
University of California, Berkeley

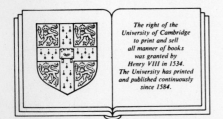

The right of the
University of Cambridge
to print and sell
all manner of books
was granted by
Henry VIII in 1534.
The University has printed
and published continuously
since 1584.

Cambridge University Press

Cambridge
New York   New Rochelle   Melbourne   Sydney

Published by the Press Syndicate of the University of Cambridge
The Pitt Building, Trumpington Street, Cambridge, CB2 1RP
32 East 57th Street, New York, NY 10022, USA
10 Stamford Road, Oakleigh, Melbourne 3166, Australia

First published 1988

Printed in Great Britain by Woolnough Bookbinders, Irthlingborough

British Library cataloguing in publication data
Swanson, Guy E.
Ego defenses and the legitimation of
behavior. – (The Arnold and Caroline Rose
monograph series of the American
Sociological Association).
1. Human behaviour
I. Title II. Series
150   BF131

Library of Congress cataloguing in publication data
Swanson, Guy E.
Ego defenses and the legitimation of behavior.
Bibliography.
Includes index.
1. Self-protective behavior – Social aspects.
2. Defense mechanisms (Psychology) 3. Social psychology.
I. Title.
BF697.5.S45S92   1987   155.2   87–3006

ISBN 0 521 34361 5

SE

Contents

v

Foreword

I first read about defenses while an undergraduate at the University of Pittsburgh. One of my teachers, William Root, helped me to understand their central place in the psychoneuroses and in psychotherapy. Later on, while in graduate school, I learned that the rates of each neurosis and psychosis have a distinctive pattern in a metropolitan area. For example, people who are both middle class and upwardly mobile have high rates of manic-depressive psychosis (Freedman, 1950) and people at the lowest levels of income and education have high rates of schizophrenia (Dohrenwend and Dohrenwend, 1974; Faris and Dunham, 1939; Hollingshead and Redlich, 1958). Each of the "functional" neuroses and psychoses is associated with a distinctive cluster of defenses. I wondered whether a given cluster of defenses is used disproportionately by "normal" people if they come from the part of the population in which a functional mental disorder related to these same defenses has its highest rates. Were that so, it could help to explain the findings from epidemiological studies.

My ideas about defenses were influenced by Faris and Dunham's great monograph *Mental Disorders in Urban Areas* (1939) and by Lasswell's (1930, 1935, 1948) psychodynamic interpretations of politics. I also learned from Fromm's *Man for Himself* (1947) and from the manuscript by Bettelheim and Janowitz that was later published as *The Dynamics of Prejudice* (1950). Each of these sources led me away from the idea that defenses are exceptional in human behavior. Each supported the view that defenses are usually a part of personal and social control and are a form of what George Herbert Mead (1934) called "self" processes.

A few years after graduate school, I met Daniel Miller. Both of us were new instructors in the University of Michigan. On that rainy October day, we were chilled and wet and were hoping that our tour of a camp for children would quickly end. We took shelter in the dining hall and got acquainted. Miller was a clinical psychologist educated at Stanford. He, too, had read Faris and Dunham and knew Mead and he wanted to study defenses and their social origins in "normal" people. A decade later we had collaborated on two studies,

The Changing American Parent (1958) and *Inner Conflict and Defense* (1960) and had each drafted a prospectus for further research on these topics (Miller, 1963; Swanson, 1961).

I am grateful to Daniel Miller for his friendship and for a post-graduate education in psychoanalytic thought. He is not responsible for my failings as a student.

I turned again to an interest in defenses in the late 1960s as a member of Michigan's Mental Health Research Institute. The Institute's directors, Gardner Quarton and John Platt, encouraged me in developing a working paper and in conducting some preliminary studies. They and other colleagues – Albert Reiss, Leon Mayhew, Monica Blumenthal, and Morris Fridell – gave that work a searching review.

These new beginnings at Michigan were the basis for research that I developed in the Institute of Human Development of the University of California at Berkeley and that I describe here. The studies I have done in Berkeley have had financial support from the Grant Foundation and from Berkeley's Committee on Research. They have been facilitated by the existence in the Institute of coded data on coping and defense (gathered under Grant HD 03617–06, changed to AG 00365) and by the colleagueship of Norma Haan. Her deeply original work on ego processes (reviewed in Haan, 1977) had helped to rekindle my own interest while I was still at Michigan.

The work I am now reporting was given its special focus by results I obtained from administering some preliminary instruments at other universities. I want to thank friends on their faculties who arranged for this administration: Gerald Ginsberg (University of Nevada), Wesley Allinsmith (University of Cincinnati), Theodore Ferdinand (Northern Illinois University), Charles Snyder (Southern Illinois University), Ernest Campbell (Vanderbilt University), and Everett Wilson (University of North Carolina).

The data I used for the present study were defined and gathered by investigators who began their work before I joined them in Berkeley's Institute of Human Development. I have only reworked information that they developed and then generously encouraged me to reflect upon as a sociologist and social psychologist. I take this opportunity to thank all of these colleagues.

The trenchant comments of two post-doctoral fellows, Susan Hales and Susan Weisskopf, and of two colleagues, Diana Baumrind and Norma Haan, led me to rethink and revise an earlier version of this report. I am indebted to them for help and opposition.

1 To anticipate what follows

Anna Freud's conclusion holds today as in 1936: The importance of ego defenses in psychoneurosis and in everyday life is well established but the "considerations which determine the ego's choice of mechanism remain uncertain" (1936: 50). I want to describe a way of thinking about defenses that may help us to identify those considerations: to understand why people differ in the defenses they use. I also present the findings from research on some adolescents and their defenses, research that was guided by this new approach.

Like everyone who studies defenses, I begin with Sigmund Freud's account. It seems to me a good one. As he says, repression, projection, and the other ego defenses are a part of almost everyone's daily behavior. Whenever these defenses appear, they constitute an exercise of self and social control over desires or situations that threaten our sense of personal soundness and self-respect. They serve to justify us despite our feeling that we do not, or may not, deserve respect. They prevent our becoming even less worthy than we feel we are.

Freud's interpretation was shaped by his observations of defenses as employed by psychiatric patients. Perhaps for that reason, he tended to mix properties of defensiveness – that is, of the degree to which people are preoccupied with defending themselves – with properties of the defenses themselves. I want to focus on the properties of the defenses as such – apart from defensiveness. I propose that, when that is done, there is no reason to think that defenses are necessarily unconscious or irrational or that they necessarily entail gross self-deceptions. On the contrary, the justifications which defenses embody are likely to be tailored realistically to protect relations of the person with himself and others, relations that he finds endangered and wants to preserve. These proposals are developed in chapter 2 along with an explanation for the pervasiveness of defenses in almost everyone's experience.

Freud himself believed that defenses are ubiquitous and inescapable because our ability to function as persons is constantly threatened, especially by biologically-given passions. There is a lot to be said for that, but it does not provide much help if we want to understand why people differ in the ways that they defend themselves: why, for example, one person tends to project his objectionable desires onto other people whereas another tends to repress such desires. Or why the same person projects at one time and represses at another. I propose that, whatever the merits of Freud's suggestion, people seem continually to defend themselves because they always and necessarily undermine the commitments they have made to themselves and others. I suggest that they always, and necessarily, subvert those commitments because they are cross-pressured, the interests and social ties that bind them to one social relationship being in competition with the interests and ties entailed in some other social relationship. If defenses are justifications tailored to social relations that are in danger and in need of preservation, then the form of justification used is likely to be determined by the nature of the social relationship concerned.

Working from these assumptions, I look afresh at Anna Freud's well-known classification of the defenses according to the character of the threat with which they deal and the level of cognitive complexity and "distortion" they embody. I try to clarify that classification and so to recast it that variations in form of defense can be associated with variations in social relations in which self-justifications may be required. In chapter 3, I suggest characteristics of social relations that might foster or make likely a particular kind of threat and therefore certain defenses rather than others. Similarly, in chapter 4, I suggest features of social relations that might make likely a cognitively complex defense rather than one that is simpler.

(It may already be evident that I will use many kinds of conceptions and observations in developing these ideas, including some provided by psychoanalytic and other clinical writers. I think that my own interpretations and findings are broadly consistent with those of clinical observers, as indeed they should be if I am to talk of defenses and to refer to the phenomena that everyone agrees are important. But I try to treat defenses within an interpretation that also contains observations on social relations and social organization and, as a result, all of these things take on meanings not always evident in traditional treatments.)

In chapters 5 and 6, the ideas and suggestions from earlier chapters are evaluated against findings on the social relations found in 118 families and the defenses observed in the behavior of adolescents growing up in those families. I should say something here about these families and adolescents and also about the way in which defenses were observed. That will lead us into the chapters that follow.

The families and adolescents

The origins of my sample of families and adolescents lie in two studies of human growth and development. These studies were begun around 1928–31 at the Institute of Human Development of the University of California at Berkeley and were carried out in the cities of Oakland and Berkeley: the Oakland Growth Study and the Berkeley Guidance Study.

The Oakland Growth Study was initiated in 1931 in the higher fifth and lower sixth grades of five elementary schools whose students would later attend a University-related junior high school. All of the children in these grades were invited to participate in a study to "find out more about how children grow." Children were included in the study if they and their parents accepted this invitation, if the family expected to remain in the area for the next seven years, and if the children actually enrolled in the junior high school that was related to the University of California. These criteria produced an initial sample of 214 children from a universe of 220. It was divided about evenly between boys and girls.

The Berkeley Guidance Study chose for its sample every third child who was born in that city from January 1, 1928, through June 30, 1929, and who was available for study at the age of 21 months. Children from 248 families out of a total of 405 were actually available.

Subjects from the Oakland and Berkeley studies were seen frequently up through the time at which they completed high school. They were studied again in 1958–60, 1968–70, and, most recently, in 1980–81. My research depends on data from 1968–70. At that date, participation was obtained from 109 subjects from Oakland (51% of the original sample) and 143 from Berkeley (58% of the sample).

The subjects in these populations proved to be fairly representative of the geographic areas from which they came (Block and Haan, 1971: 21–30), but well above the national average in income, education, and scores on tested intelligence. They were almost exclusively Caucasian and were preponderantly native-born, of northern and western European antecedents, and of Christian religious affiliation.

Careful investigations (Haan, 1964; Honzik, Macfarlane, and Allen, 1948; Macfarlane, 1971) have been made of the decline, over the years, in the number of subjects available for study. These indicate that migration from the area was the major factor. Refusal to cooperate was relatively rare. (In 1968–70, participation was related slightly to the subjects' socio-economic status ($r(246) = 0.12$, $p < 0.05$) and IQ in adolescence ($r(246) = 0.16$, $p < 0.01$). There seem to be no other relations between a subject's participating in those years and his demographic or personality characteristics.)

In 1968–70 the subjects from both samples were interviewed as were their spouses and older children. (Comparable data are not available for other periods.) There were 118 cases in which a subject, his/her spouse, and one or more of their children aged 14 through 18 were interviewed.

My own findings will concern the adolescent children who were interviewed in these 118 families. I studied the defenses of one adolescent child selected at random from those interviewed in each family. Table 1.1 gives some basic information on these children and their families.

There are about equal numbers of males and females among these adolescents. Six per cent are only children, 38% are first-born children having siblings, 34% are middle children, and 22% are last-born children. The number of children in these families ranges from one to nine with an average of 3.4.

The first item in the table is the distribution of the children by age. Although the Institute had planned to interview children aged 14 through 18, about 7% of those in my sample are older or younger. The average age is 15.7 years.

The families vary considerably in socio-economic status but are higher in their average ranking than would be true for a national sample. By Hollingshead and Redlich's (1958) criteria, 31% are rated Class I (upper middle class or higher), 25% are Class II (middle middle), 28% are Class III (lower middle), and 16% are Class IV (upper working class). None of the families was rated as Class V (lower working class).

Observing defenses

Norma Haan developed the ratings of defenses that I used (Haan, 1977). In 1957–58, when the original subjects in the Oakland and Berkeley studies were first interviewed as adults, Haan trained a group of experienced clinical psychologists to read the interviews and make global ratings of the degree to which each subject used each of ten defenses and ten coping processes. In the interviews with the subjects, spouses, and their children aged 14 through 18 in 1968–70, these ratings were made again. This time Haan added ratings for ten forms of ego fragmentation (Swanson, 1980: 208–10) as well as for various sorts of coping and defense. Her instructions read in part (Haan, 1969):

The ratings are an attempt to represent a map of most common ego functions . . . The set needs first to be viewed as a whole and then various decisions need to be made. . .

Raters were told that the pattern of 30 ratings (see figure 1.1, taken from Haan, 1977: 35) should give "a picture of the" subject's "ego functioning as he presented himself in interacting within the interview." They were instructed to

Table 1.1. *Percentage of children by demographic characteristics:* N = *118*.

Characteristic	Percentage	Characteristic	Percentage
1. Age		4. No of children in family	
19	3	9	1
18	12	8	2
17	20	7	2
16	13	6	3
15	26	5	13
14	21	4	18
13	3	3	30
12	1	2	26
		1	6
Total	99		
		Total	101
2. Sex		5. Socio-economic status	
Male	48		
Female	52	I	31
		II	25
Total	100	III	28
		IV	16
3. Birth order		V	0
Only child	6	Total	100
First-born	38		
Middle-born	34		
Last-born	22		
Total	100		

identify the ego processes that were "characteristic and most salient" for each subject. They were to determine whether these were "usually and most intensely coping, defensive, or fragmenting" and were to rate the subjects on each ego process employing a five-point scale that ranged from (1) "minimal or absent" to (5) "high." Haan noted that most subjects "could be expected" to have some ratings of 4 or 5 but that "an impoverished, self-limiting person in a bland, non-demanding environment might not have any 5's and maybe no 4's."

Each interview was rated for all 30 ego processes by the clinician who had conducted the interview and by another clinician as well. A subject's rating on

Figure 1.1. *Taxonomy of ego processes*

Generic processes	Modes		
	Coping	Defense	Fragmentation
		Cognitive function	
1. Discrimination	Objectivity	Isolation	Concretism
2. Detachment	Intellectuality	Intellectualizing	Word salads, neologisms
3. Means–end symbolization	Logical analysis	Rationalization	Confabulation
		Reflexive-intraceptive functions	
4. Delayed response	Tolerance of ambiguity	Doubt	Immobilization
5. Sensitivity	Empathy	Projection	Delusional
6. Time reversion	Regression-ego	Regression	Decompensation
		Attention-focusing functions	
7. Selective awareness	Concentration	Denial	Distraction, fixation
		Affective-impulse regulations	
8. Diversion	Sublimation	Displacement	Affective preoccupation
9. Transformation	Substitution	Reaction formation	Unstable alternation
10. Restraint	Suppression	Repression	Depersonalization, amnesic

any given ego process was the average of the scores given by these two raters. The reliability of that average was then estimated by the Spearman–Brown formula. I report the reliabilities for ratings of the defenses in appendix 1 (see table A1.5). Analyses of variance show that all of these reliabilities are significant at the 0.01 level or beyond (McNemar, 1969: 342–7). The median coefficient of reliability based on the children's interviews is 0.50. The median coefficient based on interviews with the parents is 0.68. (Most of the reliability coefficients for defenses are of the modest to moderate magnitudes that are usually obtained when skilled raters are employed to judge aspects of personality, whether the raters work from interviews or from their own systematic observations of behavior (Cronbach, 1970: 571–604).)

I present Haan's definition of each defense in chapter 5, and in that chapter – and in chapter 6 and appendix 5 – I describe some special properties of her classification and the results of a factor analysis of the ratings based upon it. At this point I want only to note that there is reason to believe that the defenses, coded from the interviews with the adolescent children, usually concern the adolescents' relations in their families.

Defenses, I shall argue, entail justifications of one's behavior in social relations, so it is important for my purposes that the defenses observed concern social relations that are also under observation, specifically, in this study, the adolescents' relations with parents and siblings. The interviews from which the adolescents' defenses were coded were clinical, life-history interviews which had exactly that focus. Much less attention was given to other topics – for example, to the adolescents' experiences at school and with friends, to their plans for the coming years, and to their attitudes towards such public issues as racial integration, the use of drugs, or the United States' involvement in Vietnam. The questions asked on these latter topics tended also to get at familial relations because adolescents were asked to describe the feelings their families would have on these public issues and their own reactions to these feelings.

I appreciate, of course, that these young people were exposed to many groups other than their families and that their relations in those groups also foster defenses. If that is a fact influencing their defenses as coded in this study, it will lower the likelihood of finding significant relations between their defenses and the social relations they confront within their families.

But it is time to move from an overview to the study itself. Chapter 2 contains a review of the nature of defenses and a basis for understanding why individuals defend as they do.

2 Ego defenses in everyday life

We would never guess from reading G.H. Mead or Piaget that people are ambivalent about becoming persons, that human selves are grounded in elaborate justifications, or that, as persons, people's strength and resilience depend upon the acceptability of those justifications. For these points we must turn to Freud.

Freud, Mead, and Piaget are close on many fundamentals. They all say that we become persons or selves because other people teach us that our desires and outlook may not be the same as theirs: because they require us to separate the two, and because they force us to take their preferences seriously. We are persons to the extent that this training takes hold: to the extent we take account of our own inner lives and of other people's – take account of motives and knowledge, attitudes and abilities, limitations and potentialities – and guide our behavior accordingly. And the consequences of this training are not limited to social relations. We come, by this means, to look at all things and at all situations from as many points of view as seem important; to pay attention to our own desires, capacities, and behavior, and to cultivate and shape them to serve our interests. Through these reflective processes – Freud's "secondary process," Mead's "reflective intelligence," Piaget's "operational intelligence" – we come to solve problems more effectively, to master difficulties, and together with other people, to shape a meaningful world.

The difficulty, Freud says, is that we are impulsive, selfish, and insatiable – inherently and constantly so – and that our impulses admit of no restraint. Over the long run, we become more effective in getting what we want if we acquire the abilities associated with being a person or self, but that will require us continually to repress imperative desires and to abandon the wish for immediate gratification. In that sense, our growth as selves is like the development of civilization. In both there emerges a discriminating judgment. That judgment rests upon our becoming responsible for the guidance of our own behavior; for shaping it to serve other people's interests, individual and collective, and not just our own. It rests, therefore, upon convictions that we deserve to be fed and respected as persons only if we want and do what is right. Freud claims that, between these convictions and the id instincts, there is opposition and conflict rather than disequilibrium . . .; there is compromise, sacrifice of need, and inner adaptation rather than a cognitively warranted, truly adjustive, existential solution to frustration .·. . (Selznick, 1969: 258)

For Freud (1930: 97), selves and civilization alike are "built up upon a renunciation of instinct." They presuppose "the non-satisfaction (by suppression, repression or some other means?) of powerful instincts." Neither can flourish unless protected against the assaults and wiles of unacceptable impulses. It is the office of the ego defenses to provide that protection. That is why the defenses are indispensable for the formation of a self and, thereafter, for its preservation.

The contrast with Mead and Piaget is clear:

There are passages in Mead [and Piaget] which suggest a belief that the cognitive taking account of the Other is a sufficient condition for the distinctively human self to emerge. It is this which the Freudian interpretation . . . denies . . . (Selznick, 1960: 256)

In Freud's interpretation, ego defenses also make possible the appearance of a psychoneurosis. That is the thrust of Otto Fenichel's magisterial analysis (1945: 20):

we have in psychoneuroses, first a defense of the ego against an instinct, then a conflict between the instinct striving for discharge and the defensive forces of the ego, then a state of damming up, and finally the neurotic symptoms which are . . . a compromise between the opposing forces.

Why do people defend themselves as they do?

Psychiatric practice and everyday experience bring us to the question about defenses that has been asked most often and that led to the research described in these chapters: Why do individuals defend themselves as they do? Why do they defend themselves differently from one situation to another and why do they differ in their characteristic methods of defense? Psychotherapists want the answers because the ways in which a patient defends help to determine the form of his neurotic symptoms. They are a clue to the nature of the patient's difficulties and to the processes by which those difficulties can be "worked through" and, perhaps, overcome. The answers are equally important to each of us as we try to understand ourselves and other people (Blum, 1983).

There are answers to this question but none is satisfactory. Freud asks the question and establishes its importance but certain of his assumptions seem now to hinder the finding of better answers. My hope is to offer a way of thinking about defenses that may help to overcome these difficulties. That is my objective in this chapter.

The nature of defenses

Why do people differ in the ways that they defend themselves? Anna Freud (1936: 50) tells us that the immediate difficulty in answering the question is conceptual.[1] As she says, there are ambiguities in the very conception of a psychological defense and each of the many lists of defenses includes "under a single heading a number of heterogeneous phenomena." These ambiguities and confusions make it difficult to identify the several defenses, to systematize them, or to explain, on systematic grounds, why it is that a person makes one defense and not another (Freud, 1936: 50, 173–7; Lazarus, 1966: 190, 296–7, 307, 310; Mahl, 1971: 195; Sjöbäck, 1973: 181–208, 239–60).

I find it helpful to think of the ego defenses as one of the several forms of justification that people give for their own behavior. People are always "giving an account" of themselves and, in most situations, they are trying to give a passably good account. Self-justifications are a normal part of "normal" behavior (Aronson, 1976: 85–140; Scott and Lyman, 1968; Semin and Manstead, 1983).

In this chapter I try to specify features of ego defenses that distinguish them from other self-justifications. I do that by looking in more detail at Sigmund Freud's account of defenses, noting certain of his assumptions that seem unjustified, presenting warrants for somewhat different assumptions, and offering a characterization of defenses and of the conditions that foster them which the new assumptions seem to sustain. I also review some major efforts to identify the systematic relations among defenses: their differences and similarities. In chapters 3 and 4 I use the assumptions proposed in this chapter to recast those systematizations and to suggest social conditions that might make more likely the use of certain defenses rather than others. Those proposals are evaluated against the new research that is described in chapters 5 and 6.

Ego defenses and psychoneurosis

Sigmund Freud (1926, 1933: 94–5) suggests that the defenses – he calls them "ego defenses" – occur in the psychoneuroses but not in the "pure" traumatic neuroses. He admits that no one ever sees a pure traumatic neurosis and that all of the psychoneuroses are in part traumatic. Nevertheless he insists upon the

---

[1] Wallerstein (1967, 1983) draws a useful distinction between defense mechanisms and defensive processes. The latter he considers as empirical events, the former as a conceptualization of those events.

distinction, saying that it is clinically real and therapeutically important. The traumatic neuroses, he writes (1924: 274),

are not in their essence the same as the spontaneous neuroses [that is, the psychoneuroses] which we are in the habit of investigating and treating by analysis . . .

In the psychoneuroses, the ego defends itself against instinctual impulses of the id "whose demands seem to it to be menacing," whereas, in the traumatic neuroses, the ego defends itself against a danger which threatens it from without (Arlow and Brenner, 1964: 24–8, 44, 53–4; Freud, 1919: 87; Greenacre, 1952).

This is a distinction that will become clearer as we proceed. It directs us to look for the sources of ego defenses in inner impulses and in the threats that these impulses can provide.

Fenichel's (1945: 148) description of one of the defenses helps us to see what is involved. He describes repression as consisting

of an unconsciously purposeful forgetting or not becoming aware of internal impulses or external events which, as a rule, represent possible temptations or punishments for, or mere allusions to, objectionable instinctual demands. The purposeful exclusion of these data from consciousness is obviously intended to hinder their real effects as well as the pain on becoming aware of them. However, although the repressed is not felt consciously it remains effective.

In this definition, the person is threatened by his having an "objectionable instinctual" impulse. This impulse might better be called a "motive" (Rapaport, 1967: 853–915) because, as Fenichel (1945: 54–5) says, it has an aim ("the very specific discharge action which dispels the physical condition of excitement and thus brings about satisfaction"), an object ("that instrument by which or through which the instinct can attain its aim"), and a source ("the chemicophysical status which causes a sensory stimulus to bring about excitement"). It also has drive: "the quantity of energy which the instinct represents" (Blum, 1953: 15). Aim and object

obviously are changed . . . under influences stemming from the environment, and Freud was even of the opinion that they originated under the same influence. (Fenichel, 1945: 12).

In repression, as in all of the ego defenses, the defender is the ego. This is the individual behaving as an actor. As an actor, an individual engages in instrumental activities: relates selectively toward the environment in its relevance for his motives. More exactly, the defender is the individual as a person or self (Schafer, 1976). This is so because he is aware of some aspects of his own behavioral processes (in defenses, he is aware of instinctual impulses and of the threat that they pose) and because he behaves instrumentally toward those processes (in defenses he tries to control them).

The impulse is a threat only because it endangers the individual's ability to behave as an ego and a self (Fingarette, 1963: 73–89). This becomes clear in Freud's treatment of anxiety.

The defenses are held to be triggered by anxiety and anxiety is, in part, an experience or expectation of helplessness as an ego or self. Freud develops this point in saying that anxiety has a meaning embedded in experiences of trauma and that trauma is occasioned by a danger to the ego's very existence or worth.

Here is Freud on danger (1926: 166):

we go on to enquire what the essence and meaning of a danger-situation is. Clearly, it consists in the subject's estimation of his own strength compared to the magnitude of the danger and in his admission of helplessness in the face of it – physical helplessness if the danger is real and psychical helplessness if it is instinctual. In doing this he will be guided by the actual experiences he has had.

(Whether the subject is correct in his estimation is immaterial for the outcome.)

What in a situation makes it traumatic? It is not our *being* helpless. It is our "actually [having] experienced" a "situation of helplessness of this kind" (Freud, 1926: 166). This experience consists in an appreciation that our helplessness constitutes a negation of our powers, integrity, and worth as an ego, often as a self (Fenichel, 1945: 117–18; Fingarette, 1963: 71–112). This negation is the meaning that danger has for us. In Freud's view, as summarized by Fenichel (1945: 117), "The ego may be regarded as having been developed for the purpose of avoiding traumatic states." If we are helpless, the ego has failed of its reason for being.

And anxiety? Freud (1926: 166) describes it in the following terms:

Anxiety is . . . on the one hand an expectation of a trauma, and on the other a repetition of it in a mitigated form . . . two features of anxiety which we have noted have a different origin. Its connection with expectation belongs to the danger-situation, whereas its indefiniteness and lack of object to the traumatic situation of helplessness – the situation which is anticipated in the danger-situation.

Anxiety can be "a direct consequence of the traumatic moment" or "a signal threatening a repetition of such a moment" (Freud, 1933: 94–5). It is "the original reaction to helplessness in the trauma and is reproduced later on in the danger-situation as a signal for help" (Freud, 1926: 166–7). Anxiety is thus an appreciation that one is, or is about to be, endangered as an ego or a self.

But why a defense? Why, for example, does not the person use suppression instead of repression: a holding back of action on the impulse until circumstances are propitious rather than "an unconsciously purposeful forgetting or not becoming aware" of the impulse or of any external events that might evoke or release it? Or why not sublimation? Or why not an abandonment of the impulse as not worth the cost of further pursuit? In answering these questions, we make more precise the kind of danger, trauma, and anxiety that an ego defense involves.

The reason the person does not abandon the impulse is that he cannot. He cannot because he finds the impulse to be imperative and inescapable, or because he lacks the ability to control it, or both. He interprets the impulse as an enduring part of his life. He cannot sublimate it because, for whatever reason, he can find no harmless aims or objects that can be substituted for the original, dangerous ones. Suppression will not do because it is the very existence of this particular impulse that is a threat to the person and not just his overt actions. When he thinks of himself as a person who has such an impulse, such a desire, he feels guilty or ashamed, compromised or terrified. If that is so, the only successful defense will be an ego defense, a person's defense of his integrity against his very own motives.

It is true that a person's motives become threatening to him because they can lead him into a dangerous course of action: especially into actions that other people strongly disapprove. It is also true that something in the environment may threaten his personal integrity irrespective of his motives and he may try to ward off that threat. But the feature of a threatening situation that occasions an ego defense rather than some other is the person's belief that, whatever else he may have to do to counter external threats, his security as a person also depends on his controlling those of his desires that are unjustified: unjustified in his own eyes and not simply in the view of other people.

And that returns us to Freud's distinction between the psychoneuroses and the traumatic neuroses. In both cases the "motives of defense are rooted in external influences" (Fenichel, 1945: 130) Both kinds of neurosis are embedded in danger, trauma, and anxiety. Both entail defensive activities by the ego.[2] The difference is that, in the psychoneuroses, the person truly feels

---

[2] The difference between the traumatic neuroses and those based upon the neurotic conflict is highlighted by Fenichel (1945: 541): 'one element that is characteristic of traumatic neurosis [and that] is missing in actual neuroses: the charactersitic repetitions of the trauma in dreams and symptoms. These repetitions represent attempts to achieve a belated mastery . . . of the unmastered amounts of excitation. Repetitions occur in all psychoneurotic phenomena, too, but there they are of another nature . . .' In the psychoneuroses, the repetitions are (*ibid.*, 542): 'due to the tendency of the repressed to find an outlet . . . What happens is that a repressed impulse tries to find its gratification in spite of its repression; but whenever the repressed wish comes to the surface, the anxiety that first brought about the repression is mobilized again and creates, together with the repetition of the impulse, a repetition of the anti-instinctual measures . . .' Repetition in the psychoneuroses (*ibid.*, 543) 'is not intended to be a repetition. When the excitement is "repeated," it is done so in the hope that its outcome will be different, a gratification instead of the preceding failure. But this intention fails, and what actually occurs is a repetition of the frustration . . .' In the traumatic neuroses, the repetition 'is characterized by different features. The ego's attitude toward the repetition is a very ambivalent one. The repetition is desired to relieve a painful tension; but because the repetition itself is also painful, the person is afraid of it and tends to avoid it. Usually, therefore, a compromise is sought: a repetition on a smaller scale or under more encouraging circumstances.

that the danger would not exist were it not for his own motives and he believes that the danger can be controlled or removed if his motives, or their significance, are different. In the traumatic neuroses, he feels that his motives make no difference, that no desire of his has led to the danger he encounters: has led the tornado to strike, the dog to attack, the bombardment to start, his car to crash, or his projects to fail.[3]

By the time a person is four or five years of age, and certainly in adolescence and adulthood, defenses have a further characteristic that is important: the person tries to control certain of his impulses not merely because those impulses lead to trouble but because he himself disapproves of them. He sees them as more than dangerous. They are illegitimate, reprehensible, humiliating.[4]

Given these feelings, an ego defense can be effective only if the person does more than control the objectionable impulse. He must deal with the impulse in such a way that he reinstates himself in his own eyes. Without that reinstatement, he is divided against himself and he therefore has difficulty in functioning.

Effective defenses provide this reinstatement in two ways. First, they control the impulse itself by affirming that standards and motives by which the person claims to live and deserve acceptance are more important to him, and are stronger determinants of his conduct, than are his deviant desires. Second, they "defend against the affects" – the panic, shame, or guilt – entailed in a traumatic self-accusation. They do this by providing warrants that make the person acceptable to himself, and to others, despite his having the objectional impulse or despite his seeming to have it.[5]

A defense cannot provide these warrants unless it meets rational and normative criteria. It must sustain the person's claims to have certain abilities,

[3] Certain phenomena that resemble the ego defenses can now be seen as different. Two recent examples are found in the work of Brehm and of Aronson. Brehm (1972) has written of psychological reactance: the individual's desire to retain and exercise his freedom to act and his struggle against limitations on that freedom. Defense is involved here, and even defense of ego and self, but the immediate threat comes from the environment, not from the inappropriateness of one's motives. Aronson (1972: 89–139) discusses psychological dissonance as an instance of a need for self-justification and, in that sense, as defensive. Many studies of dissonance do seem to fit that designation and all desires to justify oneself entail cognitive dissonance. It is also true, however, that all instances of cognitive dissonance do not turn on a desire to justify oneself. Psychological dissonance refers to the experience of having incompatible meanings, experiences, or desires. Dissonance experiments do not require that any of the subject's desires be unjustified or unacceptable but only that there be a problem of the subject's reconciling those of his desires that are at cross-purposes. This is not the distinctive feature of the problem that gives rise to an ego defense. Ego defenses involve inner conflicts, but not just any inner conflicts.

[4] This may be true of children younger than age four. We simply do not know.

[5] People differ in the extent and the manner in which they deal with these two aspects of defense (Fenichel, 1945: 161–7; Freud, 1936: 31–41).

commitments, and objectives – this is in the face of evidence that he and others believe to negate those claims. An ego defense must take that negative evidence into account and must rest upon evidence and arguments that lead to an opposite conclusion (Toulmin, 1958: 211–52). If these evaluations and arguments are to be successful as a part of his defense, the defender – and other people as well – must find them believable. That implies that defenses must meet established standards for reasoning and for the making of claims concerning the rectitude of actions.[6]

These, then, are the considerations behind my focus upon ego defenses as justifications that people use when self-accused (which always means that they also anticipate accusations by others): when they accuse themselves of failing to meet requirements that they want to believe they support. Defenses are therefore forms of problem-solving and of coping but are different from other forms of either.

Problem-solving means dealing with difficulties in, or blockages to, behavior as a process for dealing instrumentally with an environment. Coping is one aspect of problem-solving. It means dealing with those real or anticipated threats to one's ability to function as an ego which difficulties in behavior may pose (Lazarus, 1968: 341): the threat, perhaps, that one will be left unsatisfied or in pain or exposed to ridicule, and so on. Coping means so handling anxieties concerning these threats that one can continue with problem-solving and perhaps thereby eliminate the threats themselves. Ego defenses are a form of coping and one distinguished by their nature (they are self-justifications) and by the nature of the threat (the self-accusations of failing to meet standards that one professes to oneself and others to uphold).

---

[6] Defense is sometimes contrasted with "coping," or subsumed under it. For Haan (1963) or Kroeber (1964), coping and defense are both ego processes, the difference being that coping is rational, realistic, and adaptive whereas defense is the opposite. This seems close to a distinction between psychological "health" and "pathology." Lazarus (1966: 258–318) provides a different formulation. For Lazarus, coping refers to "strategies for dealing with threat" (151) and threat is taken to be an anticipation of harmful events or, if these events are already present, of their continuation (30–84). In Lazarus' thought, coping is to be distinguished from problem-solving, the latter being a more inclusive term (151). Coping is that activity within problem-solving that deals with problems as problems – as obstacles to one's successful functioning and therefore as threatening. (Problem-solving also includes the holding up of behavior while devising a plan, the analysis of a situation that is independent of one's feelings, the allocation of facilities and resources for the purpose of solving the problem, the evaluation of preliminary solutions, the suppression of lines of action that might interfere with the one of greatest importance, the taking of initiatives to seize opportunities or to create them, and so on (Arlow and Brenner, 1964: 39).) Coping is an attempt to overcome an obstacle or to compensate for it. The means are many. In coping, the person may attack, avoid, ward off, endure, make do, sublimate, transcend, move ahead courageously . . . whatever. Lazarus considers defenses to be a form of coping: "psychological maneuvers in which the individual deceives himself about the actual condition of threat" (1966: 266).

Later in this chapter I take up some alternative ideas about the nature of ego defenses. Most of them add features to the core definition just given.

Ego defenses in everyday life

We are now in a position to see why it is that ego defenses are a part of the everyday behavior of clinically normal people and why they are an inescapable part of that behavior. They are ubiquitous and inescapable because they are inherent in people's being socially interdependent.

Interdependence is related to social influence, power, or interaction but is not quite the same. A person exercises influence when he modifies another's behavior. A person has power if, by virtue of his own qualities, he can influence someone else. People interact when they not only influence one another but when their influences are mutual: when the influence of each is in some way contingent upon the influence of the other.

Interdependence is a special case of interaction. Its distinctive feature is that each of the persons who are interacting needs the others for what they do. People may try to escape from one another's influence or power or even from interaction with them. In interdependence people are drawn to one another and to a mutuality from which each is fed.

We are looking here at commonplace events: at people who need each other and who, no matter what their purpose – trade, alliance, marriage, friendship – arrive at some reciprocal terms on which each will give to the others and will get from them. Those terms, implicit or explicit, constitute an agreement. People honor this agreement in order to get things they want. They no longer relate to each other directly but, instead, through the terms of the agreement.

Five features of agreements are of special importance for an analysis of defensive processes. One of these features, the reciprocal exchanges which they require, is already before us. We should note, in addition, that agreements are interpersonal, normative, and collective, and that deviance from them is possible and probable.

Agreements are interpersonal in that participants present themselves to one another as wanting certain things and as able to do certain things for others. They also claim to understand reciprocal arrangements, to be able to meet their terms, and to want things that will not, of themselves, subvert such an arrangement. They claim to want what others can provide and to be so dependent on these prospective partners that they are unlikely to look for other partners before meeting the terms of an agreement. People develop agreements by presenting themselves to one another as persons or selves: in terms of their knowledge of their own motives and skills and understanding and of their ability to do things that will advance the interests of others.

Agreements transform giving and getting into normative relations, into the fulfillment of duties and the exercise of rights. Rights and duties are inherent in reciprocity. Reciprocation is a condition for the survival of interdependence among particular participants. Under an agreement one gets because one has a right to do so – because one is taken to be a person who can and will meet justified claims that others make. And one gives as a duty: to insure that others will honor one's justified claims. The "justification" is in the agreed-upon reciprocation and in the participants' acceptance of their relations as being, on balance, good.

Agreements are collective in character because they embody reciprocal arrangements that specify the interests that participants have in common as well as their special interests. These include the things that participants must do to sustain their joint enterprise, the things that they may do to benefit from it, and the procedures by which interaction must be conducted to be legitimate.

Agreements are an order of fact independent of the participants taken individually. Participants can judge their own and others' actions against the terms of their agreement, can refer to those terms in adjudicating disputes, and can employ agreed-upon procedures to reach joint solutions to new problems.

If people enter agreements because they need one another, why is deviance both possible and likely? Primarily because people always have competing claims on their time, energies, and commitments and because their desires are subject to change. No social relationship fulfills all the desires of its members. As a result, the members always have competing interests and have wishes that are potentially subversive. Every agreement is in some degree a compromise between all of the things that people would like from a relationship (and which, on balance, are worth having) and what they actually get. Therefore the parties to an agreement always have grounds for a renegotiation of their agreement should an opportunity arise. And opportunities are always present. No agreement is entirely clear as to the actions that sufficiently fulfill its terms. There are always matters of discretion – for example, how quickly a person must reciprocate; how many unanticipated obstacles he must try to overcome in order to fulfill his obligations; whether substitutions can be made in the means or manner in which a requirement is met.

Given all of these cross-pressures, ambiguities, and contingencies, there is almost always some likelihood that people will exceed their rights or scant their duties or will consider the possibility of renegotiating or abandoning the agreement. Some deviance will be accidental; some intentional. In every social relationship, tendencies to deviance will be endemic.

That brings us back to the ego defenses. A person defends when he has a motive that he finds unacceptable but that is also active, unavoidable, and ineradicable. His dilemma lies in the cross-pressures of his wanting something and of his truly wanting not to want it. The essence of defense is to demonstrate one's loyalty to the standards by which the motive is unacceptable and to show that one's having the deviant motive does not compromise one's fulfillment of obligations.

Godfey Lienhardt (1961: 249) catches the nature of an ego defense in some observations on the Dinka, a tribal people living along the headwaters of the Nile. When the Dinka pray, they often claim the favor of the spirits by saying that they, the Dinka, have blameless lives and faultlessly meet all of their ritual obligations. This is untrue and the Dinka know it.

Do the Dinka then think that they can deceive the divinities? That interpretation would be naive . . . The very presence of these denials [of wrongdoing] is a confession of their faults. When a man states that it is not *true* that he did this or that, in this context, he implies something other than the statement that he never did it at all . . . he states that he does not wish it to be true: he wishes it had not happened, and his intention, publicly expressed, is that it should not be ultimately true. In other words, whatever he may have done or said on specific occasions does not, and is not to, represent his permanent dispositions, and his permanent dispositions and intentions are what constitute the real, existential truth of the situation he depicts. . .

Before summarizing my argument, I must concede that ego defenses may be fostered by conditions other than social interdependence. All I can properly argue is that social interdependence seems to embody a set of conditions sufficient to generate these defenses.

My argument comes to this:

- People who are interdependent really need each other. They find their relationship to be, on balance, necessary and rewarding.
- They are committed to certain standards: to the terms of the agreement on which that relationship rests.
- They have desires that are deviant and that persist.
- Because the agreement commits them to reciprocal actions, people become suspicious of themselves when they sense that they have unacceptable desires.
- Because the agreement embodies a view of themselves which they presented to others, and to themselves, as being true, they now have reason for self-doubt. They have presented themselves as being certain kinds of persons: as able to make and fulfill agreements; as trustworthy. Their very integrity as egos or selves comes into question when they find that they are not what they had assumed. They know a kind of existential dread.
- Because agreements are normative in character, people see themselves as shameful or guilty and not simply as in error.
- Because agreements are collective and, in that sense, independent of the parties to them, participants find that the terms of a possible defense are objectively given. A successful defense will be one that a participant, and his fellows, will find consistent with standards to which all parties can refer. The defense cannot

be arbitrary. It cannot be a fabrication. It must meet the criteria of fact and logic which those standards demand.

Ego defenses, I propose, are a part and parcel of social interdependence. But they are not usually salient for the parties involved. For most people, most of the time, the charges they are answering prove of little importance. People's deviant motives are not usually so powerful that they interfere with their meeting the terms of agreements. What is more, people usually pay most attention to what it is that they want from social relations. They find that it suffices to give only passing attention to the various specific requirements that must be met in order for them to get what they want – including the requirement that they behave defensively. Thus they try, in passing, to behave in ways that are legitimate and thereby to minimize the importance of any charges of misconduct.[7]

Some disagreements on the nature of ego defense

The fact that ego defenses have so often been studied in connection with the psychoneuroses, and from a psychoanalytic perspective, has colored discussions of their nature and origins. It has even obscured some of the key observations that arose in careful reflections upon psychiatric cases (Abend, Porter, and Willick, 1983; Brenner, 1981, 1982: 72–92; Sandler and Freud, 1983; Wallerstein, 1983; Willick, 1983). I think in particular of the following statements, each a commonplace in the literature: defenses include, or are applications of or derivations from, some biologically-given processes (Freud, 1936); defenses are merely instances of processes general to all of learning or behavior (Bandura and Walters, 1963); defenses are necessarily rooted in events occuring in infancy or early childhood; defenses are inadequate and irrational (Haan, 1963, 1969, 1974; Kroeber, 1964); defenses entail gross self-deception (Freud, 1936; Lazarus, 1966: 273).

Each of these statements seems to me wrong or misleading and I work from different assumptions. I treat ego defenses not as biologically given but as socially fostered and socially constituted; not as instances of just any process of learning or behavior but, specifically, of social interdependence; not as limited in their origins in infancy or early childhood but as continuously created and recreated in social relationships at all periods of life; not as irrational or

---

[7] This is part of people's efforts to behave in such a manner that they can, if called upon, account for what they do (Blum and McHugh, 1971; Garfinkel, 1967; Goffman, 1971; Scott and Lyman, 1968).

inadequate – although they may be something of both – but as at least intended to meet logical and normative criteria; not as necessarily entailing gross self-deceptions – although self-deception may be involved – but as always responsive to the realities in social situations. I need to give my reasons for thinking that the assumptions alternative to mine are less adequate.

On biological interpretations

There are many suggestions concerning a biological constitution or origin for defenses. Most of these make one of two points: (1) constitutional factors have a direct role in producing certain defenses or (2) constitutional factors can serve as precursors and prototypes of defenses. Each point requires at least brief consideration.

(1) Constitutional factors as the causes of particular defenses

A few writers still suggest that defenses are innate patterns of human behavior. A more common argument is that genetic factors have a role in the formation or choice of defenses (Sjöbäck, 1973: 255–6).

The argument that defenses are innate assumes that people have an inborn knowledge of themselves and their environment. Given the overwhelming evidence against the existence of such knowledge, this argument need not be considered further.

The argument that defenses have some genetic sources proves usually to be modest. It proposes that some genetically determined characteristic can preclude, or make possible, the use of a particular defense or defenses. An example is Hartmann's (1939: 14) suggestion that "native" intelligence helps to determine "the choice and success of the defensive process."

Each such argument has to be judged on its own merits and some will doubtless appear plausible. It is important to note, however, that arguments of this sort do not take us far in understanding why people defend at all or why they defend as they do. To illustrate by using Hartmann's proposal, a person's "inherent" intelligence is surely not, of itself, the reason he defends and, although it might be true that some level of such intelligence is required for certain defenses, the presence of such a level of intelligence would not preclude a person's employing defenses that demand less intellectual capacity.

(2) Constitutional factors as the precursors and prototypes of defenses

As Sjöbäck (1973: 250–4) observes, hypotheses about constitutional precursors or prototypes of defenses can be grouped along three lines as follows:

(1) . . . defensive processes may be regarded as analogous to the ways whereby the individual defends himself against dangers in the external world; *e.g.*, by means of flight or fight.

Or

(2) We come across assumptions that certain basic somatic functional modes can be regarded as prototypes of defensive processes . . .

For example, ideas that

projection is modelled upon the spitting out of unpleasant-tasting objects, and that introjection is connected with swallowing . . .

or that

projection has its roots in anal expulsion, and urethral elimination . . .

or that

swallowing is the prototype of repression.

Sjöbäck describes the third of these sets of hypotheses as follows:

(3) A third angle of approach to the precursor question would be one which would lead to propositions concerning primitive *mental processes*, per se, assumedly functioning as precursors of defensive processes; this, irrespective of such mental processes' hypothetical origins . . . Hartmann . . . mentions . . . some simple basic responses to stimulation, such as "the neonate's closing of the eyelids when exposed to light," and "definite flight reactions."

Whatever the validity of these sorts of argument, they do not answer questions about the nature, systematics, or use of the ego defenses. They say, in essence, that certain defenses depend upon a person's having learned certain things at some earlier time and that his learning of those things depends, in turn, upon potentialities that are biologically given. We can see, however, that the activities these authors cite as developed through learning have only a remote connection with ego defenses. They are components of many behaviors other than defenses (*e.g.*, flight is involved in running from an enemy, swallowing is a part of eating and drinking, closing the eyelids occurs in sleep). Without the many further assumptions that would be required to link such behaviors specifically to ego defenses, these proposals are only a bit more useful than saying that in order to read one must first be able to see.

On general psychological interpretations

Perhaps, however, the ego defenses could be interpreted comprehensively by means of general psychological theory. If so, they could be understood as special cases of learning, cognition, motivation, performance, or other processes that appear in all behavior or in all human behavior. That has been the approach of several psychologists (Gardner and others, 1959: 127–36; Horowitz, 1972; Lichtenberg and Slap, 1972) and it is one that Freud himself sometimes employed.

The well-known studies of displacement by Neal Miller (1944, 1948), Dollard and Miller (1950: 157–191), and Fitz (1976) and the investigations of regression by O. H. Mowrer (1940) are typical of this perspective.[8] In dealing with this displacement, Miller reasoned as follows:

The pairing of noxious stimuli with . . . responses that an individual, because of past positive reinforcement, is strongly disposed to make gives rise to an approach–avoidance conflict, the outcome of which is dependent upon the relative strength of the approach and avoidance responses. Miller's conflict model is the best known attempt to predict, on the basis of learning-theory principles, what the outcome is likely to be. According to this model, inhibitory (fear or anxiety) responses and the responses with which they compete generalize to stimulus situations similar to those in which they were originally learned, the strength of the generalized responses being a function of the similarity between the original and the new situations. Miller assumes that the generalization gradient for an inhibitory response is steeper than that of the response which is inhibited and that, consequently, at some point on the stimulus dissimilarity continuum the approach tendency becomes the stronger and is therefore manifested in overt activity. A series of studies with animals . . . supported Miller's basic assumptions . . . (Bandura and Walters, 1963: 15–18).

Mowrer, who claimed only the status of an "analogue" for his results, created conditions in which "regression" might occur. In the main part of his experiment, each of five rats was placed individually in a box. The floor of the box was a grid through which electric shocks could be administered. Mowrer turned on the current and slowly increased it until the animal was highly agitated. He kept the current at that level for 15 minutes. Mowrer found that each rat came to assume a position of sitting quietly on its hind legs with its forepaws raised about the grid. In that position, the pain was minimized. After six days of this kind of training, each animal was put into the apparatus again, but this time the box contained a pedal that was easily moved and that shut off the current. All of the animals soon learned to do this and they abandoned sitting upright when the current came on. The final step was taken after three

[8] It might be thought (Blaney, 1977; Peterson, 1979) that Seligman's (1975; Garber and Seligman, 1980) studies of helplessness and "depression" in man and other animals provide a further example of this sort of work on defenses – including, perhaps, a defense like turning against the self (see appendix 4). That seems not to be the way Seligman himself understands his work (1975: 89, 93; Abramson, Seligman, and Teasdale, 1978). He does stress, however, that helplessness, in his sense, is a condition of the organism as an ego or self (1975: 96–99; Abramson, Seligman and Teasdale, 1978) and some of his key methodological suggestions turn on this assumption (1975: 80–1).

days of training (30 trials in all) in the modified box. Each rat was now put in the box where it found that the pedal as well as the floor carried a shock, this having to be suffered in order to turn off the current. Four of the five animals "promptly regressed" to sitting on their hind legs with their forepaws raised.

There is no doubt that the experiments by Miller and Mowrer deal with some of the behaviors that are also entailed in defenses. Displacement is a kind of substitution – one occasioned by "noxious stimuli" – in which an initially attractive object with which such stimuli are associated is abandoned for an object that has lesser attractions but fewer dangers. Regression can be a reversion, occasioned by aversive conditions, from a more adaptive line of behavior that was learned more recently to a line of behavior that was learned earlier and that is less adaptive.

It is crucial, however, that neither Miller's studies nor Mowrer's operationalize all of the key features of the defenses that these investigators hope to understand. The features they omit indicate the limits of their approach (Bandura and Walters, 1963: 18–21). As we have seen, an ego defense wards off a threat to the individual as an ego or self, not immediately as an organism. There is no hint in Miller's studies, or Mowrer's, that that distinction is involved. The threat in an ego defense comes from a motive. In Miller's studies, and in Mowrer's (although not in all investigations that use the same approach), the threat comes from the environment. In ego defenses the individual is threatened by one of his own motives because he personally finds it incompatible with standards that he has made his own. He finds himself dangerous, or otherwise unacceptable, because he has this motive and he tries therefore to find ways of living with himself, and of functioning in the environment, despite his unacceptable desire. In the ego defenses, as commonly described in the clinical literature, the motive is unacceptable not simply because it poses a threat but because it is considered shameful or morally wrong or a violation of social standards concerning adequate and competent behavior. Miller's and Mowrer's studies do not concern such phenomena.

To lose these several features of ego defenses is to lose what seem to be their defining properties. To try to conceptualize these defining properties as being but special cases of the general properties of behavior seems therefore inappropriate. General theories in psychology necessarily deal with those variables that are involved in, or are features of, all behavior or of all behavior in a particular species (Swanson, 1965a). When one deals with phenomena whose very definition entails other sorts of properties, one must look outside general theories of behavior for schemes in which such properties have a systematic rather than an arbitrary place.

The ego defenses entail many properties not found in all behavior, properties requiring a theory which, unlike general psychology, provides a means by which they can be systematized. Among these properties, at least implicitly, are self conceptions and processes; an individual's awareness of his own motives; his judgment that his own motives, as such, are sources of danger; his hope of reinstating himself in his own eyes and in those of others despite his having some unacceptable motives. A social interpretation of defenses helps us to deal systematically with these crucial properties.

On a grounding of defenses in infancy

Are defenses necessarily rooted in events of infancy or early childhood? As ordinarily defined, the ego defenses imply some measure of awareness of our inner life, of standards by which we and others judge our desires and feelings, and of the connections between motives and overt behavior. Our best understanding is that this awareness is not present at birth, that it is acquired gradually through our participation in social relations, and that it does not become well-established, even in a simple form, until age four or five. Whatever their precursors in infancy, it is unikely that the defenses, as we usually think of them, are present in infancy at all. By contrast, there seems nothing in the nature of defenses to preclude their appearing in connection with concerns that originate later in life and that have no immediate connection with concerns or defenses that appeared earlier. I will develop this point later in this chapter when I discuss the place of unconsciousness and self-deception in defensive activities.

On the inadequacy of defenses

It is often claimed that ego defenses are inadequate in the sense that they do not eliminate the sources of our inner conflicts. That is true. But it is also intrinsic to the situation in which defenses arise that these conflicts seem – perhaps are – inescapable and irreconcilable. Defenses do take account of the forces immediately involved in such conflicts. They do enable us to go on acting in a coherent fashion and one which promises to afford us whatever gratification seems possible. In that sense they are adequate – sometimes ingeniously so.

On irrationality in defenses

On the same grounds, ego defenses seem rational rather than irrational. They are founded upon an assessment of the relevant facts and this assessment can be quite accurate. They are a means that is often well-tailored to the ends that it serves. It is true that a person's objections to his own motives may, from some point of view, appear ill-founded and that the strength of his objections may seem to be unwarranted. Those, however, are judgments about the quality of his assessments and are not characteristics of the defenses themselves.

I think that inadequacy and irrationality come to be associated with defenses, not because these are intrinsic properties of any defense but because defenses were first studied systematically in psychiatric patients whose inner conflicts were intense and whose *defensiveness* was consequently high. If a person's inner conflicts are intense, his behavior is likely to seem less adequate and less rational than is otherwise the case. What we see then are high levels of *defensiveness* and not just defenses. The person's conflicts are salient, taking up much of his energy and attention. He is torn and strained. He is less able to control unacceptable desires or is so preoccupied with controlling them that he is less able to deal with other aspects of his life. He may continue to assert the primacy for his behavior of his agreements with others, but this primacy is under heavy attack.

On defenses and self-deception

Finally, there is the assertion that self-deception, especially unconscious self-deception, is an intrinsic characteristic of any ego defense. I shall propose that unconscious self-deception is no more a necessary property of ego defenses than is irrationality or inadequacy (Erikson and Pierce, 1968: 1031; Gur and Sackeim, 1979). Like irrationality and inadequacy, unconscious self-deception seems to me an accompaniment of high degrees of intensity in a person's inner conflicts, and of defensiveness, rather than a necessary property of defenses as such (Sackeim and Gur, 1979).

Do defenses necessarily involve self-deception? A person who represses is not telling himself a lie. In repressing, he affirms that his real, his true, allegiance is to the standard or course of action that runs counter to some objectionable impulse. And he means what he says. At the same time, however, he wants to release that impulse. It is only "on balance" that he wants to prevent its expression or, at least, its direct and explicit expression. He tends to talk, think, and act as if the impulse is not a part of what he wants to be for himself or others and he tries to prevent the impulse from contravening these commitments. It is hard to see in these circumstances that the person misleads either himself or others as to his "real" intentions.

Whether a defense involves self-deception seems to depend on the intensity of the inner conflict that it resolves (Lazarus, 1966: 237–42). If the contest between social standards and objectionable desires is sharp and close, the person is likely to try to augment his control over those desires by telling himself that the desires count for little beside his social commitments. This is misleading. If he comes to believe what he says – and such a belief may be warranted – he will no longer be self-consciously aware of the continuing attachment he has to the desires. They will come to have the status of unconscious processes (Schafer, 1976: 225–7, 234–5).

What is being claimed when something is said to be unconscious? In the case, let us say, of repression? Certainly not that the defender has "forgotten" his dangerous desires or their objects. Standard accounts of defenses stress that, in one sense, he is sharply aware of those things. What is claimed is that he has placed his desires in a context which he regards as justifiable and in which their meaning is so changed that their implications will not be acted upon in thought or overt action, and he now points to this outcome as proof of his essential goodness of character. The meanings these desires may have in other contexts are put to one side. And the person is usually not able to say how he came to this conclusion or even that he has done so or that he had to. And, like self-deception, unconsciousness seems to be more likely when people have to act under great pressure.

My point in all of this is to suggest, first, that unconsciousness and self-deception are likely to accompany high degrees of defensiveness such as the ones that are found in psychiatric patients or in anyone who experiences high degrees of inner conflict and, second, that they are not necessary features of the ego defenses themselves. One test of this second point is to see whether an assumption of unconscious self-deception is necessary to explain the concomitants and derivatives usually associated with a defense.[9]

Suppose we make such a test, employing repression as an example. We want to know the consequences of dropping the word "unconsciously" from Fenichel's description of repression as "an unconsciously purposeful forgetting or not becoming aware of internal impulses or external events . . ." Fenichel does not mean that the person who represses has actually forgotten or is actually unaware of these impulses and events, but only that he presents himself, to himself and to others, as if he had.

Consider now a man who feels greatly tempted to take bribes and who wants, even more, to be an honest public official. Suppose that he purposely arranges his activities so that it is more difficult for people to offer him bribes and so that it is easy and necessary for him to concentrate fully on his work. He knows what tempts him. He rejects and avoids it and holds fast to the lines of

---

[9] On the role of unconscious processes in the psychoneuroses and the defenses they entail, see Arlow and Brenner (1964: 26–28, 44, 53–4).

action that he claims to prefer. That seems to me repression in all respects except that of unconscious self-deception.

Certainly the pattern is not merely that of suppression: an effort to prevent a desire from appearing overtly, whatever the reasons. Rather there are the key ingredients of any ego defense (efforts to show oneself that one is acceptable despite having a desire one finds unacceptable) and ingredients of a specific form of ego defense (an effort to see that the desire is not the subject of thoughts or imaginings or of overt implementation).

Consider, next, the likely concomitants and derivatives of this man's defense against temptation as compared with the ones that clinicians have associated with repression. In this man's situation, as in repression, "although the repressed is not felt consciously [*i.e.*, is not something that the man thinks about all the time] it remains effective" Fenichel, 1945: 148). In the case of the official, it is likely that his control over temptation will sometimes be loosened by events, perhaps by an opportunity to receive money in what can seem an expression of appreciation rather than an inducement to extend a favor. In those circumstances, as in repression (Fenichel, 1945: 148):

Conflicts arise . . . that are connected with what had previously been repressed. Then there is a tendency on the part of the repressed to use the new event as an opportunity for an outlet . . .

And we would not be surprised if the official seemed not to react as might an honest but less tempted man in matters that touch upon his problem: if he failed to see the humor in jokes about bribery or if he took less than a normal interest in expensive cars or if he was exceptionally and, by most standards, unnecessarily rigid in following procedures for the letting of bids and the drawing up of contracts or if he read and re-read letters of commendation from his superiors or burdened his children with stories of how the work of honest public servants proved alone to protect the public interest. As Fenichel says (1945: 149):

repressions may either betray themselves by voids – that is, by the fact that certain ideas, feelings, attitudes that would be expected as adequate reactions to reality are actually missing – or they may betray themselves by the obsessive character with which certain compensating ideas, feelings, and attitudes that represent derivatives are clung to . . .

What we select as defining characteristics of defenses, or of anything else, depends upon what we want to explain. What I have tried to show in this example is that the consequences that we usually want to explain on the basis of repression do not require an assumption of unconscious self-deception. My proposal is that this assumption can be excluded in treating the essentials of ego defenses. That proposal may seem better justified after I have treated other defenses in later sections of this study.

The systematics of defenses

Our basic question remains: Why does a person defend as he does? Why one defense and not another? I claim that it is helpful to think of the ego defenses as grounded in social interdependence and as occasioned, and even constituted, by it. That implies that variations in the defenses should be produced in some systematic way by variations in the social relations of which they are a part.

Existing studies offer two suggestions about the systematics of the defenses. One is that defenses can usefully be clustered according to the nature of the danger with which they deal. The other is that there are hierarchical relations among defenses with some defenses being more complex or developmentally advanced than others and with some defenses implying a greater degree of pathology or distortion than others. These suggestions are consistent with the findings of several studies. If we examine these suggestions, and think about the social relations that might be associated with one or another variety of threat, or with one level in a developmental hierarchy rather than another, we can move toward an answer to our basic question. (Norma Haan, 1977, offers other bases for grouping defenses. These have proven useful for her purposes but they do not specify the systematics of relations among defenses. I discuss her categorizations in appendix 6.)

I discuss types of threat and the defenses likely to be associated with each of them in chapter 3. In that chapter, I also describe the kind of social relations likely to provide one sort of threat as against another and the indicators of those social relations that I chose for a study (reported in chapters 5 and 6) of defenses used by adolescents when relating to their parents. I follow the same pattern in chapter 4 where the focus is on a classification of defenses by their degree of complexity. When defenses are cross-classified by the type of threat that each one helps us to defuse and by their relative complexity, and when the types of threat and levels of complexity are linked to social relations thought likely to produce them, we have a theory with which better to explain why people defend as they do. Chapters 5 and 6 contain findings on the usefulness of that theory.

3 Defenses and sources of danger

Defenses associated with two types of danger

Anna Freud (1936) gives a standard account. She describes four clusters of defenses according to the sources of anxiety and danger with which they deal. The first and second of these sources receive the most attention in this chapter and in the ones that follow.

First, there are defenses against one's desires when the defenses are occasioned by anxiety about conscience or superego. They have come to be called "defenses against conscience."

Defenses are always directed against the "irruption of instincts," but a person's "reasons for feeling a particular irruption . . . to be dangerous may vary" (p. 54). Some irruptions are threatening not because they would be dangerous in themselves but because the person, having presented himself to others and himself as being trustworthy because free of certain desires, feels guilty or conscience-stricken when these very desires appear. In Anna Freud's words (1936: 55):

The characteristic point about this process is that the ego itself does not regard the impulse which it is fighting as in the least dangerous. The motive which prompts the defense is not originally its own. The instinct is regarded as dangerous because the superego prohibits its gratification and, if it [*i.e.*, the instinct] achieves its aim, it will certainly stir up trouble between the ego and the superego.

A second occasion for defense is anxiety about the reactions of others. Anna Freud calls this "objective" anxiety. She says that it is found most commonly in little children. In objective anxiety, the person does not fear his desires as such and has not defined himself, to himself, as *not* having such desires. Instead, he "regards the instincts as dangerous because those who bring the child up have forbidden their gratification and an irruption of instinct entails restrictions and the infliction or threat of punishment" (1936: 57).

A third occasion for defense is found in dread of the strength of the instincts themselves. The person fears that they will destroy or submerge his ability to function as an ego or self. Freud sees this dread as always being present in experience but, "under normal conditions, hardly noticeable." It is most likely to be seen in "full force" under rather extreme conditions in which

a sudden accession of instinctual energy threatens to upset the balance of the psychic institutions, as is normally the case, owing to physiological changes, at puberty and the climacteric, and occurs for pathological reasons at the beginning of one of the periodic advances which occur in psychosis. (1936: 60).

The fourth and final occasion for defenses is the person's anxiety concerning a lack of harmony or integration among his desires. Freud associates this state with "later life" (1936: 60). The ego, she says, has a need for synthesis: "some sort of harmony between its impulses." It has problems in deciding which "of two opposing impulses is warded off or admitted or what compromise is arrived at between them."

Anna Freud thinks that the first and second of these occasions for defense – anxiety aroused by "conscience" or by "objective" dangers – are by far the most common and, because subsequent research supports her judgment, they will be the focus of the treatment of danger in this study. We need, however, to remove an ambiguity in the distinction she draws between them. By removing it, we can improve our classifications and explanations of defenses.

If, as Freud maintains, conscience arises from our relations with other people, and if these relations involve penalties for our behaving in ways that others disapprove, then defenses against conscience must also be defenses against objective, external threats. And if, as she claims, all defenses protect us against our condemnation of ourselves for having undesired impulses, then defenses against objective anxiety are also defenses against conscience. An examination of particular defenses may help us to clarify the grounds for Freud's distinction.

To perform that examination, we need some definitions and illustrations of defenses. Figure 3.1 presents these for the ten defenses that I studied in the research described in later chapters.

First, a note about the contents of figure 3.1. None of the definitions in that figure can be considered authoritative although each catches features that are commonly associated with a particular defense. There is no such thing as a standard definition for any defense and the differences, even among definitions that are frequently cited, can be substantial (Sandler, 1962; Ornston, 1978). What clinicians generally have in mind by a given defense is more a vaguely bounded roster of attributes than a set of "formal, necessary and sufficient criteria for category membership" (Rosch, 1978: 35). They regard formal definitions, or selected illustrations, as being more or less close to some prototypes – to relatively clear cases of category membership – rather than as definitive (Cantor, Smith, French, and Mezzich, 1980; Palmer, 1978: 288-90).

Figure 3.1. *Some definitions and illustrations of ten defenses*

Denial – Denial of present or past facts and feelings that would be painful to acknowledge and focusing instead on the benign or pleasant. Basic formula: there is no pain, no anticipation of pain, no danger, no conflict. (Haan, 1977: 305)
From 1927 onwards, Freud's elaboration of the notion . . . relates essentially to the special case of fetishism. . . . he shows how the fetishist . . . simultaneously disavows and acknowledges the fact of feminine castration. . . . (Laplanche and Pontalis, 1973: 119)

Displacement – the attachment of an affect to something other than its proper object . . . *e.g.*, hatred of a father is attached to a walking stick used by the father; anger aroused by punishment is transferred to a pet . . . (English and English, 1958: 158)

Doubt and indecision – Subject is unable to resolve ambiguity. He doubts the validity of his own perceptions or judgments, is unable to make up his mind, and is unable to commit himself to a course of action or presentation of incidents. He hopes that problems will solve themselves or that someone will solve them for him. He states his problem and then qualifies it to death. He worries about whether he has answered questions correctly and is uncertain about whether he has treated others the way they should be treated. His makes strenuous efforts to avoid uncertain situations because he is aware that he becomes easily stalemated. (Haan, 1977: 303)

Intellectualization – analysis of a problem in purely intellectual terms, to the neglect or exclusion of affective or practical considerations. It is often a defensive reaction to avoid affect. A person will endeavor to name and define instead of avowing the feeling: "I have an Oedipus complex" instead of "I hate my father." (English and English, 1958: 268)

Isolation – a process similar in effect to repression, but differing in that the underlying impulse or wish is consciously recognized, although its relation to present behavior is not . . . (English and English, 1958: 279) particularly evident in psycho-analytic treatment . . . (subjects who make a radical separation between their analysis and their life, between a specific train of thought and the session as a whole, or between a particular idea and the ideas and emotions surrounding it). (Laplanche and Pontalis, 1973: 232)

Projection – The process of ascribing to others one's own acknowledged desires or faults. This is presumed to be a defense against a sense of guilt or inadequacy. (English and English, 1958: 412)

Rationalization – the process of concocting plausible reasons to account for one's practices or beliefs when these are challenged by oneself or

Figure 3.1 (*cont.*)

---

others; or the tissue of justifications thus produced. No conscious criterion warns us that we are thus rallying to the defense with reasons unconnected with the true motivations; we appear to ourselves to believe that we are giving real grounds. (English and English, 1958: 438–9)

Reaction formation – establishment of a trait or a regular pattern of behavior that is directly opposed to a strong unconscious trend; or the pattern itself . . . Development of aggressive behavior as a means of repressing or denying fear, or of great sympathy as a means of repressing sadistic impulses, are examples . . . (English and English, 1958: 449)

Regression – Subject resorts to evasive, wistful, demanding, dependent, ingratiating, non-age appropriate behavior to avoid responsibility, aggression, and unpleasant demands from others and self. He encourages others to indulge him . . . (Haan, 1977: 304)

Repression – the exclusion of specific psychological activities or contents from conscious awareness by a process of which the individual is not directly aware. (English and English, 1958: 458)

All of this means that the materials in figure 3.1 must be taken as provisional. They may suffice for our immediate purposes, but will have to be enriched before trying, in later chapters, to specify the likely range of meanings that experienced clinicians have in mind as they classify people's defenses.

That said, we can continue with the grounds for Anna Freud's distinction between defenses against conscience and against objective anxiety. I begin with the latter because the bases for that category are clearer.

In Anna Freud's discussion, the classification of a defense depends on (1) whether a prohibited desire was or was not expressed directly toward the person or persons who were its target(s) and (2) whether it was or was not expressed in a manner likely to impair relations with the target person(s) (Miller and Swanson, 1960: 194–255). (Figure 3.2 notes the possible combinations of these two conditions and the defenses that *can* meet the criteria of one or another combination.) In her thinking, defenses against objective anxiety are those in which a prohibited impulse was expressed directly and in a manner likely to jeopardize relations with other people. In figure 3.2, this is the combination given under IIB.

As indicated in figure 3.2, projection is often placed among the defenses against objective anxiety. So, if less frequently, are denial, rationalization, and regression. In these four defenses, the person can express deviant impulses

Figure 3.2. *Some clusters of ego defenses by the nature of the defensive situation*

Defensive situation	Illustrative defenses
I. Deviant impulse not expressed directly toward target	
A. But expressed in a manner likely to protect relations with others	Displacement Reaction formation
B. Impulse not expressed directly or indirectly	Repression Doubt and indecision
II. Deviant impulse expressed directly toward target	
A. In a manner likely to protect relations with others	Intellectualization Isolation
B. In a manner likely to impair relations with others	Projection Rationalization Denial Regression

directly and in socially unacceptable ways and can also justify this behavior. Thus, in projection (see the definition and illustration in figure 3.1), he may charge others with having faults like his own, or faults that are greater. By that means he inhibits them from blaming him too greatly and/or he trivializes the importance of his own failings. In denial – or better, "disavowal" (Laplanche and Pontalis, 1973: 118–21) – he retains questionable desires, or pursues a questionable course of action, on the grounds that, if properly understood, his wishes or behavior will not be judged dangerous to him or to the relations he has with others. In rationalization, he tries to show that he behaved as he did for reasons that do not call into question his solidarity with others, that the meaning of his act makes it socially innocent. In regression, he avoids or abandons a course of action that is prohibited, but he demands that other people, in turn, take care of him and indulge him in expressing some of his other desires. By this means, he demonstrates his basic dependence upon, and solidarity with, other people. Looking back over all four of the defenses just described, we can see that in none of them does the defender acknowledge that his desires or behavior were, in themselves, unjustifiable.

In what sense do these four defenses ward off "objective" anxiety? Surely not in the sense that the danger encountered is purely external. The person himself questions what he has done and believes that this question must be answered satisfactorily. If it is not, he will be self-condemned as well as unacceptable to others. These defenses enable a warding off of objective anxiety in that the person, having expressed a prohibited desire, directly and in a manner that he and others question, gives priority to restoring his relations with others and himself. In doing so, he treats other people as, in part, the keepers of his conscience. Their acceptance of his conduct is one condition for his being acceptable to himself. The objective danger is in their rejection of his actions.

The six other defenses in figure 3.1 are frequently treated as defenses against conscience. They have in common that the person tries not to let an impulse threaten his solidarity with others and he does this in order to be acceptable to others and to himself. Anna Freud suggests that a person is likely to use one of these justifications when he views a socially prohibited desire as, perhaps, wrong in itself; when, in her phrase, "the superego prohibits its gratification." The person then tries not to express that desire or not to express it directly.

These justifications are defenses against "conscience," not in the sense that the person anticipates no external threat but in the sense that he gives priority to fulfilling his obligations to others by maintaining, and not jeopardizing, his solidarity with them and, by so doing, he feels acceptable to himself. He behaves as he thinks one should and, in that way, demonstrates his commitments.

In two of these six defenses, doubt and repression, there is almost no expression of the forbidden impulse. The person who defends by means of doubt and indecision avoids situations and choices in which prohibited desires might be expressed. If avoidance is impossible, he tries not to take any definitive action. In repression, he goes further in preventing the forbidden desire from passing over into action: he excludes it even from self-conscious awareness.

In two other defenses, displacement and reaction formation, the impulse may be expressed, but only indirectly. In displacement, it is expressed toward a target that is not prohibited; in reaction formation, the "energy" associated with the forbidden desire is "drawn off" by the person's energetic pursuit of acceptable courses of action.

In the last two defenses, intellectualization and isolation, there can be some direct expression of a prohibited desire, but only in so qualified a way that it is not something anyone need take seriously. Thus, in intellectualization, the person may mention this desire as one of a host of considerations he must review in deciding what to do, but he stresses that, whatever he does, it will be right and proper. Or, in isolation, the person says, in effect, that, although he has a forbidden desire, he will not allow it to become a significant factor in the social relations he wants to preserve: the desire "is deprived of its affective cathexis; so that what remains in consciousness is nothing but its ideational content, which is perfectly colourless and is judged to be unimportant" (Freud, 1909: 196).

Social sources of danger

Anna Freud's typology has taken hold among researchers and most of the subsequent studies of the reasons for people's defending as they do have distinguished sources of anxiety about conscience from sources of anxiety about "objective" dangers. In all of these studies, the sources were sought in social relations. In most of these studies, the people being investigated were children or adolescents and the social relations giving rise to anxiety were those between the youngsters and their parents. My own research also deals with defenses made by adolescents and with sources of anxiety that adolescents encounter at home. I will now describe the procedures I used in identifying those sources of anxiety.

Sources of anxiety about objective dangers

Everyone has desires that he finds unobjectionable and expresses directly only to discover that people to whom he is committed take his behavior amiss. That, as we saw, is the situation Anna Freud believes conducive to the use of defenses against objective anxiety. The likelihood of a person's defending in that situation presumably depends upon the degree to which people accept him despite behavior they find objectionable. It is certainly the case, for example, that parents differ in their acceptance of such behavior by their children. If they think that some degree of deviant behavior is a necessary part of a young person's finding his way to a fulfilling and acceptable style of life, or if they see it as occasionally necessary for catharsis, then they can accept him and his conduct. They will, of course, want to see signs that he has a basic commitment to "proper" social relations. In defenses like isolation or intellectualization, the youngster can give some direct expression to his desires and can, simultaneously, indicate his basic solidarity with his parents.

If, on the other hand, the parents are less tolerant of conduct they dislike, focusing on what seems to them the negative features of a youngster's behavior and judging him primarily according to his current embodiment of their preferred standards of conduct, then his objectionable behavior creates a rupture in his solidarity with them and his defenses must justify the restoration of solidarity. (Such defenses can include projection, denial, rationalization, and regression.)

In my own research on the sources of defenses, I have used two indices to distinguish these two styles of parental response. The first catches parental permissiveness or acceptance of the direct expression of a child's desires including those that are possibly deviant. The second reflects the parents' positive support for such direct expressions.

Permit direct expression of desires
This index was developed by Eliane Aerts in connection with her own study of families in the Institute's samples (Aerts, 1979). She instructed coders to rate interviews with parents according to what she called "the respect" that parents accord their children as whole persons.

When they describe their children, parents may or may not predominately use comparisons with other children or with their image of the ideal child. . . .

As Aerts' detailed instructions to coders indicate, the central question is how parents regard their children's expression of tastes and desires they do not approve. Raters were to indicate each parent's most characteristic manner of describing his/her children:

- Describes more in comparison with other children in the family or outside it than as a distinctive individual.
- Describes more in terms of his embodiment of, or deviance from, standards thought desirable for children of his age and sex than as a distinctive individual.
- Describes in a way respectful of his integrity as a person, a human being: his disappointments, his enthusiasms, his uncertainties, his attempts to make judgments, form opinions, be himself.

The focus of Aerts' coding is her third alternative: respect for the child's integrity as a person. If this alternative is checked, it means that the parents accept the child despite, and including, his sometimes objectionable conduct. If either of the first two alternatives is checked, the parents accept the child only if his behavior fits standards that the parents believe important and the parents honor the child's struggles to develop as a person only if they are expressed in such approved courses of action.

For my own purposes, I treated Aerts' first two alternatives as one and combined her ratings for mothers and fathers into a single code to indicate whether both parents, one, or neither seemed respectful of their children's integrity as persons: accepting them even though their conduct was sometimes undesirable. (The agreement between Aerts' coders in producing the ratings as used in my reworking of her code is high: $r(90) = 0.87$, $p < 0.01$).

Support expression of desires
This index is based upon the interviews with the parents. These were coded for the degree to which members of the family give one another spontaneous and

sensitive help. Each family was placed in one of two categories based on a combination of ratings from the interviews with the parents: those in which the ratings from the interviews with both parents fall in categories 3 or 4 below and those in which they do not.

1. Members of this family serve the needs and interests of others only when they are *pressed* to do so.
2. Members of this family serve the needs and interests of other members when they are *requested* to do so.
3. Members of this family provide for individuals' needs in their family *as these needs appear*. They do not anticipate these needs, but, once a need becomes apparent, they give freely and willingly of their own resources.
4. Individuals in this family take the initiative in providing for the needs and in promoting the interests of the others. They *anticipate* others' needs and provide for them on the basis of this foresight and forethought.

The Spearman-Brown reliability coefficient for this rating (based on the composite scores of the parents as judged by two independent coders) is 0.90.

I thought that parents rated on these two indices as permissive or supportive of the direct expression of desires would be more likely than others to have children who used such defenses as isolation and intellectualization (section IIA of figure 3.2). Children reared by parents who received the opposite ratings should be more likely to use defenses against objective anxiety (section IIB of figure 3.2).

Sources of anxiety about conscience

Everyone has interests and desires that he finds unacceptable or, at least, unacceptable if expressed directly. If he finds these desires unacceptable, other people are likely to have the same reaction. That is the situation Anna Freud describes as the source of defenses against conscience.

The direct expression of such desires is not acceptable. Whether they must go unexpressed or can be expressed indirectly will depend, in part, on the degree to which other people with whom the person wants to preserve a social relationship will permit at least an indirect expression. Parents, for example, may judge such interests and desires as normal and even, in some measure, desirable in their children or they may not. Thus, some parents assume that children differ from one another in their interests and they encourage their own children to define and pursue those personal interests. The parents may not approve of all of a child's interests or desires but may, nevertheless, see even objectionable desires as valuable because they are a part of the child's moving toward maturity. They ask only that the child make clear that his primary commitment is to the maintenance of social solidarity; that he avoid direct and socially disruptive expressions of his feelings. Defenses such as displacement and reaction formation can provide for such indirect and socially acceptable expressions of possibly objectionable desires.

There are parents who do not encourage children's pursuit of personal and possibly objectionable interests. If that is so, a child has little choice in defending except to prevent any expression of his feelings, direct or indirect. Such defenses as doubt and indecision and repression can then be appropriate.

An index catching these distinctions – *approve individuated interests* – came to light in the course of an earlier study of the adolescents in the Institute's samples (Swanson, 1974). On that occasion, I had the help of Norma Haan and Marjorie Honzik in scouring the Institute's files for indicators of warmth and trust in the relations between parents and children. One factor that emerged from a varimax factor analysis of those indicators seems to tap the parental practices just described. It seems to reflect the parents' trust of their children, the degree to which the parents themselves pursue personal interests and encourage the children to do likewise, and the children's acceptance of their own individuality. The parents do not see the children's exercise of free choice in these matters as threatening social solidarity. Rather they seek to foster this form of a child's individuality (Lukes, 1973).

Three indicators have high loadings on this factor: both parents have their own interests and pursue them; the mother trusts the children to be able to act on their own without close supervision; and the children are judged as "not giving" – that is, the children are comfortable with pursuing their own needs and interests even if, on occasion, this means giving lesser weight to the needs and interests of others. High scores on this factor indicate parental approval for individuated interests and individuated styles of life in children and their willingness to bear the risk that some of these desires will be "deviant".

I interpreted high scores on this index as representing conditions that would make more likely a child's use of defenses like displacement and reaction formation (section 1A in figure 3.2) whereas low scores would signify conditions that would make more likely the use of such defenses as repression or doubt and indecision (section IB of figure 3.2).

We might wonder whether there is some relationship among the three indices just described. The only significant relationship is that between *permit direct expression of desires* and *approve individuated interests* and it is modest: $r(94) = 0.21$, $p < 0.02$. Given the high reliability of these two indices, this correlation suggests that these indices catch rather different aspects of the parents' orientations towards their children.

Other sources of anxiety about objective dangers and conscience

Previous studies of children's defenses against conscience and objective anxiety have found them associated with three facts about the children's parents: the methods they use in disciplining children, their socio-economic status, and the entrepreneurial or bureaucratic setting in which the principal breadwinner works. These earlier studies have used a simple dichotomy of defenses against conscience or objective anxiety rather than the four-fold typology presented in figure 3.2. As a result, their definitions of anxiety about conscience or objective dangers do not always coincide with mine. I decided, however, to add the three independent variables found important in those studies to the ones already listed in this chapter and to explore their power to predict the defenses of children in my own sample.

Methods of discipline

Comprehensive reviews of the relevant research (Aronfreed, 1968; Hoffman, 1970; Maccoby and Martin, 1983; Parke and Slaby, 1983; Yarrow, Waxler, and Chapman, 1983) have shown that certain methods of disciplining children relate to the strength and form of a child's conscience. Miller and Swanson (1969: 213–55) report associations between these methods of discipline and an adolescent's use of certain defenses.

The principal associations are with methods of discipline that Hoffman (1970) calls "power assertion" and "induction." In power assertion, parents control the child through capitalizing on their own superior physical power or their control over material resources. In induction, they give explanations or reasons for requiring the child to change his behavior (for example, the parents point out the physical requirements that the situation sets for appropriate behavior or they speak of the consequences that the child's conduct will have for other people or for the child himself). Hoffman also includes under induction the parents' appealing to the youngster's pride or to his strivings for mastery and his desire to be grown up and to show concern for others. Hoffman's survey of existing research reveals that the use of induction, especially when the parents are clearly affectionate toward the child, is correlated with the child's exhibiting an internalized standard. This means that the child has a moral standard that he experiences as his own and perhaps as shared with some other persons or some group and it means that he tries to live by this standard even when there are no external dangers from his flouting it.

Miller and Swanson (1960: 213–55) discovered in their sample of adolescent boys that repression, a defense against conscience, was associated with mothers' employing induction as a method of discipline and with their rewarding their sons on frequent occasions. By contrast, boys tended to use denial, frequently considered a defense against objective anxiety, if their mothers used power assertion as a means of discipline and if the mothers rewarded their sons only occasionally. (Miller and Swanson also found repression more likely among boys from middle-class homes and found denial to be more common among boys of lower verbal intelligence and among those from working-class families.)

In the present study, information on the disciplining of children was available in a questionnaire given to the parents. They were asked an open-ended question: "When you think your children are doing or are about to do something wrong, what do (or did) you usually do?" That was followed by a list of methods of discipline and the parents were asked to indicate the frequency with which they used each of them. I transformed these ratings into ipsative scores in order to remove the effects of the frequency with which parents disciplined children irrespective of the methods that they used. These scores were then subjected to a varimax factor analysis. (Appendix 2 gives the procedure by which the ipsative ratings were derived and were then transformed to permit a factor analysis.)

Three significant factors emerged. The first has high loadings from three methods of discipline: "discuss and examine the various aspects of the issue with them," "point out the way other people could be affected," and the parent's saying that he does *not* tell his children "how angry I'll be if they do wrong." The second factor is defined primarily by two styles of discipline: "stop them, control them" and the parent's *not* telling his children "how pleased I'll be if they do right." The third factor has high loadings from three disciplinary procedures: "attempt to teach them what's right and wrong," "tell them how pleased I'll be if they do right," and the parent's *not* telling the child "about the bad things that could happen" to him if he continues to behave as he has. In Hoffman's terms, the first and third factors catch aspects of induction, namely, reasoning and positive appeals, and the second factor indicates the use of power assertion.

The family's economic position

Socio-economic status (SES)
As we saw in the previous section, there is evidence associating a child's use of defenses against conscience with his being reared in a middle-class home and evidence associating his use of defenses against objective anxiety with his being

reared by working-class parents. These correlations are usually interpreted to mean that a family's socio-economic status leads the parents to have orientations toward rearing children which are, in turn, conducive to the children's use of some defenses rather than others. SES was therefore taken as an independent variable for my work, the ratings being based upon Hollingshead and Redlich's (1958) criteria.

Entrepreneurial or bureaucratic status
Miller and Swanson (1958: 120–45) show that many of the differences found between families of different social classes in their socialization of conscience are produced by differences between what they call "entrepreneurial" middle-class families and "bureaucratized" working-class families. The distinction between entrepreneurial and bureaucratized families derives from the setting in which the breadwinner works and it cuts across considerations of socio-economic status. In Miller and Swanson's terms (and as applied to families like all of those in the present study – families in which the parents are native-born and were reared in a city), occupations are entrepreneurial in the case of persons who are self-employed or who obtain half or more of their incomes from profits, fees, or commissions, or who work in organizations having fewer than three levels of supervision, or whose primary responsibility on the job is that of selling the product or service or, more generally, of obtaining customers or capital (Miller and Swanson, 1958: 67–80; 1960: 63–6). They regard all other occupations as relatively bureaucratized.

As Miller and Swanson picture them, entrepreneurial occupations – especially entrepreneurial middle-class occupations – foster higher levels of responsible independence and initiative than do bureaucratized occupations *and also* promote a person's progressive control over his possibly deviant impulses.[1] Miller and Swanson suggest that entrepreneurial parents, especially entrepreneurial middle-class parents, are more likely than others to instill this style of behavior in their children. As is obvious, such a pattern of conduct and socialization is particularly compatible with defenses like those in rows IA and IIA of figure 3.2: defenses in which approval of individuality and even acceptance of deviance are assumed. This pattern is least compatible with defenses like those in row IIB of that figure: defenses which imply a direct expression of a deviant impulse and also a lack of respect for the child's integrity as a whole person (Miller and Swanson, 1960: 390–1). For these reasons, the occupations of families in my sample were coded as entrepreneurial or bureaucratic and that distinction was taken into account, along with

[1] Two points about these findings that seem unclear to Kohn (1971).

socio-economic status, in looking for the social correlates of children's defenses.

A note on the completeness of data

Information was not sufficient to code all 118 families on all of the indices reviewed in this chapter. The indices and the number of cases for which a code seemed possible are as follows:

1. Permit direct expression of desires   94
2. Support direct expression of desires   111
3. Approve individuated interests   114
4. Methods of discipline   74
5. Socio-economic status   118
6. Entrepreneurial or bureaucratic status   108

4 Social foundations of complexity in defense

Ego defenses are helpfully classified by the nature of the danger with which they deal – danger from objective threats or conscience – and by the complexity of the considerations they take into account.[1] Roy Schafer (1968: 60) provides a fresh statement of the psychoanalytic view of these differences in complexity:

The hierarchic conception of defences as being layered, of a series of defenses from the most archaic ones to the easily accessible preconscious ones, refers to *a continuum of conflicted positions*. It is this continuum of conflicted positions that is the empirical clinical datum on which defence theory is based. Freud's relatively early formulation of the matter still holds, I believe:

. . . (We) shall do well . . . to assume that to every transition from one system to that immediately above it (that is, every advance to a higher stage of psychic organization) there corresponds a new censorship.

Schafer's statement, like Freud's, mixes together the complexity of the considerations that defenses treat and the intensity of the conflicts they are employed to mediate. In this chapter I focus on the first of these concerns, presenting some relevant theory and the operational definitions used in my own research when employing that theory. I take up intensity of conflicts in chapter 6.

The argument in this chapter can be summarized as follows:

- Defenses are our efforts to restore ourselves to acceptability in our own eyes and in other people's.
- To be effective in defending, we must take account of the actual social relations we have with others and ourselves. This means, first, that we must deal with the disruption of these relations by our deviant desires or acts and, second, that we can maintain or repair social relations only if we build upon the specific grounds for social solidarity that these social relations afford.

---

[1] In recent years, there have been several attempts to systematize the defenses according to their formal properties (Chandler, Paget, and Koch, 1978; Holland, 1973; Moser, von Zeppelin, and Schneider, 1969; Smelser, 1967, 1984; Suppes and Warren, 1975). None of these seems to generate a systematic treatment of most of the defenses that are commonly discussed in the clinical literature and none seems to provide a treatment of defenses that preserves either their critical substantive features or their status as social accounts.

- Given these assumptions, an appropriate defense will be one that is congruent with the nature of the strains on solidarity in a particular social relationship and with the grounds for solidarity which that relationship affords.
- Appropriate defenses will vary in cognitive complexity because the social relations concerned also vary in complexity.
- This leads us to look to difference in the complexity of social relations for conditions that engender, or make likely, the use of defenses that differ in complexity.

I move, in this chapter, in five steps. First, I review evidence and arguments suggesting that it is fruitful to view defenses as being arranged in some sort of hierarchy. Second, I suggest a hierarchy of social relations that might be associated with the hierarchy among defenses. Third, I identify main forms of social solidarity and strain associated with each level of this hierarchy of social relations. Fourth, I suggest how the nature of solidarity and strain at each level determines the ego defenses that will be appropriate in justifying deviant impulses and conduct. Finally, I present the indices that I used to get at the hierarchy of social relations within the families in my sample and to relate it operationally to the defenses used by children reared in these families.

Hierarchies of defenses

One way to arrange the defenses is by the level of cognitive and affective development that each implies (Bertini, 1960; Bogo, Winget, and Gleser, 1970; Chandler, Paget, and Koch, 1978; Donovan, Hague, and O'Leary, 1975; Engel, 1962; Friedman, 1967; Gardner, Holzman, Klein, Linton, and Spence, 1959; Gedo and Goldberg, 1973: 89–100; Goodenough, 1976; Haan, 1977: 54–8; Lichtenberg and Slap, 1972; Luborsky, Blinder, and Schimek, 1965; Miller and Swanson, 1960: 194–212, 256–71; Minard and Mooney, 1969; Schimek, 1968; Smith and Danielsson, 1982; Whiteman, 1967, 1970; Witkin and Goodenough, 1976). Another is to arrange them by the degree of distortion that they entail (Gill, 1963; Lampl-de Groot, 1957; Loewald, 1952; Menninger, 1963; Miller and Swanson, 1960; Schafer, 1968: 60; Vaillant, 1971, 1977).

To use a defense like intellectualization, a person must be well advanced in cognitive development. He must be able to hold up his behavior while conducting a systematic review of many possible courses of action and while considering the consequences of each one. He must match these consequences, singly and in combinations, against his desires and his responsibilities. A defense like denial requires less ability. The person needs only to reject the idea that his personal limitations, or any problems posed by his situation, will prevent his realizing his desires. Children of two or three can perhaps deny but intellectualization is likely to appear only in late childhood or adolescence.

Most of the defenses can be arranged in a rough order according to the level of development that each seems to entail. There are, however, anomalies. Anna Freud (1936: 51–2) calls attention to the case of repression and to turning against the self:

Repression consists in the withholding or expulsion of an idea or affect from the conscious ego. It is meaningless to speak of repression where the ego is still merged with the id . . . Accordingly, . . . repression . . . could not be employed until relatively late in the process of development . . . Such processes as regression, reversal, or turning round upon the self are probably independent of the stage which the psychic structure has reached and as old as the instincts themselves, or at least as old as the conflict between instinctual impulses and any hindrance which they may encounter on their way to gratification . . .

But this . . . does not accord with our experience that the earliest manifestations of neurosis which we observe in young children are hysterical symptoms, of whose connection with repression there can be no doubt; on the other hand, the genuine masochistic phenomena, which result from turning round of the instinct upon the self, are very rarely met with in earliest childhood . . .

More generally, the level of complexity of a defense consists in the range of considerations that the defense takes into account in an orderly fashion (Chandler, Paget, and Koch, 1978; Elkind, 1976; Whitman, 1967, 1970). In defending, we justify our acceptability as participants in social interdependence. We develop as social participants by learning to deal in an integrated way with relations of interdependence in which our rights and responsibilities are increasingly diverse and differentiated. Thus a greater complexity in defenses is required and fostered as we come to justify our participation in more diverse and differentiated social relations. Figure 4.1 notes some steps in this progression. It draws upon an informal coding of clinical discussions for its placement of defenses. (Many defenses are described as having both simple and complex forms. The more complex form is used in placing a defense in figure 4.1.) These placements will be given a firmer theoretical grounding later in this chapter and in chapter 5.

In at least one defense, doubt and indecision, a person exhibits interdependence by neither acting upon his suspect desires nor giving them up. He stays with the group in anticipation that some of his needs will somehow be satisfied and that he will be spared the consequences of choosing. In another defense, regression, a person exhibits interdependence chiefly by staying in the group and turning to other members to ask that they meet their commitment to accept him as he is, his personal needs included. As the figure indicates, it is

Figure 4.1. *A developmental hierarchy of ego defenses*

	Person takes responsibility for:				
Defense	Staying with others in this group for the satisfaction of his needs	Acting responsibly	Fulfilling obligations and other desires while keeping up social solidarity*	Fulfilling obligations and other desires in integrated actions that minimize threats to social solidarity	Pursuing an integrated style of life across diverse situations while minimizing threats to social solidarity
Intellectualization	+	+	+	+	+
Reaction formation	+	+	+	+	+
Isolation	+	+	+	+	
Projection	+	+	+	+	
Rationalization	+	+	+	+	
Displacement	+	+	+		
Repression	+	+			
Denial	+	+			
Doubt and indecision	+				
Regression	+				

*Adapted from Miller and Swanson (1960: 207)

considered an advance in development when we learn – as in repression or denial – to go further and to take responsibility for acting responsibly. It is again an advance if, in acting responsibly, we learn not only how to meet the obligations that are clearly ours but also to pursue our other interests in a manner that maintains or restores our solidarity with other people. That ability seems implicit in a defense like displacement. Our level of development is accounted even higher if we are able skillfully to integrate our fulfillment of obligations with our pursuit of other interests so that both are accomplished by the same course of action and with a minimum of threat to social solidarity. That level of skill appears implicit in such defenses as isolation, higher forms of rationalization, and, as I shall argue in chapter 5, in projection. Finally, it is taken as an indication of still greater ability in interdependence if we are able, as in intellectualization or some forms of reaction formation, to pursue general styles of life in which all of the skills and distinctions already mentioned are employed across many and diverse situations.

Defenses can also be ranked by the degree of the "distortion of reality" which they entail. The argument is, first, that the cognitively more complex defenses are less distorting and second, that higher levels of anxiety make it impossible for an individual to employ the more complex defenses because these defenses require him to be sufficiently composed if he is to make elaborate distinctions and to exercise a refined self-control.

Hedegard (1968) has found in a review of the literature that clinicians are in rough agreement about the relative amount of "distortion" typical of the several defenses and she has shown in an experiment that the likelihood of a person's using a more distorting defense increases with the amount of anxiety experienced. To measure defenses, she used a modification of the Defense Preference Inventory constructed by Blum (1956). Subjects were asked to look at pictures showing events in the life of a dog named Blacky (Blum, 1949) and to choose from a number of statements that tell what Blacky is thinking and feeling. There is, for example, a picture of Blacky watching his mother and father as they pay loving attention to Blacky's sibling, Tippy. The subject is asked to choose from among a set of statements, each statement being designed to represent a particular defense or the absence of defense (Hedegard, 1968: 37–40):

Here Blacky is feeling so angry and jealous he would like to physically hurt Tippy. (no defense)
Though Blacky is quite angry at being left out, he feels that he ought to join the group and pay attention to Tippy also. (reversal)
Blacky is pleased to see Mama and Papa being affectionate to Tippy, since he feels that Tippy deserves a turn at getting affection. (reaction formation)

As Blacky watches Mama, Papa, and Tippy together, he is sure that right now he couldn't care less what happens to any of them. (isolation)

Blacky believes that insight into his own jealousy of Tippy will enable him to handle himself better in competitive situations later on. (intellectualization)

It seems to Blacky now that Tippy must be confessing to Mama and Papa feelings of envy toward Blacky. (projection)

Right now Blacky is feeling so furious and jealous of Tippy that he even feels like angrily kicking the stones in front of him. (displacement)

Discouraged and frustrated with himself as he is, Blacky feels he doesn't deserve the attention Tippy is receiving. (regressive denial)

Hedegard trained six male undergraduates as hypnotic subjects. In the course of training each subject, and while he was under hypnosis, Hedegard administered the Blacky pictures. She asked the subject to tell, for each picture, some life experience of which he was reminded. After all the pictures had been presented, the subject's responses were reviewed to pick one which seemed a prototype of "an anxiety experience, *i.e.*, the subjective experience of internal discomfort and fear together with uncertainty about the outcome of the situation." In a later session, the subject, again under hypnosis, and now connected to a psychogalvanometer, was asked to relive this experience.

Galvanic skin responses, invariably large to huge, were noted. He was then told that this experience was called "anxiety" and that he could also experience this feeling in connection with the light going on . . . in the room. Since the light was controlled by a rheostat this could be made a continuous process. He practiced this, with the practice monitored by GSR recording and his subjective reports of his experiences. Each S(ubject) reacted with what seemed to be extremely high levels of anxiety.

Next, he was told he could experience different levels of anxiety associated with different levels of illumination in the room. These levels were the numbers 0, 40, 70, and 100 on the rheostat. This was practiced and repeated until S's responses were clearly differentiated. Again, GSR changes, E(xperimenter)'s observation, and S's subjective report were used as criteria of the success. The anxiety responses were then attached to any presentation of the numbers alone. Finally the cues were made effective during the waking state by posthypnotic suggestions, for which S had amnesia. The levels of anxiety were described as follows:

    0   lack of anxiety, feeling neutral
   40   moderate anxiety
   70   fairly strong anxiety
 100   very strong anxiety (Hedegard, 1968: 48)

During the actual data collection, the subject was awake. He was shown each Blacky picture and the Defense Preference sentences under varying degrees of illumination of the room. The order of presentation of all these stimuli was varied across subjects.

Hedegard found (1968: 67) that, when experimentally indicated anxiety was low, subjects employed intellectualization or a mild form of displacement, reaction formation, or isolation. Under moderate anxiety, they chose a sentence indicating projection or one of the more distorting forms of isolation. Under high anxiety, they selected extreme forms of projection or displacement or chose denial or regression. Reference to figure 4.1 shows that the choices made under increasing anxiety tend to be of defenses at the lower levels of complexity. Hedegard herself (1968: 34–5) notes that projection is the principal exception. It is a relatively complex defense which tends to appear under high anxiety.[2]

Hierarchies of defenses and social relations

Figure 4.1 give us a hierarchy of defenses according to their cognitive complexity. A similar ordering of defenses emerges from clinical observations and from systematic research such as that of Hedegard. This second ordering is inspired by the notion that defenses differ in the degree to which they distort reality. It proves, however, to depend almost entirely upon assumptions concerning differences in cognitive complexity for the placement of defenses. (The placement of projection is the one exception.)

Why does a person who seems to be able to use all of the defenses use those at one level of complexity rather than those at another level? (This is likely to be an older child or an adolescent or adult.)

In the argument given at the beginning of this chapter, I suggested that people use defenses that are appropriate to the social relations in which they are trying to justify themselves and that, other things being equal, they will use cognitively complex defenses in connection with socially complex relations. Social relations are more complex as they entail more distinctions and differentiations in the ways their participants relate to one another and perhaps in the development of broadened principles by which those many relations can be centrally integrated: can be coordinated and controlled (Selman, 1980: 142–7). Cognitive activities are more complex as they involve the making of more discriminations and differentiations and the integration of

---

[2] Miller and Swanson (1960: 256–71) report that the use by adolescent boys of defenses of the sort that Hedegard associates with low or moderate anxiety is more likely among middle- than among working-class subjects. Chandler, Pager, and Koch (1978), who make a Piagetian analysis of the cognitive complexity of defenses, find that, whereas most children who can perform concrete operations can detect and understand such defenses as repression and denial, it is generally the children who can perform formal operations who can detect and understand rationalization, displacement, and turning against the self and even more complex defenses such as projection and introjection.

these distinctions on some common grounds. It would be surprising, therefore, if justifications responsive to the properties of complex social relations did not require a greater cognitive complexity.

A hierarchy of complexity in social relations has come to light from studies of the growth and development of groups, both large and small. I will describe that hierarchy as pictured in those studies, show how it can be used to identify levels of social relations that exist simultaneously within an established group, and suggest its connections with the complexity of the ego defenses that participants are likely to use. I conclude this chapter by describing the methods I used to identify different levels of social relations in the families I studied, levels I then related to the defenses employed by adolescents who were reared in those families.

Stages of collective development

Consider the life course of a self-developing group as an example of collective growth, that is, an example of increasing complexity in social relations. Self-developing groups occur frequently and spontaneously. At times they are purposely created to serve the interests of psychotherapy, formal education, the facilitation of their members' "personal growth," or the ability of management in a formal organization to deal with novel problems. The self-developing groups that have been studied most often are found in universities and take the form of clinical courses in the analysis of groups and interpersonal relations (Farrell, 1976; Tuckman, 1965). I use these latter groups as a convenient source of illustrations.

In the typical case, the number of students in such a university course is limited to about 20. The instructor begins by giving his students a list of materials to be read during the term and the dates on which they will be discussed in class. Some of the materials are theoretical interpretations of group growth and process. Some are case studies of specific groups. One of these case studies is assigned as the subject to be discussed at the second meeting of the class and students are asked to determine what is happening in the group under study and why its members are behaving as they are. The instructor then says that the events which take place in the class itself are also important materials for the members to analyze: "Part of our task will be to understand what we find ourselves doing as a group, to understand why we do it as we do" (Mills, 1964: 11–12). He announces the dates for examinations and papers. That done, and except for "brief answers to questions concerning assignments, his presentation of further assignments, and his occasional Socratic questions directing the students' attention to a further examination of

Figure 4.2. *Stages of collective development*

VIII. Administrative system
 VII. Regime
  VI. Political community
   V. Constitutional order
  IV. Work group
 III. Charismatic center
  II. Social interdependence
   I. Interdependence

their own group," the instructor falls silent for the remainder of the term. That is the setting in which collective development begins.

The students may feel puzzled or abandoned but most of them stay with the course and try to make it work for others and themselves. That in itself is important for collective development. It signifies their need for one another and for the relationship in which all participate. It signifies willingness to take actions that may prove necessary and to run the attendant risks. In the words of figure 4.2 (where some main stages of collective development are listed), it constitutes the students' acceptance of their interdependence.

Interdependence is, of course, a fact of their situation and some students recognize that fact at once and accept it. Others acknowledge their interdependence only after failures and confrontations that are caused by their attempts to move ahead on their own.

The second stage in figure 4.2 marks the students' discovery that they are socially interdependent and their acceptance of that relationship. To get what they severally want when interdependent, they must develop arrangements through which they can work together. Whether they know it or not, they must develop a plan or, as I called it in chapter 2, an "agreement": a set of personal and common objectives and also the arrangements by means of which they can jointly implement those objectives. This seems something that they come only gradually to learn. These new activities require that they come to coordinate not only their bodily movements but the expression of their desires and the pursuit of their plans. They must, in short, relate to themselves, and to one another, as persons, in the relevance that this may have for their present situation.

The specialists who study these developing groups notice that certain participants facilitate the creation of a plan and, thereby, of social interdependence. They have called some of these participants "critics" and others "independent enactors." To create a plan, especially in this ambiguous situation, many suggestions and demands have to be evaluated. People need some idea of the terms under which their fellows will accept any of the relationships that are possible: an idea of what they can expect to get from others under each relationship and what others expect in return. Critics are participants who reject or modify proposals. Independent enactors are participants who form the winning coalition in support of one plan rather than others. The plan, as embodied in the support of the independent enactors, then becomes the focus of collective action: the collectivity's agenda. The participants now have a plan and a rudimentary organization to sustain and implement it.

A further note on the plan. Given the way in which it arises in a self-developing group, a plan consists of a set of conditions under which desires of the several participants will be fulfilled and joint action will be undertaken. Personal and common interests are thus contained within the plan, and are ordered in their relevance for one another. As we saw in chapter 2, participants thereafter relate to one another not directly but in terms of the plan. In those terms, the benefits each and all can expect are contingent on their contributions to others, individually, and to the collectivity as a whole. Because the participants, or some of them, have committed themselves to enact and support these terms as legitimate, they now have a normative relationship through the plan. As we saw in chapter 2, exchange is thereby transformed from giving and getting to the exercise of rights and the fulfillment of duties.

A third notable step in collective development is the formation of a charismatic center. What happens is this. People find that, to implement a plan, they must coordinate their efforts and they must make certain that what they do is consistent with their joint objective. They must also afford the plan a sustained support. For that reason, the relatively uninvolved participants are encouraged to take a more active, committed role: to become independent enactors.

Perhaps because they are seen as having proposed and established the plan, the original set of independent enactors are now encouraged by other participants to serve in coordinating and controlling its implementation. In most small groups, one of these enactors comes to receive the greatest encouragement. He is frequently the person judged to have done the most to create the plan. As the writers on these processes tell us, this person is thereby transformed into a "hero." He and his ideas are now the focus and basis for collective action: a charismatic center.

A fourth stage in collective development entails the formation of a work group. A collectivity that has a charismatic center has what is necessary for joint or collective actions as contrasted with merely individual or interpersonal actions. As collective actions are undertaken, further developments seem always to occur: routinized arrangements emerge for making decisions and also a division of labor in implementing collective choices. A collectivity having these features seems to be what many writers call a "work group" (Mann, Gibbard, and Hunt, 1967).

A group is an arrangement through which people take joint action. This arrangement will always include a charismatic center, individual or collective, and provisions for collective decision-making. These latter provisions involve some weaving together of participants' claims on the collectivity and their obligations to it.

All social relations are, in some measure, both associations and social systems. As associations, they are unions of people who come together and stay together for the benefits they severally obtain. As social systems, they are joint or collective enterprises whose participants do things to sustain and foster their relationship: adjudicating disputes, coordinating their activities, allocating the costs and benefits of collective life, and so on. As an association, a social relationship is a facility through which people pursue personal and special interests. As a social system, it is a union that participants serve as the agents of common interests.

Collective decision-making involves an integration of these two aspects of social relations – these complementary sets of requirements. For sustained and effective action – for "work" – a collectivity must have routinized provisions for serving both the personal and collective interests of its participants (Swanson, 1971).

It must also have a division of labor through which collective choices are implemented. As Bales and Slater (1955) first stressed, collective actions force the members of a group to pay attention to the two poles of any course of problem-solving, one outer and one inner, and to their coordination. In collective action, this means that people pay attention to the outer environment from which they jointly obtain resources and facilities and also to the nurture of an inner solidarity with one another which makes it possible for them to act in concert. For reasons which Bales, Slater, and others amply discuss, these poles become the foci for two roles that are at once complementary and competitive: task leadership and social-emotional leadership. The separation of these two basic aspects of the collectivity's task, and the institutionalization and coordination of these types of leadership in enduring roles, make it possible for a collectivity routinely and efficiently to undertake collective action.

The fifth step in collective development is the rise of a constitutional order.

When a charismatic center takes form, it is embodied in the ideas, acts, and person of the hero. A work group consists in a division among members of responsibility for carrying out of these ideas and acts and in the rise of two poles of leadership, these usually played by different members. In short, the group's objectives, values, and organization are gradually being separated from the person of the hero.

We have yet to learn just how this occurs, but several processes seem possible and likely. First of all, there are disagreements and dissatisfactions around the existing arrangements for making collective decisions. We shall see later on in this chapter that some of these arrangements – including some that are quite common – embody conflicting provisions about the weight to be given the members' personal and special pursuits as against their duties to the group as a whole. In any case, members are likely to try to renegotiate arrangements for decision-making if it seems to their advantage. For reasons like these, they come to see the nature of the group, and therefore its leadership, as less than fixed: as matters susceptible to evaluation and change. Second, people who work together in a division of labor are necessarily coordinated with one another by means of their understanding of what the group is trying to accomplish and of the relevance of their own and others' contributions for those ends. Even if they are coordinated by a supervisor, they, and he, must have some grasp of what is wanted and why. No supervisor can monitor all the judgments that people must make in dealing with contingencies encountered in their work. Each person has to make unanticipated choices. If these are to benefit the group, each participant must understand the ends that are collectively sought. For these reasons, the members of a work group will come, in practice, to focus upon collective ends as distinct from the person of the group's leader or leaders. If disputes arise about the appropriateness of a member's efforts, he has, in these ends, a standard for judgment that is independent of the leaders'.

Third, there will be disagreements and conflicts over the interpretation of the group's objectives and over the proper method for implementing them. If the hero takes sides, as some members will press him to do, then opponents can succeed in their purpose only if they differentiate between the hero as an individual and the objectives and standards associated with him.

In college courses on group development, a fourth process is evident. Members who were less active in the early stages of the group's formation now seek a position of respect. They cannot claim status as the group's founders but they can claim a dignity equal to that of the hero and the original independent enactors on the grounds that they subscribe fully to the group's objectives and that their participation is essential to the group's activities. Obviously, that claim can be honored only if the group's objectives are distinguished from the persons of the group's formulators.

Whatever the processes may be, a separation is effected. The hero is dethroned as a necessary part of the charismatic center and is then accepted back into the group as a valued member. The group's objectives and its basic procedures for making and implementing decisions are defined as transcendent over persons and over lesser procedures and all persons who subscribe to these transcendent principles, and who do their share in bringing them to life, become equals: equals "under the law."

Levels of complexity in social relations and in ego defenses

Figure 4.2 continues on to three further stages but the five already in hand are the ones I plan to connect with ego defenses in this chapter and the next. (Appendix 3 discusses the remaining stages and the relations of all eight stages to some important theories concerning the stages of personal development.) We need here to note five properties of the levels of collective development and then to link particular levels with particular ego defenses.

First of all, the same levels of collective organization, or levels very like these, have been observed in the development of many sorts of groups. My examples are taken from college courses in group growth and development but similar stages are reported for small naturally occurring groups, for the development of relations in psychotherapy, and for the "life histories" of social movements, of complex organizations, and of massive changes in a society's social arrangements (Bellah, 1964; Swanson, 1970, 1971). In short, levels or stages of this sort have been observed in diverse social situations.

Second, social relations at earlier levels do not disappear when relations at later levels are developed. To take an example, most of the families I have studied are organized at the level of a work group or constitutional order but their members continue to be interdependent, socially interdependent, and organized to some extent around one or more chief figures or heroes. The appearance of higher levels provides a new, superordinate basis for people's earlier relationships but does not destroy those relationships.

Third, the continued existence and relative independence of earlier levels of social relations is evident when relations at one level are strained but relations at other levels operate with reasonable effectiveness. Thus we sometimes see families in which people's relations of interdependence are unsteady and yet their relations as a work group are reasonably effective: on a personal level people do not trust one another but they carry out their formal roles in the family's division of labor in a dependable and effective manner. As we

Figure 4.3. *Defenses by level of collective development*

Level of collective development	Likely defenses
V. Constitutional order	Intellectualization Reaction formation*
IV. Work group	Projection Rationalization Isolation
III. Charismatic center	Displacement
II. Social interdependence	Repression Reaction formation# Denial
I. Interdependence	Doubt and indecision Regression

*Complex forms
#Simple forms

sometimes say, their relations are correct but they are not warm. We also see families in which the situation is reversed, families in which levels of personal trust and attachment are high but the performance of specialized roles is erratic, even when these roles have been defined and accepted.

Fourth, social relations at each level have a distinctive basis of solidarity. When people are interdependent, their collective life is organized around their need for one another and especially their relations with the independent enactors. In social interdependence, solidarity rests primarily on the personal ties among the independent enactors as these ties are organized in the enactors' coalition with one another and in the existence of a network of rights and duties. In unity around a charismatic center, solidarity is founded upon the hero's ability to function as a leader and, concomitantly, upon other people's willingness to accept and sustain his leadership and to take initiatives to support common interests and to take care of themselves. And so on.

Fifth, social relations at each level are distinctive in the kind of strains among participants that are likely to threaten solidarity. That is the immediate basis for linking particular levels of collective development or complexity with defenses of a particular degree of cognitive complexity. Those connections are given in figure 4.3.

Varieties of social solidarity and strain

I want to propose now that strains in social relations at a particular level of social complexity can express and generate the desires that threaten solidarity at that level and can therefore lead people to defend themselves. The form of strain, and of the defense used to justify the threatening desires related to it, are determined in part by the form of solidarity that is jeopardized. This is the rationale for the relations expressed in the rows of figure 4.3.

In the remainder of this chapter, I describe the form of solidarity and strain peculiar to each level of collective relations, link it to the use of certain ego defenses (these links to ego defenses are made briefly in this chapter and in more detail in the next), and, finally, present the indices that I employed to identify the presence or absence of strains at particular levels of collective relations in the families I studied. In the next chapter, I present the associations between these indices and the defenses used by adolescents reared in those families.

Level I. Interdependence

Many students of developing groups find that, even when the claims people make on others are legitimate, those claims necessarily call in question the very relationship on which they are founded. We need to look at each of the levels of social relations, paying special attention to such inherent sources of strain on solidarity. They put people in the kind of situation that requires an ego defense, a situation in which a person has a desire that may undermine social relations that he wants and is committed to support.

As we have seen, the solidarity of social relations at level I (interdependence) consists in people's mutual need for one another, in their mutual acceptance of one another as having certain needs, and in their mutual commitment to gratify these needs within the relationship. Solidarity consists, then, in the dependability and beneficence of this network of interpersonal ties. In groups, such as families, in which people tend to deal with one another as whole persons, solidarity in interdependence requires that people stand ready to accept each other as whole persons and to facilitate their pursuit of diverse and changing interests.

Relations of each participant with each of the others need not be equally close. In the typical case, in the typical family, for example, some participants are especially important for the others. In a family, these are likely to be the parents. The network is organized especially around these people.

When solidarity is high, each participant feels at ease with the others, drawn to them, desired and desirable, an object of stable, dependable support; secure in a relationship that can sustain and shelter. But solidarity is never complete.

Relations of interdependence contain large ambiguities. People come together because they need one another but the extent of their mutual needs is unclear and must be discovered. Because each participant honors another as someone on whom he depends, as someone who is, or does, what is important, each is encouraged by another to be himself. But there will certainly be lines of behavior that others will reject. Each person must therefore be cautious about doing what the relationship seems also to encourage. He must be especially cautious if his needs or resources change, possibly making him a person whom others no longer value.

There are also ambiguities concerning the extent of obligations. What exactly has the person accepted to do for others? If he does what he is disposed to do, is it adequate? The relationship provides no clear standard. Disappointments are inevitable.

Relations of interdependence are personalized. People need one another for what they, in some sense, are. If they fail one another, or drift apart, it is likely to be taken as a rejection of the partners' personal adequacy or desirability. And some failures are certain as are some competing interests. Even the most devoted participants will sometimes be unavailable to their partners or unable to do what those partners need to have done. Every participant has some interests that go unfulfilled in a given relationship. When he looks elsewhere to pursue them, it reflects on the adequacy, and perhaps, on the stability, of the existing relationship.

Solidarity in interdependence is grounded, thus, on particular kinds of ties among participants and these make likely certain strains on solidarity. The likelihood that the strains are overcome depends on the dependability of the ties and the amount of gratification obtained from them. To put it another way, it depends on the degree to which people in interdependence trust and value one another.

Students of group growth and development find that a concern with trust and mistrust is central in the early stages of collective organization. Participants make great efforts to test one another's trustworthiness and trustfulness. As writers on this topic suggest, participants seem especially concerned with establishing whether they can trust one another in the broad sense that Erik Erikson (1950, 1959, 1968) has in mind when he talks of the problem of "basic trust" as against "basic mistrust" in relations with oneself and others. Prelinger and Zimet (1964: 64–5) generalize Erikson's thought in this way:

Trust may be defined as a deeply ingrained conviction that one's needs, material and emotional, will be satisfied: that the world and the people in it are basically good, abundant in their supplies, and well-meaning. But it also implies a personal feeling of "being all right" oneself, and of being considered all right by significant others; a feeling that one can cope with the world and with oneself, and that one is at home in one's body. Finally, it implies a confident feeling that requirements and even frustrations coming from the outside generally make sense.

Basic mistrust may be defined as a sense of always living precariously, that good things never last, that one does not know if one's needs will be satisfied tomorrow and rather doubts that they will be. That the world contains many hidden dangers, that people are out to exploit or even "get" you; that oneself is bad and empty, can't cope, and is doomed to suffer failure and injury; that the world is an unsafe, unpredictable, threatening and cold place.

Level II. Social interdependence

In social interdependence, solidarity depends especially upon the regularization of giving and getting between pairs of persons and across a network of complementary normative claims: across a set of rights and duties. It rests upon the independent enactors' support for the network.

The network usually contains one or a few people on whom the others chiefly depend. It is vulnerable to changes in their abilities or commitments. In most families, for example, the parents are the chief figures in social interdependence and, in most of them, variations in network solidarity have traditionally been related more to the father's performance than the mother's; not because he was the more important figure in the family's inner life but because the entire family depended upon him as the chief breadwinner and because his work and other outside contacts could lead to his developing competing interests.

In a system of social interdependence, each participant experiences the relationship – that of a family, for example – as a network of rights and duties; a system of interpersonal relations and a collective enterprise. He finds, for example, that his rights are the basis for claims that others will honor and for his limiting some of the claims made upon him. He learns that the honoring of his rights may be contingent upon duties that other members owe to one another: perhaps that he has to get in line and wait when there are earlier claimants. He discovers that some claims take precedence over others and that some members of the collectivity, in some circumstances, have rights that usually take precedence: in a family, for example, the rights of the parents (the independent enactors), the breadwinner, a new baby, anyone who is sick. His rights are the basis for his autonomy, but they exist only as a part of a collective plan or agreement and in a contingent relationship with his performance of duties.

As Erikson says, if a participant has worthwhile rights, and is secure in them, he has a basis for self-reliance, dignity, and a lawful independence. If he can fulfill the rightful claims of others, he affirms his importance in the social order. There are, however, difficulties. Every participant wants things, or wants them at times, and under circumstances, that exceed his rights or that conflict with the rights of others. He and others constantly "set him right" and he therefore has many occasions for shame at his own ineptitude and for doubts concerning the goodness and dependability of social relations.

People's attachment to one another in social interdependence consists, then, in their being secure in a system of worthwhile rights. The students of developing groups say that this experience is captured in Erikson's discussion of autonomy and that, when this security is undermined, the experience is what Erikson calls "shame and doubt." In Prelinger and Zimet's (1964: 66) summary:

Autonomy can be defined as a sense that one is capable of being and may be the originator of one's own actions; that one has a will of one's own and can exercise it; that one "stands on his own feet"; that one is in control of oneself and exercises his control comfortably; it includes a sense of pride and independence, of being able to hold one's ground in the face of others.

Shame and doubt refers to a sense of being easily exposed as powerless, incapable, weak, and bad. It includes a wish to hide from others, to cover up one's despicability and worthlessness. One's own plans and actions are surrounded by doubts concerning their justification, value and efficacy. Self-consciousness and a lack of self-confidence are present; inability to make up one's mind.

Level III. Charismatic center

At level III, social solidarity depends especially upon the effectiveness and dependability of one or a few people – the hero or heroes – in articulating collective interests and in mobilizing other people on behalf of those interests. In his role as hero, a person must be treated as being set apart; as representing legitimate, common concerns; as above partisanship. He must protect himself, and must be protected, from undue influence; he must not be forced or manipulated to do other than what his proper exercise of his "office" would imply.

The participant in a relationship under a charismatic center knows about rights and duties, has some sense of the collectivity as a differentiated network of interlocking relationships, is able to use this network, and accepts it as, on balance, beneficial. This dependable, lawful, and supportive social order provides him with grounds for a high and yet realistic sense of ambition and independence. He seems confident of his ability to do what is required in order to promote his own interests and to fulfill obligations. He seems – Erikson's words are again appropriate – "more together," "self-activated," "in free possession of surplus energy."

There are, thus, confidence and skill and there are explorations and initiatives. These draw upon, and symbolize, the strength of the social order. They also threaten it.

The person gets support for initiatives and explorations. The common purpose has been identified and participants are encouraged to take initiatives that advance that purpose – to serve as independent enactors. The difficulty is that these initiatives implicitly challenge the role of the hero. At level IV (work group), there are institutionalized actions that participants can take to support the common enterprise without their raising questions about competing with the hero for his position as articulator of the collectivity's action. At level III there are not.

As students of group development sometimes observe (*e.g.*, Slater, 1966), social relations at level III embody features of a classic "Oedipal" situation (Spiro, 1982; Swanson, 1987). A person learns that his personal and special interests can be pursued successfully only through support from a social relationship and learns that this relationship depends upon, among other things, the successful functioning of one or more leaders serving the relationship as a whole. "Oedipal conflicts" involve a participant's efforts to do things that may undermine the ability of the leaders to perform the duties of their "offices": efforts, perhaps, to obtain special favors, to have a relationship with one leader that subverts his official activities or his ties to the other leader(s), or efforts to supplant a leader. "Successful" resolutions of these conflicts occur if the person finds that his interests will be sufficiently gratified through the relationship providing that he commits himself to supporting the leaders in their roles and avoids doing things that might undercut their service to the relationship as a whole.

Once again, observers have found in an Eriksonian formulation a statement of the conflict inherent in a level of social relations. At level III it is his contrast between initiative and guilt. In Prelinger and Zimet's (1964: 67) summary:

Initiative refers to: evidence of ambition, energetic driving in pursuit of accomplishment, a tendency to solve problems by attack, pleasure in attack and conquest, striving towards goals lying in the future, but also to active, curious exploration and active, expansive movement; rivalrous, and jealous competition.

Guilt is . . . understood specifically as guilt over enjoyment derived from acts of "making," and over the aggressive components of active competition. Excessive guilt would be manifested by self-restriction, overconscientiousness in planning enterprises, and paralysis of action.

With *men* the accent would lie on intrusion of a physical, intellectual, and social sort, on "making" by invading, monopolizing, and manipulating of people and things.

In *women* the emphasis would lie on "making" by inception, maternal inclusion, or creation. Also on seductive, bitchy, bodily-narcissistic demandingness for attention to her as a physical being.

Negatively, in both sexes may be found: fear of damage, confinement, weakness, losing out to rivals, or a sense that all these should occur or have already occurred. In women also: being found unattractive, unlovable, repulsive.

Level IV. Work group

Solidarity at this level turns primarily upon the effective integration of people's activities through a system of decision-making and a division of labor under the charismatic center. As we have seen, certain instabilities seem inherent at this level of collective action because members are likely to have principled differences among themselves and with the charismatic leader, differences concerning their prerogatives to pursue personal and special interests as against collective interests and concerning prerogatives associated with specialized roles. In the very pursuit of their rights and duties, and in the exercise of their specialized rights and privileges in implementing group decisions, participants will tend to exceed the actions that will benefit the group and to infringe on one another's specialized spheres of authority.

We have also seen that the subordinate or peripheral members of a developing group are likely to resist its operation as a work group, and to do so exactly because the establishment of a division of labor may leave them in a permanent status as second-class citizens. A division of labor opens up broad responsibilities and opportunities in collective service, a set of meaningful careers in the group. Subordinate and, especially, peripheral members fear being shut out from these opportunities.

When people are organized as a work group, they have something specific to do that is personally and socially rewarding and this enables and motivates industriousness: serious, systematic effort. Working under the group's charismatic center, and within a system of decision-making and a division of labor, enables each member to be an independent enactor without undermining the group. But there are special dangers as well. We have noted the struggles over the definition of rights and of spheres of responsibility and discretion, and the fears of subordinate and peripheral members that they will be treated permanently as inferiors. These latter fears tend to become associated with people's fears that they really are inferior. Subordinate and peripheral members have not had opportunities to become competent in carrying sustained responsibilities. It will take time to gain the skill, understanding, and outlook that are required. While these people are learning, they are inadequate by their own and others' standards. They are likely to feel inferior and to wonder whether they will ever be any good at the activities that carry high prestige.

Many of the dilemmas of subordinate and peripheral members, as contrasted with those in more central positions, seem captured by Erikson's contrast of inferiority with industry in his fourth state of psychosocial development. Once again, the relevance of this contrast for relations in work groups has been noted by students of developing groups and Erikson's formulation has been summarized by Prelinger and Zimet (1964: 68):

Industry refers to an active orientation towards producing things and thus to win recognition. There is eager absorption in the productive situation and determined striving towards the completion of things: "stick-to-it-iveness." There are sincere attempts to be useful and to do useful things. Skills are acquired, practiced, and valued. There is marked interest in learning how things are done in the surrounding culture from the points of view of know-how and/or rules.

Inferiority refers to a despairing of one's tools and skills, leading to a sense of being unable to be like others, of being doomed to mediocrity or of being crippled, mutilated, and isolated.

Such feelings of inferiority also threaten social solidarity. They imply that a social order is deeply inadequate and unsatisfying to participants and these latter feelings also must be defended against by participants if they want to maintain their relations with others.

Level V. Constitutional order

The basis of solidarity in a constitutional order is people's commitment to serve the group's broad interests and objectives and to do so, not in this way or that, but in whatever manner seems appropriate in the circumstances. They have the right and duty to exercise this wide discretion.

The studies of small, self-developing groups show that people in this situation display characteristic uncertainties and ambivalence. Because their responsibilities are open-ended, they feel pressed to do a great deal indeed – far more than any formal duty requires – to demonstrate their solidarity. At the same time, they feel empowered and duty-bound to protect their independence of action and judgment on the group's behalf and are wary of what may prove undue attempts to influence them. Finally, they face difficulties because they lack clear, specific guidelines. What should they do and what should they not? They cannot be quite certain of the value of any given course of action in meeting their diffuse obligations. They cannot be quite certain that what they do will not, in some broader context, prove to threaten the group's real interests. They must try to operate within the "spirit" of the law while lacking the guidance of its letter and must therefore be cautious.

The definition of the group's real interests requires some judgment about its situation in the wider world. A responsible member of a constitutional order must take simultaneous account of the group's inner life and of the risks and opportunities and obligations afforded it by its broader situation.

Erikson's discussion of identity associates it with diffuse commitments to a group's essential goals as contrasted with a feeling of obligation to perform one or another particular role in a group or to model oneself after particular individuals. Thus he writes of identity (1959: 102) as "a maintenance of an inner *solidarity* with a group's ideals and identity" and of identity formation as beginning (1959: 113) "where the usefulness of identification ends."

He also stresses the requirement, in identity formation, of the person's having a position in, and an understanding of, the wider world from which he can contribute to the broad interests of each group in which he participates as a fully-qualified member. His contrast of identity diffusion with identity catches the special anxieties associated with a person's needing to have a generalized orientation for his life and conduct and with his not, as yet, having found it. And he suggests that most people in most societies realize an identity through involvement in the institutional systems and values of the society as a whole, an involvement which (1968: 31–2) "secures them what joint verification and what transitory salvation lies in doing things together and in doing them right – a rightness proven by the bountiful response of 'nature,' whether in the form of prey bagged, the food harvested, the goods produced, the money made, or the technological problems solved ... only such consolidation offers the coordinates for the range of a (historical) period's identity formations and their necessary relation to a sense of inspired activity ..."

In Prelinger and Zimet's summary of Erikson's description (1964: 69):

Identity refers to a sense of inner sameness and continuity in time, and of inner homogeneity at any given time. Specifically it implies a sense of being at home in one's body, of "knowing where one is going," and of an assuredness of recognition by others. All this is based on good integration between inner drives and wishes, and social conditions, specifically in terms of work, sex, relationships to peers, and the community.

Identity diffusion implies a sense of discrepancy between one's appearance and being, doubts concerning one's sexual identity, an inability to choose a career because of conflicting interests and doubts, an inability to relate to others as an equal partner or to compete with them, a feeling of emptiness, lack of a coherent philosophy of life and of a goal for one's existence. No commitments are made and a state of paralysis with regard to the making of choices exists.

Ego defenses and social solidarity and strain by levels of complexity in social relations

The grounds for social solidarity, and for strains on solidarity, vary from level to level in figure 4.2. So, therefore, do the ego defenses that are most likely to be appropriate. These connections are discussed at length in the next chapter but a brief overview at this point may help us to grasp the interpretation as a whole. Ego defenses will be considered appropriate in dealing with social strains at a given level if they meet the requirements, at that level, for affirming solidarity with others despite possibly deviant desires or conduct. To show what I mean, I begin with level V, constitutional order, and proceed to each simpler level of social relations.

Level V. Constitutional order

Solidarity is high in a constitutional order if people are devoted to the group's broad objectives and if they try continuously to find ways to promote those objectives within the family and in relations with society at large. The way to show that one is truly devoted to a constitutional order is to make continuous efforts on the group's behalf, efforts that go beyond the routine. That creates a defensible position. If doubts about one's motives arise, these efforts are evidence that one's commitment to the group is wholehearted.

Two of the defenses in figure 4.3 may lend themselves to this sort of demonstration. They are intellectualization and a complex form of reaction formation. Intellectualization can entail one's taking exquisite and constant care to make the right choice and do the right thing, considering all the consequences of all possible courses of action and tailoring one's actions to one's findings. Reaction formation can involve one in constantly taking constructive initiatives on the group's behalf; contributing to its life and prospects beyond what is formally required.

Both of these defenses can also enable one to exercise rights provided in a constitutional order. People in such an order have the right, not merely the duty, to exercise discretion on behalf of the group's essential standards and purposes. Both defenses can enable one independently to make choices on the group's behalf.

Level IV. Work group

A work group has high solidarity if people support and employ certain procedures for making collective choices and are faithful in performing some specialized service on the group's behalf, carefully coordinating their contributions with those of others. A person's position is defensible if he can show that he routinely does these things and that any other interests he may seem to have do not interfere with his careful fulfillment of his responsibilities. In that context, those interests are permissible.

Three defenses in figure 4.3 can be used to express this posture toward a group. Isolation can serve and also projection and rationalization. In these defenses, people can point to their record of sustained service as the basis for concluding that desires or behavior which seem deviant should not be taken seriously. In each, people note that they have the right to pursue interests and actions that do not interfere with the performance of their duties and also the right to exercise discretion on the group's behalf in the performance of their specialized duties. Isolation involves the person in separating out from the rest of his behavior those aspects that might be objectionable and in claiming, in effect, that the latter should not be taken seriously – given the other and acceptable things he does. Projection can consist in a person's claiming that deviant behavior arose from his exercising his rights and that given those rights and given his demonstrated faithfulness to the group his deviance should not be taken seriously. In rationalization, the person claims that the real meaning of his behavior is consistent with his commitments. He meant well, however it may seem. That becomes believable if he can point to a long record of appropriate participation in the group.

By providing people with roles through which to sustain the group and obtain personal gratifications, a work group affords its members a basis for justifying themselves. Members can make the claim that their sustained and faithful service shows their real commitments and that, beside that service, what seem to be deviant behaviors should be considered accidental or incidental. All of these defenses draw on such a record. On the other hand, isolation, projection, and rationalization would not seem likely to serve the demands for justification in a constitutional order. None involves an assertion of initiatives or contributions that go beyond any specific requirements.

Level III. Charismatic center

When a collectivity is organized under a charismatic center, but is not a work group or constitutional order, solidarity consists in people's support for the hero's acts on behalf of common interests and their avoidance of actions that might undermine the hero's position and service. Members are required to care for the group as a whole, and serve it, but they do so legitimately only if directed and empowered by the hero. They lack the independent authority that comes from their having responsibility for some broad role in the collective enterprise or from a general authorization to act for the collectivity at their own discretion. As a result, their efforts to take responsibility for the group are likely to be suspected of posing a challenge to the hero. The members' problem is compounded by their being authorized to pursue at will those of their interests that do not impinge on the common, corporate interest. Since the boundaries between what is personal and what is corporate are not clear, the possibility of inadvertent transgression is high.

One defense in figure 4.3 lends itself to dealing with this situation. In displacement, the person deals with situations in which it is not so much his impulses as their targets that may be unacceptable. Impulses that might undermine the hero's position can often be directed toward other targets, thus rendering them acceptable and affirming social solidarity.

Because there is no basis in organization under a charismatic center for an ordinary member's exercising discretion in the group's interest, or proving his devotion through the sustained performance of a specialized role enacted in the common interest, defenses like those considered when I discussed constitutional orders or work groups are not appropriate. On the other hand, organization at this level does distinguish between purely personal interests and corporate interests and gives people permission to pursue the former at their own discretion. That makes it possible to use a defense such as displacement that embodies a freer expression of possibly deviant impulses than is usually available at simpler levels of collective organization.

Level II. Social interdependence

Social interdependence is importantly different from organization under a charismatic center, but there are similarities as well:

- In both cases, members have some relatively limited obligations and, apart from these, have the right to pursue their interests as they will. In social interdependence, the obligation is to fulfill specific duties incurred through agreements with particular individuals. Among those individuals, the independent enactors are the most important.
- In both forms of organization, the authorized pursuit of personal interests can lead toward an undermining of collective solidarity. This is so in social interdependence because such a pursuit implies that existing agreements do

not encompass all of a person's interests and that his loyalty to those agreements may be uncertain.

What defenses might be appropriate given the nature of solidarity and the forms of strain found especially at this level of social relations? Repression, a "primitive" form of reaction formation, and denial seem to lend themselves to these features of social interdependence.

Solidarity in social interaction does require that participants meet their obligations. The obligations are specific. Failure to meet them immediately raises questions about the viability of the relationship. Unlike the situation in more complex forms of social relations, there is not the possibility here of claiming that one's behavior as a whole, rather than some particular act, is a proper index of one's performance on obligations. In social interdependence, and from the standpoint of the specific duties it entails, participants must reject any impulse that seems deviant. That is what repression involves.

In repression, a person shows himself – and, indirectly, others – his true commitments by preventing an unacceptable impulse from influencing his behavior, going to the extent of rejecting it even from his thought. He focuses instead upon doing what is "right."

In a form of reaction formation that clinicians call "primitive," he goes further. He not only does what is required, but he does it with excessive care.

But social interdependence also affords limits to the claims others can make. One's own duties and their rights are specific; limited. In denial, a person says that the claims others want to make on him, or the limits they want to set on his behavior, are excessive; that people are wrong in thinking that what he wants or hopes or does will, in fact, lead to difficulties; that his solidarity with them hinges on his fulfilling limited obligations and is not jeopardized by his doing what he will in other respects.

Level I. Interdependence

As we have seen, people in interdependence are drawn together by mutual needs for things that the others seem spontaneously to offer. There are, however, great uncertainties about the conditions under which those things will be produced and the likelihood that each will find the others attractive. On the one hand, participants are encouraged to be themselves and they encourage others to do likewise. It is by each being himself that the others are drawn to him. On the other hand, no one has a clear sense of the claims he can make on any of the others without jeopardizing the relationship or of the claims that others may want to make on him. Questions of basic trust are salient.

In this situation, one person can protect the relationship by being cautious. There may be further things one can get from other participants, but that must be determined without driving them away. Two defenses in figure 4.3 seem suited to deal with these circumstances. They are doubt and indecision, and regression. They have some properties in common. In a situation of ambiguity, the person who is uncertain about the justifiability of his desires either does not act upon them (doubt and indecision) or stops acting upon them (regression), but he does not relinquish his desires because there may be grounds on which they will prove acceptable. He shows his solidarity with others by not disrupting his relations with them and by demonstrating his dependence on them: demonstrating that he will not pursue possibly justifiable objectives if these give rise to strains (doubt and indecision and regression) and also (in regression) by asking others to continue valuing him for what he is and to help and take care of him.

Indices of strain in social solidarity

We come, finally, to indices of the strain associated with the form of solidarity found at particular levels of complexity in social relations. I describe, for each level, the indices I used in studying families and the defenses of their adolescent children. Each family will be classified as having strained or unstrained relations at each of the five levels of organization, one or a few distinctive operational definitions being employed for each level. (As indicated in table A1.1 of appendix 1, there are no significant correlations among these several indicators.) I shall assume that, in families where strains at a particular level of social relations are especially strong, the children will be especially likely to justify their deviant tendencies – tendencies that are always present – by showing their basic commitment to social solidarity.

Level I. Interdependence

Solidarity at this level consists in the existence of mutual, interpersonal needs among participants, in the dependability of those participants in serving one another's needs, and in degree of mutual trust they feel and foster. The likely strains on this form of solidarity are interpersonal indifference, dislike, or lack of acceptance, and erratic and undependable behavior and lack of trust. As in all forms of solidarity, the behavior of the independent enactors (in a family, the parents and, perhaps, the oldest children) in these matters is especially important.

I defined four indices as possibly tapping strains of this sort in the families I studied. The first captures something of the parents' personal dependability; the second, the parents' need for, and acceptance of, the child in my sample; the third, the trust, attraction, and stability in the marriage; the fourth, the level of acceptance and trust between the parents and between them and the children. (It is possible that the indices appearing later in this particular series incorporate the relevance for the family's functioning of indices appearing earlier.)

Personal stability of each parent

The interviews with the parents had been rated on many dimensions of personality according to Block's (1961) Q-sort procedure. A cluster analysis of these dimensions produced several uncorrelated factors, one of them having to do with personal stability. It is defined by ratings of the parents as being stable rather than unstable, as operating on an "even keel" rather than being changeable, and as not being worrisome rather than being worrisome. A score on this cluster was calculated for each parent.

Parents' acceptance of this child

Interviews with the parents had been coded for parental feelings about each of the children. Ratings of these feelings prove to comprise a well-defined factor which seems to indicate the degree to which the parents show acceptance of each child. Specifically, the quality of the parents' relations with the child, and the adequacy with which the parents understand him, are rated very good rather than distant; the parents are highly approving of the child's interests and activities rather than being "hardly approving" of anything he undertakes; the parents are judged to enjoy the child very much rather than hardly at all. A factor score was calculated for each parent's acceptance of the particular adolescent in the family whose defenses I sought to explain.

Strength of marital bond

The parents filled out a questionnaire which asked, among other things, for their feeling about their marriage. A factor analysis of their answers produced an orthogonal factor on strength of marital bond. Five items had high loadings on this factor: being exceptionally happy with the marriage rather than having extreme marital conflict, feeling extremely friendly rather than extremely hostile, being very satisfied with the marriage rather than very dissatisfied, and seeing the emotional tone of the family as spontaneous rather than somber. A score on this factor was calculated for each parent.

Closeness of familial ties

This is again a factor score. It was derived from a varimax factor analysis of feelings and ties expressed by parents and children when asked, in interviews, about their relations with other members of the family. (More details about its construction appear in Swanson, 1974.) High scores mean that the mother and the children in a family report that they feel close in their relations with the father and that the children say their mother is supportive. A single score on this index was calculated for each family.

Level II. Social interdependence

I propose two indices for strains in social interdependence within families: hierarchical organization and the defensiveness of each parent.

Hierarchical organization

In most families, the parents are the independent enactors. As a social network, a family shows properties common to all networks – for example, hierarchy, centralization, and their opposites (Burt, 1982) – and the roles assumed by the parents are highly determinative of the network's pattern. When the family is organized in a hierarchy, one parent has appreciably more discretion than any other member. This opens up the possibility that this leading figure will sometimes act arbitrarily or otherwise infringe on the rights of others. In either case, other members are less likely to feel secure in their rights or assured that limits on their duties will be honored.

The families of my sample were coded for their arrangements for making decisions, using categories employed in several other studies (Swanson, 1971) and presented in figure 4.4. A coder read the interview with the father and placed the family in one of the seven categories in the figure. A different coder read the interview with the mother and classified the system of decision-making as described in her report. For present purposes, a family was considered hierarchical if either coder placed it in patterns 5, 6, or 7. All other families were considered egalitarian. According to the Spearman-Brown prophecy formula, the reliability of coders in placing a family in one of these two categories (as based upon check-coding) if 0.84 ($p < 0.001$).

Parental defensiveness

When independent enactors are defensive, strains in social interdependence are likely. This is so because defensiveness involves high levels of tension concerning rights and duties, and social interdependence consists exactly in a

Figure 4.4. *Patterns of decision-making in families*

Below are seven models of ways families make decisions. We would like your impression about how this family makes its decisions. Read through all seven of the models and choose the *one* that *best* describes this family. Put a *1* in the blank beside that model. Then put a *2* beside the model that is the *next best* description of the family.

Note that each model focuses on the parts the *parents* play in making family decisions. Models 1–4 describe families in which the parents have joint responsibility for most decisions and models 5–7 describe families in which *one* parent has final decision-making responsibility, at least under some circumstances.

1. In this family, it is hard to see the existence of standard procedures for the conduct of business. Often things are done or not done, pretty much as the moment dictates. The parents may or may not consult with each other before coming to a decision or before setting out on some course of action. If either dislikes what the other is doing, his main recourse is to block his partner or to withold resources (*e.g.*, money, time, encouragement) that are necessary for the support of his partner's activities. Similarly, he will often find that, rather than consultation or discussion, the principal means to get his partner to take some action is to make resources available to the partner, earmarking them specifically for the purpose he intends.

2. In this family, "decision" is too strong a word for the parents' standard way of doing business. Rather they talk over problems, and talk around them, until a kind of common view emerges. This view is then the basis for action. They don't go ahead until a common view emerges.

3. In this family, both parents have to talk about the problem and agree upon a solution *before* they announce their decision to the family and/or before they begin to carry it out.

4. In this family, both parents often consult with each other about what the family will do. If they consult with each other, they will reach agreement on a solution before they announce their decision to the family. However, each parent alone also has the right to decide upon a course of action, announce his decision to the family, and even begin carrying it out without first consulting his partner. Each partner always has the right of review over any action which has been initiated by the other parent without prior consultation. This means that, if he wishes, he may question the action of his partner and may hold up the implementation of this action until they have consulted together and reached an agreement about the final course of action.

5. This family is identical with the one described as model 4 except that, should the parents disagree on something important, one of them, but not the other, has the right to break the tie and get things moving again.

6. In this family, one parent is seen by all as being the "head" of the family. Although that parent does make the final decision, each parent has a special sphere of responsibility and competence. Thus, if one parent is finally the "governor" of the family, the other has a legitimate role as his "counselor."

Figure 4.4 (*cont.*)

This counselor's advice will nearly always be sought and taken into consideration before a final outcome is decided upon by the "governor." The "counselor" expects to be consulted on important family matters and generally is.

7. In this family, one parent is, without question, the "head" of the family. This "governor" has the final word in deciding what action the group shall take and how it shall be taken. There is no established or regular consultative procedure in this family. The other parent sees himself as playing a subordinate role to the "governor" in family affairs and does not expect to be called upon for advice, although this advice may be sought by the "governor" upon occasion.

network of rights and duties. The independent enactors are the key figures in that network.

A highly defensive person questions the moral rightness of his own behavior and, by implication, the rightness of others' behavior. His demands on himself and, at least indirectly, on others are so extensive, and so constant, as to press on the limits of what is reasonable or justifiable (Miller and Swanson, 1960: 123–35). Perhaps he justifies himself by finding extenuating circumstances in the misconduct of others. Or perhaps he tries to buttress his control of his own deviant desires by demanding that everyone join him in the meticulous support of collective standards. This implies that they do not presently meet these standards.

Other participants will, of course, question the enactor's outlook. When they do, they are questioning, and thereby undermining, the focus of solidarity in social interdependence and, in that context, will view themselves with anxiety and reproach.

High levels of defensiveness can also be taken as indices of the presence of ego-centered needs: personal needs that the defenders try to satisfy "regardless of the effect on the attainment of the group['s] goal" (Fouriezos, Hutt, and Guetzkow, 1950: 683). Defensiveness indicates the presence of such needs in each of two senses. First, it indicates that people have unresolved desires which they recognize as subversive of their relations with others. Second, it indicates that they are preoccupied with these desires, and with justifying themselves for having them, even at the expense of carrying on other aspects of their relations with others. In both meanings, ego-centered needs destabilize a system of rights and duties: the defenders are not able to give proper attention to the performance of their own duties or properly to honor the rights of others.

Neither the highly defensive enactor nor the people with whom he relates are settled into a system of rights that they can exercise with comfort: a system that can serve them as the secure foundation for autonomous action. All parties become preoccupied with the possibility that they have exceeded their rights or scanted their obligations, or that some participants may do so. They therefore become preoccupied with feelings of shame and doubt.

It might be thought that degree of defensiveness as just defined also reflects or includes degree of neuroticism: the extent and intensity of the person's anxiety about his impulses and the extent to which he develops disabling symptoms in response to that anxiety. This seems unlikely in principle and appears to be incorrect in fact. It is unlikely in principle because defensiveness can be pervasive in a person's behavior at low or moderate levels of underlying anxiety and because even high anxiety may be accompanied by few disabling symptoms. It appears actually to be incorrect because there are no significant correlations between the defensiveness of the parents in my sample and their scores on Block's (1965: 112) indices of neuroticism, specifically his scales for psychoneuroticism, overcontrol, and undercontrol. In addition, the correlations between parental defensiveness and their scores on the several scales of the MMPI are few and scattered. A report of these findings appears in appendix 1: in tables A1.2 and A1.3.

In my study, the defensiveness of each parent can be estimated from the range of their use of defenses that were described in chapter 1. These ratings were factor analyzed separately for fathers and for mothers. In each analysis, three significant varimax factors emerged (table 4.1).

Factor I for fathers and II for mothers seem identical. The defenses that load most heavily on these factors are denial and repression. As we have seen before, denial and repression are relatively simple defenses, but not the very simplest.

Factor II for fathers and factor I for mothers have high loadings primarily from defenses that can be moderately complex: rationalization, projection, and displacement. A simple defense, regression, also loads heavily on both. Three of these four defenses are likely to be defenses against objective anxiety.

Factor III for fathers is defined primarily by a high loading of intellectualization and by weak loadings of displacement, denial, projection and repression. Factor III for mothers has high loadings of the two simplest defenses, doubt and indecision, and regression.

My index of a parent's defensiveness is the number of factors, from 0 to 3, on which he has scores at or above the median score for parents of the same sex. I examined the relations between the defenses used by the children and this indicator of fathers' defensiveness, mothers' defensiveness, and, by summing the scores for each child's parents, the defensiveness of the parental pair.

Table 4.1. *Factor analysis of parents' defense scores*

Defenses	Fathers			Mothers		
	I	II	III	I	II	III
Isolation	50	26	36	66	27	13
Intellectualization	−00	07	76	66	−02	04
Rationalization	30	53	43	70	18	20
Doubt	16	45	38	09	04	75
Denial	76	16	09	15	62	07
Projection	23	63	03	68	24	15
Regression	06	63	19	54	10	65
Displacement	36	60	−02	53	29	35
Reaction formation	48	23	18	21	52	13
Repression	73	15	−10	06	80	13
Eigen-value	3.8	1.4	1.1	4.0	1.5	1.1
Cumulative percentage of variance	38	52	63	40	55	67

Level III. Charismatic center

As I suggested earlier, one or both of the parents in a family are the persons most likely to expect, and be expected, to serve as the hero or heroes. Therefore it should be a strain on a family's solidarity around a clear and strong charismatic center if the parents, though present, are unable to serve in this capacity. One index of that situation is provided by a rating of the role appropriateness of the parents' personalities. A second is their prowess as breadwinners.

Role appropriateness of parental personalities

This index was derived from the parents' answers on the California Personality Inventory (CPI), a paper-and-pencil test administered to parents when they came for their interviews. The CPI was originally developed to measure characteristics of clinically normal adults, especially personal strengths and adaptive skills. A varimax factor analysis of the parents' responses produced two well-defined factors for fathers and two for mothers. The same factors have been found in many studies with this inventory (Megargee, 1972: 110–12). One of them brings together personal qualities that have been associated in previous research with the orientations of persons who serve as the task leaders of groups; the other, qualities shown to be those of social-emotional leaders. As Parsons (1955) has suggested and Zelditch (1955) has shown, the role of adult males and husbands is defined cross-culturally as that of task leadership and the role of adult females and wives as social-emotional leadership. I shall assume, therefore, that these CPI factors can serve as gross indicators of the role appropriateness of the parents' personalities (more exactly, their appropriateness for parental roles as traditionally defined).

The first factor has high loadings from the CPI scales for dominance (aggressive, confident, persistent, and planful; persuasive and verbally fluent; self-reliant and independent; having leadership potential and initiative), sociability (outgoing, enterprising, and ingenious; competitive and forward; original and fluent in thought), and intellectual efficiency (efficient, clear-thinking, capable, intelligent, progressive, planful, thorough, and resourceful; alert and well-informed; placing a high value on cognitive and intellectual matters). The second factor is defined by high loadings from scales for a sense of well-being (energetic, enterprising, alert, ambitious, and versatile; productive and active; valuing work and effort for its own sake), self-control (calm, patient, practical, slow, self-denying, inhibited, thoughtful, and deliberate; strict and thorough in their own work and in their expectations for others; honest and conscientious), making a good impression (cooperative, enterprising, outgoing, sociable, warm, and helpful; concerned with making a good impression; diligent and persistent), and achieving through conformance (capable, cooperative, efficient, organized, responsible, stable, and sincere; persistent and industrious; valuing intellectual activity and intellectual achievement). Husbands were rated as relatively lacking in skills and orientations appropriate for their role if their wives had higher scores than they on factor I; wives if their husbands had higher scores than they on factor II. Note was also taken in my analyses of cases in which a wife or husband had higher scores than his/her spouse on both factors and of cases in which the absolute scores of one or both spouses on one or both factors were one standard deviation or more above or below the average for this sample of parents.

Ability as a breadwinner
A man or woman's ability as a breadwinner, both in absolute terms and relative to that of his/her spouse, has been shown in many studies to be related to his powers as a spouse and parent. It may well affect his ability to serve as a charismatic center. In my own sample of families, the husband's work is almost always the sole source, or provides by far the largest share, of the family's income (a state of affairs that would be less likely in families founded more recently!). In any case, this fact eliminates the possibility of comparisons of the relative contributions to income by the two spouses. What I could do, and did

do, was examine the correlations between fathers' occupations and the defenses used by their children and the correlations between each parent's education and those defenses.

Level IV. Work group

Strains leading towards feelings of presumptuousness and inferiority and, thence, to defenses, are inherent in the operations of a work group. That being so, we can operationalize level IV by identifying a family as organized at the level of a work group but not at that of a constitutional order. (As I have shown elsewhere (Swanson, 1974), families can be classified as work groups or constitutional orders on the basis of their procedures for making decisions.)

There are, however, work groups whose members seem under special pressures to defend themselves. These are groups that empower members to pursue personal and special interests and that simultaneously press them to treat such pursuits as illegitimate. Conflicts of that sort can also be coded from a family's procedures for making decisions (figure 4.4).

The rest of this section reviews the typology of decision-making in families and describes the rules I followed in using it to distinguish between work groups and constitutional orders and to identify families that both permit and forbid their members to pursue personal and special interests.

Work groups vs. *constitutional orders*

All of the families in my sample except those coded as "1" in figure 4.4 are probably organized at least at the level of a work group. This means that they are organized to make decisions or otherwise to formulate collective choices (the families coded "1" are not), they have some division of labor in their activities (if only by age and sex), and one or more people serve as charismatic centers. We need, of course, to separate families that function as work groups from those which also operate as constitutional orders. This can be done using the patterns of decision-making in the figure.

The mark of a constitutional order in a family is the subordination of its action as a work group to the group's general or common purposes as distinguished from the subordination of that action to the person of the hero or heroes. In organizational terms, this means that the family is able to make decisions, that the common or collective interest is distinguished organization-ally from the interests of individual members and subgroups, and that no one person or subgroup has a monopoly on the right to define or to speak for the common interest. As I have argued elsewhere (Swanson, 1974), these criteria are usually met by the patterns of familial decision-making numbered 2, 4 and 6 in figure 4.4. In these patterns of decision-making, collective decisions are taken: there are formal mechanisms for developing an authoritative course of action. In addition, each of these types of family works from the premise that diverse points of view are legitimately involved both in the evolution of the authorized course of action and in the development of actions based upon it. (In type 2, both parents are involved in discovering "a common view" which is then the basis for action. In type 4 the arrangements are more formal: decisions are attained and implemented and individual differences are expected and honored. In type 6, one parent is the head but the other has a special role, that of a "counselor" who "expects to be consulted on important family matters," whose views must be "taken into consideration" before the head makes a decision, and who has a special "sphere of responsibility and competence" in implementing as well as making decisions.) In sum, these patterns of decision-making (1) provide a formal and legitimate place for the expression of individual views and for the development of a common view, (2) distinguish between special and common interests, and (3) if there is a clash between them, subordinate the former to the latter. In this sense, there is a "rule of law" and of collective purposes that is distinguished from the personal views of the participants and to which all parties are equally subject. That is the essence of a constitutional order.

Families of the types numbered 3, 5, and 7 in figure 4.4 are likely to be organized as work groups but not as constitutional orders. In types 5 and 7, one person has the right to define or speak for the common interest and neither of these types makes a clear organizational distinction between the collective interest and that of the family's head. In type 3, there is a method for defining the collective interest but not for expressing special interests or for distinguishing them from the collective interest.

I have followed the convention of classifying a family as a constitutional order if the ratings of decision-making from the interviews with *both* parents were any combination of types 2, 4, and 6. Families coded as type 1 in the interviews with both parents were treated as being neither work groups nor constitutional orders. All other ratings of familial decision-making were classified as identifying families organized as work groups that were not constitutional orders. According to the Spearman-Brown prophecy formula, the reliability of coders in placing a family in one of these three categories is 0.60 ($p < 0.001$). (This is a somewhat lower reliability than has been obtained in previous uses of the typology in figure 4.4 (Swanson, 1971). This may be due to deficiencies in the training of the coders, but the design of the interviews themselves was probably important. The parental interviews were not drawn up to elicit the information required for this particular code and, although coders usually found the required information, it sometimes was not explicitly given.)

Empowering and prohibiting the pursuit of personal interests

I turn now to the use of this same typology of decision-making to identify families that lead members to think that their pursuit of personal interests is both warranted and unwarranted: that there are strong grounds for both conclusions. I suggest in a previous study (Swanson, 1986a) that these conditions are met in patterns of decision-making that I have called hierarchical associations and egalitarian social systems. What do these conceptions involve?

As we saw earlier in this chapter (when the idea of a "work group" was first presented), every social relationship is both an association and a social system. It is an association in so far as it serves the diverse personal and special interests of its participants, a social system in so far as it embodies their common and joint concerns. But some social relationships are so organized as to downplay one or the other. I will discuss this dichotomy using the typology in figure 4.4 to provide illustrations.

Models 3, 6, and 7 emphasize people's acting in terms of what they have in common. All play up the value of the family as a social system and play down its service as an association. In model 3, decisions are made through the development of a consensus between the parents, with them acting as equals. In models 6 and 7, one parent has the authority to decide for the family, but may consult other members. In practice, such a parent's action is likely to be legitimized as being in the common interest and not merely, or primarily, in his own interest. Once again, we have patterns of decision-making in which legitimate action is that based upon common interests.

Contrast the models just described with models 1, 4, and 5. As I have shown elsewhere (Swanson, 1971), each is helpfully understood as making a place for the participants' pursuit of special as well as common interests. By that means they legitimate the family's functioning as an association. Model 4, for example, is a kind of "federal" system. The parents do define and solve common problems, and do so as equals, but, in addition, each is free to follow his own bent and make decisions unless the other objects, at which time consultation and an effort at agreement will follow. Model 5 is similar except that one parent has the right to break deadlocks when some decision must be made. Model 1 is a looser version of 4.

In common observation, and in political theory, egalitarianism poses severe problems for social systems (*e.g.*, model 3 in figure 4.4); hierarchy for associations (*e.g.*, model 5 in this figure.). In social systems, collective interests always take precedence. Egalitarianism tends to subvert that principle in two ways. First, collective interests are defined as those to which all or a large majority of members agree. When agreement is wide and deep there is no problem. When this is not the case, each member, or small minorities, have the power to prevent the group taking action. (One thinks, for example, of hung juries or the difficulties that plagued popular decision-making in many city-states in classical Greece or medieval Italy or the disastrous effects of this sort of system for national efforts in early modern Poland (Sartori, 1968).) Second, egalitarianism makes it difficult for groups to develop a legitimate and continuing leadership that can represent the group as a whole and insure the steady implementation of its preferences. As a result, implementation depends heavily on the continuous mobilization and motivation of the whole membership – a state that is always difficult to sustain. To summarize, egalitarianism in social systems gives great practical weight, and great legitimation, to the personal and special interests of participants (Lukes, 1973) while affording preponderant legitimacy only to collective decisions. The result is that participants are likely to be severely conflicted – and to have to defend their actions.

Similar conflicts are generated in hierarchical associations. In associations, legitimate decisions are those that serve special as well as common interests. Common interests are defined as those required for the pursuit of an array of special interests. Some form of hierarchical structure – of continuing leadership, for example – may be required to implement the group's decisions but it is likely to be seen as giving an illegitimate preponderance to collective interests and as illegitimately defining what those interests should be. (The continuous distrust in large federal systems of any growth in the discretion of central authorities provides a ready example (Swanson, 1959).) The participants in hierarchical associations can, by right, pursue personal and special interests and use the group as a facility for that purpose, and can also give greater weight to collective interests: a conflict of rights and duties that should generate defenses.

There is some indirect evidence that the conflicts associated with these patterns of decision-making are linked to the defenses I have placed at level IV (and level V as well). As I have reported elsewhere (Swanson, 1986a), phobias are more common among clinically normal adolescents and among college undergraduates who are reared in families organized as egalitarian social systems or hierarchical associations. Research by others has shown that phobic reactions are more likely than other symptoms of anxiety to appear among people who employ these more complex defenses.

In the present study, I followed conventions developed earlier (Swanson, 1971), and classified a family as an association if the decision-making patterns based on interviews with both parents consisted of any combination of models 1, 2, 4, and 5. I classified families as social systems if the parental interviews yielded any combination of models 2, 3, 6, and 7. All other combinations were treated as intermediate cases.[3] As we have seen, families were classified as hierarchical if either parental interview yielded a code for model 5, 6, or 7 and otherwise as egalitarian.

Level V. Constitutional order

The essentials of a constitutional order, and an index for its presence in families, are now before us. As in work groups, people functioning in a constitutional order discover that some organizational strains are inherent in their relations. And strains associated with hierarchical associations and egalitarian social systems may operate at this level as well as at level IV. These people are authorized and obligated to exericse a wide discretion on behalf of a group.

As a practical matter, we can recognize that the leaders of a group are more likely to think and act in terms of the broadest purposes, and to do so more often, than are the run of the other members. In families, these leaders are likely to be the parents and, as they grow older, the first-born children. As many studies show (*e.g.*, Swanson, 1974), first-born children tend more than others to be pressed into "managerial" positions in families, to be urged to look at things from the point of view of the family's broad interests, and to accept broad responsibilities. That is one reason for my examining the effects of birth-order on the defenses of the children in my study. Another reason is given in the chapter to follow.

Other indices of strain in social relations

It might be thought that, apart from specific strains associated with particular levels of social relations, any tendencies of parents to be anxious or neurotic could be associated with children's defensiveness and any parental strengths as persons might mute their children's need to justify themselves. Haan (1974) has shown that the ratings given to children and adults on coping processes and defenses are related to the subjects' scores on the California Psychological Inventory (CPI) and the Minnesota Multiphasic Inventory (MMPI). We have seen that the CPI is designed to measure personal strengths of normal adults.

---

[3] As I report elsewhere (Swanson, 1987), a decision-making structure that leaves the associational and social systemic aspects of a group unintegrated, if coupled with the absence of close, supportive social relations, is associated with a major role for "pregenital" tricksters in the myths of primitive peoples and with the presence of "pregenital" tricksters among the children in families.

The MMPI is a well-standardized measure of several forms of neurotic and psychotic tendency.

It seemed possible that children's defenses would be related to their parents' scores on such inventories. The files contained the parents' scores on the CPI. For my research, estimates of the parents' MMPI scores were derived from their CPI protocols using tables and formulae developed by Rodgers (1966; n.d.) and reported by Megargee (1972: 255–256).

The files also contained scores for the parents on three aspects of personality derived from the MMPI by Jack Block (Block, 1965; Block and Haan, 1971: 125–6): neurotic overcontrol, neurotic undercontrol, and psychoneurotic tendencies.

Block (1965: 155) thinks of an undercontroller as being

Unduly spontaneous, with enthusiasms neither held in check nor long sustained; his decisions are made (and unmade) rapidly and his emotional fluctuations are readily visible: he disregards, if he does not disdain, social customs and mores; he tends toward immediate gratification of his desires even when such gratification is inconsistent with the reality of his situation or his own ultimate goals . . .

Undercontrollers are better considered as acting up than as acting out; as unruly or as showing off and not simply as unaware of the impulses that their behavior expresses.

By contrast, an overcontroller

appears to be constrained and distant, with minimal expression of his personal emotions; he is highly organized and categorical in his thinking, tending to adhere rigidly to previous understandings; he can continue to work on uninteresting tasks for long periods of time; he is overconforming, indecisive, and with narrow and relatively unchanging interests; he delays gratification even when pleasure is a sensible course of action, not threatening of long-range intents.

Block's Psychoneurotic Scale discriminates people who (Block, 1965: 111)

have small adaptive margins and consequently react to their stresses in rigidified or chaotic ways . . . they are unable to respond effectively to the dynamic requirements of their situation.

They may be expected to appear as (Block, 1965: 111–12)

more anxious, more maladjusted, less appropriate, less attuned to this world, and, not least, as possessing personal attributes which society agrees are undesirable.

This scale is bi-polar, the other end identifying persons who are ego-resilient, that is, persons who (Block, 1965: 111)

react to the press of new and yet unmastered circumstances in resourceful, tenacious, but elastic ways . . .

In my research, I have examined the possibility that parental scores on the CPI, MMPI, and on Block's indices are related to the children's defenses. The results appear, along with others, in the next chapter.

Other potential correlates of complexity in defense

The nature of social solidarity and of strains in solidarity provide one basis for anticipating the complexity of the defenses that members of a family (or other group) are likely to use. It is also obvious that the age and general intellectual level of these children and the educational and intellectual level of their parents might be positively related to such complexity. All of these possibilities were explored in the studies reported in the chapter that follows.

The following indicators of intellectual level were employed:

Tests of intelligence

Both Weinstock (1967a) and Haan (1963: 10) report that one defense, intellectualization, is positively related to a person's scores on tests of intelligence. Miller and Swanson (1960: 391–2, 432, 440) found that, among adolescent boys, either lower socio-economic status or corporal methods of discipline, if they were combined with lower intelligence scores, were related to the use of denial. In the present study, the possible role of scores on intelligence was explored by using the parents' scores on Wechsler's test (WAIS) and the children's scores on the Wechsler test appropriate for their particular age (WISC or WAIS).

Piagetian indices

Scores on two Piagetian indices of cognitive level were also available, but only for parents and children deriving from the Oakland Growth Study. Because the numbers of cases are small, any results can be only suggestive. The indices are Inhelder and Piaget's (1958) Pendulum Problem and the Correlations Problem. These indices are scored separately and a combined score is also derived.

Indices of level of moral judgment

Children and parents from the Oakland Growth Study were given two further tests that measure specific kinds of cognitive complexity: Kohlberg's (1969) index of levels of formal moral reasoning and Haan's (1977: 119–27; 1978) index of levels of interpersonal moral reasoning. Kohlberg's well-known index is intended to reflect advancing levels of abstract analytic reasoning in moral matters. Haan's seems to focus on what might be called "moral maturity" or "wisdom about moral situations." People who get high scores on her index view moral rules as a means for nurturing the lives of individuals and groups and they seek those principles of morality that enable people to overcome difficulties in their relations and to create, or recreate, a fruitful community of interests. As in the case of the Piagetian indices of cognitive development, there are scores on the two moral indices for only a few of the subjects and any results from the use of these indices will be no more than suggestive.

What should we expect to find?

If the arguments in this chapter are correct, we should find a direct association between the organizational complexity of the social relations that are under strain in a family and the cognitive complexity of the defenses used by the children in that family. We have also seen that such a relationship might appear between complexity of defenses and early birth rank, greater age, and higher socio-economic status or intelligence scores.

I have, however, suggested more specific relations between strains in familial relations and complexity of defenses, the relations given in figure 4.3. Strains in the social relations associated with some rows in figure 4.3 are operationalized by more than one index. Thus there are four possible indicators suggested for strains in interdependence, two for strains in social interdependence, and both relative and absolute indicators are suggested for the role appropriateness of parental personalities when considering organization under a charismatic center. My expectation was that defenses in a given row would be associated with one or more of the indices of strain specified for that row, taken singly or in combinations, rather than with some index specified for another row. There seemed no strong reasons for a more precise prediction.

A note on the completeness of data

As in chapter 3, information was not available on all the indices I have described. The indices and the number of cases for which codes proved available are as follows:

1. Personal stability of each parent: father   108
   mother   115
2. Strength of marital bond: father   108
   mother   115
3. Parents' acceptance of this child: father's   108
   mother's   115
4. Closeness of familial ties   114

5. Parental defensiveness: father   104
                                                     mother   104
6. Role appropriateness of parental personalities   82
7. Father's occupation and education   118
8. Methods of familial decision-making   100
9. California Personality Inventory and indices
   derived from it: fathers   83
                                              mothers 103
10. One of Wechsler's tests of intelligence: fathers 100
                                              mothers 114
                                             children 118

Interrelations among indices

This chapter and chapter 3 offer several indices that will be related to defenses in the chapters that follow. Appendix 1 presents the statistically significant ($p < 0.05$) correlations among these indices. For the most part, these are modest in size ($r = 0.2$ or 0.3). None of the indices is so highly correlated with another as to suggest they are getting at approximately the same underlying variable. Findings from these analyses will be taken up as appropriate in later chapters when effects on defenses of particular indices are controlled by the effects of other indices with which they correlate.

5 Interpretations of ten defenses: theory and evidence

Ego defenses ward off accusations that we make against ourselves. We charge ourselves with threatening social ties that we want to sustain; we accuse ourselves of corruption, disloyalty, lack of character, bad faith. Ego defenses enable us to see ourselves as deserving respect in spite of our feelings to the contrary.

We have found that defenses differ according to the situation in which these accusations arise: according to whether we have desires that we reject, whether we have expressed them directly, and whether we expressed them in socially acceptable ways. These distinctions were the focus of chapter 3.

Defenses also differ in cognitive complexity. In chapter 4 we found a basis for defining social relations that foster and entail progressively higher levels of cognitive organization, and we found a basis for relating these to defenses.

In this chapter, all of these ideas come together in interpretations of the ten ego defenses that were coded for my sample of adolescents. (In appendix 4 there are interpretations of four other defenses as well.) Figure 5.1, derived from chapters 3 and 4, associates each defense with a unique pattern of social relations. To test the predictions contained in that figure, one needs a method for estimating the variance unique to each defense. I shall propose such a procedure. In testing predictions, I must rely upon descriptions of social relations in the families in which the adolescents in my sample were reared. There are, of course, other social relationships that may lead these youngsters to defend as they do and I describe a procedure for taking some of these into account. Finally, I must sketch the assumptions I made about the way in which the clinical psychologists who rated the adolescents' defenses are likely to have worked. They based their ratings on the definitions and coding procedures developed by Norma Haan and described in chapter 1 but, as trained clinicians, they are likely also to have drawn on their wider knowledge of conceptions of these defenses contained in clinical accounts. After these preliminaries, I can take up each defense and present the relations between the variance unique to it and the pattern of social relations associated with that variance in figure 5.1. In chapter 6, I describe some combinations of these defenses that are frequently found in my sample of adolescents, interpreting each combination and reporting its social correlates.[1]

Estimating unique variance

There are substantial correlations among the defenses as coded by clinicians using the definitions and procedures developed by Norma Haan and described in chapter 1. In table 5.1, we find that correlations among the defenses of the 118 adolescents in my sample range from 0.07 to 0.59 with an average value of 0.38. (The findings for their fathers and their mothers are very similar.)

This is implied by the arrangement of defenses in figure 5.1. The placement of more than one defense in a particular row or column of that table suggests that these several defenses have features in common and that they are associated with similar features of social relations. It is likely, therefore, that the defenses themselves will be correlated.

Correlations are also made likely by Haan's procedure for rating defenses from interviews. Raters were instructed to distinguish defenses generally from coping processes and ego fragmentation. Haan's instructions for making these distinctions, and her definitions of particular defenses, associate defenses with defensiveness. Figure 5.2, adapted from one of Haan's reports (1969: 15), contains these distinctions. In that figure, defenses are distinguished as entailing adaptations that are poorly articulated with a person's "real" situation. Thus they are described as "compelled, rigid, channeled," as "essentially distorting of the present situation," as involving "a greater quantity of primary process thinking" and partaking of "unconscious elements," and as operating on the "assumption that it is possible to magically remove disturbing affects." Given this procedure, the ratings of one defense are likely to be correlated with those for others.

If ratings from Haan's procedures are to be used in evaluating the predictions contained in figure 5.1, we must find a way to identify the variance unique to each defense. This is so because each defense is associated in figure 5.1 with a distinctive pattern of social relations as represented by a distinctive conjunction of the rows and columns in this figure.

The approach I shall take is to estimate the variance unique to each defense by removing the variance it has in common with all of the other defenses that

---

[1] All defensive behaviors entail what Parsons (1951) calls "passive" rather than "active" dominance: that is, the defender stresses more his readiness to accede to just claims than an opposition to just claims. The four columns in Figure 5.1 correspond to the four major variations of passive deviance in Parsons' paradigm (1951: 259). Reading from left to right, these are perfectionistic observance, submission, evasion, and compulsive independence.

Figure 5.1. *Defenses by sources of danger and complexity in familial relations*

Strains in family at level of:*	Impulse expressed directly toward target?#			
	No			Yes
		Some expression authorized?#		
	A. Yes	B. No	C. Yes	D. No
V. Constitutional order	Reaction formation (complex form)		Intellectualization	
IV. Work group			Isolation	Projection Rationalization
III. Charismatic center	Displacement			
II. Social interdependence	Reaction formation (simpler form)	Repression		Denial
I. Interdependence		Doubt and indecision		Regression

#Operational definitions by columns (from chapter 3):

A. Parents approve individuated interests in children: (*e.g.*, trust children, pursue personal interests and encourage children to do likewise, children accept their own individuality)

B. Scores below the mean on the index just described for A

C. Parents permit children the direct expression of desires (will accept the child even if his behavior does not fit standards the parents prefer) *or*

   Parents support children's direct expression of desires (parents anticipate needs and interests and facilitate children's acting on them or parents facilitate children's acting on needs and interests as these become apparent)

D. Low scores on one of the indices just described for C

*Operational definitions by level (from chapter 4):

IV and V. Codes based on patterns of familial decision-making (work group *vs.* constitutional order; hierarchical associations and egalitarian social systems *vs.* others)

III. Role appropriateness of parents' personalities based on CPI factors

II. Hierarchical network

   Parents' defensiveness: number of scores above the mean on three defense factors

   Father's occupation and education as rated by Hollingshead and Redlich (1958)

I. Personal stability of each parent (*e.g.*, stable *vs.* unstable, operates on even keel *vs.* changeable, not worrisome *vs.* worrisome)

   Parental acceptance of this child (*e.g.*, approving; understand him)

   Strength of marital bond (*e.g.*, exceptionally happy *vs.* extreme marital conflict, extremely friendly *vs.* extremely hostile, very satisfied with marriage *vs.* very dissatisfied)

   Closeness of familial ties (mother and children feel close to father, children say mother is supportive)

Table 5.1. *Intercorrelations among children's defenses*

Defenses	Intellectualization	Rationalization	Doubt	Denial	Projection	Regression	Displacement	Reaction formation	Repression
Isolation	39	47	44	49	38	50	51	48	56
Intellectualization		43	07	30	41	23	36	22	24
Rationalization			16	54	52	54	49	23	33
Doubt and indecision				29	21	40	15	20	28
Denial					50	59	50	24	59
Projection						46	55	26	36
Regression							47	18	53
Displacement								48	42
Reaction formation									31

Figure 5.2. *Properties of ego functioning*

Coping mechanisms	Defense mechanisms	Ego fragmentation
1. Behavior involves choice and, thus, flexible, purposive behavior. It is an autonomous emergent organization.	1. Behavior is compelled, rigid, channeled, perhaps conditioned behavior.	1. Behavior is repetitive, ritualistic and automated.
2. Behavior is pulled toward the future and takes account of present situation.	2. Behavior is pushed from the past.	2. Behavior operates on assumptions which are privatistically based.
3. Behavior is oriented to the reality requirements of present situation.	3. Behavior is essentially distorting of the present situation.	3. Behavior is a closed system and nonresponsive to present situations.
4. Behavior involves secondary process thinking, conscious and preconscious elements.	4. Behavior involves a greater quantity of primary process thinking and partakes of unconscious elements.	4. Behavior is primarily and unadulteratedly determined by biologically-based needs.
5. Behavior operates with the organism's necessity of "metering" the experiencing of disturbing affects.	5. Behavior operates with assumption that is possible to magically remove disturbing affects.	5. Behavior gives evidence that individual is flooded by affect.
6. Behavior allows forms of impulse satisfaction in open, ordered and tempered way.	6. Behavior allows impulse gratification by subterfuge.	6. Behavior allows unmodulated gratification of some impulses.

92 *Interpretations of ten defenses*

were rated. This can provide only an approximation to the measure one would ideally want. On the other hand, an approximation is all we can ever obtain because the ideal measure requires many things that will never be available. For example, ideally, we should have a measure of every possible ego defense and its correlation with each of the others. Only with that information could we remove all of the covariance that is relevant.

I have measures of ten defenses and one or more of these comes from each of the main sectors of the rows and columns of figure 5.1. If the figure as a whole is reasonably exhaustive of the factors that distinguish ego defenses from one another, we have reason to expect that the estimates of unique variance derived from the covariances among these ten defenses are at least useful approximations to ideal estimates.

Unique variance can be estimated by removing the covariance through formula

$$U = X - \tilde{X}$$

where

U = the unique score on a defense
X = the original score on that defense from Haan's code
$\tilde{X} = FA'$

$$\tilde{X}_{ij} = \sum_{k-i} p^f_{ik} \, a_{kj}$$

p factors
j = original variable
F = factor score $(F = XA(D_u + AA')^{-1})$
A = factor loading from a principal factor analysis
$A' = A$ transpose

For my analyses, these unique scores were set to standard form with a mean of 50 and a standard deviation of 10.

Familial and other relations

If the arguments in chapters 1 and 2 are correct, ego defenses are ways of adapting to certain problems encountered in social relations. What I know of the defenses of the adolescents in my sample comes from the coding that Haan arranged, a coding based on typed transcripts of interviews with these youngsters. As we have seen, the interviews dealt mainly with the respondents' relations with their parents and siblings, making it plausible that any defenses they displayed concern those relations. But any other social relations in which the youngsters engaged, including those with the interviewer, may have played a part in determining the defenses they employed. Although we cannot know all the relationships that were relevant for a particular adolescent's behavior, we can be fairly certain that some features of his social situation outside the family as well as within it need routinely to be taken into account. I think especially of his age, sex, birth rank, and socio-economic status. Many studies have shown that older children tend to use defenses that are cognitively more complex. If that is so, and if we want to study associations between complexity of children's defenses and the social relations of those children in their families, we must control for age. Similarly, controls for socio-economic status seem important because, as I show in the next chapter and in appendix 3, middle- and working-class children have been found to differ in their characteristic defenses. Associations between particular defenses and a child's sex or birth rank are not well established, but these social positions are associated with so many aspects of behavior and personality that it seems important to see whether they relate to defenses in this study, especially since they have not been examined in previous research for possible associations with the variance unique to particular defenses.

These considerations determined the way I analyzed data on each defense. I worked in four steps. First, I examined whether the defense was related to the social conditions that define the row(s) and column(s) in figure 5.1 with which that particular defense seemed likely to be associated. Second, I checked relations between scores on that defense and the adolescents' age, sex, birth rank, socio-economic status, and the entrepreneurial or bureaucratic setting in which their families' breadwinners earned a living. I also checked relations between the defense and other variables described in chapters 3 and 4 that did not characterize the social conditions described in the rows or columns of figure 5.1 (*e.g.*, the parents' personality characteristics or scores on tests of intelligence or their methods of disciplining children). Third, I explored the possibility that scores on the defense might be related to social conditions defined in figure 5.1 other than those hypothesized to be the most likely associations. Fourth, I focused on any significant relations uncovered in steps two and three and analyzed the data to see whether these would change any significant findings obtained in step one. I also looked for cases in which significant relations from step one would change any of those uncovered in steps two or three.

The principal result from this last step is given at once in order to facilitate the reading of this chapter. All defenses prove to have significant relations to variables defining the social conditions hypothesized to be the ones related to these defenses and to variables considered either in step two or step three. With one exception – that of doubt and indecision – none of the relations obtained in steps two and three remains appreciable when the key independent variables identified in step one are controlled whereas the significant trends obtained in step one continue to be present when those from later steps are controlled. (I mean that the main trends connected with variables from step one continue to be evident when some variable from step two or three is controlled but that the reverse is not so. The results do not always remain statistically significant because the number of cases in cells may become very small.) In the interpretations to follow, I assume that this finding is taken into account and do not elaborate upon it.

How do clinicians define each defense?

In suggesting the social conditions with which a particular defense will be associated, we must make some assumptions about the meaning Haan's coders gave to that defense. Haan's own definitions certainly carried weight, but were not necessarily determinative. As we saw in chapter 2, there is no standard definition for any defense but, instead, a "vaguely bounded roster of attributes." Since Haan's coders were trained as clinical psychologists, they were familiar with many descriptions of defenses and had impressions from their own work as therapists. Therefore, my own interpretation of each defense takes account of a range of well-known definitions, including Haan's, and it is in the light of the range of attributes contained in these definitions that I make suggestions about social situations that might foster the use of that defense. Some of these definitions were given in chapter 2. I begin the discussion of each defense by presenting further definitions and discussing the sorts of phenomena to which they point.

Interpretations of ten defenses

We can turn now to interpretations of the unique variance of the defenses in figure 5.1 and to evidence from my sample of adolescents. I offer an interpretation of each defense as related to the nature of solidarity, and of strains in solidarity, at the level of social relations associated with this defense in the rows of figure 5.1 and to the likelihood that a child's parents will accept his deviant desires or conduct as that likelihood is represented in the columns of the figure.

I take up the defenses in the order presented in the figure, moving from the most complex to the simplest (that is, from the top of the figure to the bottom) and, at each level of complexity, moving across the figure from left to right. When a defense has more than one definition, and these suggest different levels of cognitive and social complexity (see reaction formation), I have found that it facilitates exposition to begin the discussion at the lowest level in figure 5.1 with which the defense might be associated.

My initial placement of each defense in figure 5.1 was based upon features referred to in many definitions of that defense. As we examine a wider roster of typical definitions, additional placements are sometimes indicated. Figure 5.3 anticipates and summarizes the results of that examination.

My interpretations assume, as stated in earlier chapters, that everyone has desires against which he defends and that he tends sometimes to express, directly or indirectly. The presence of such desires is not measured in this study, only some social conditions that may affect the kind of defenses used to handle the dangers they pose.

What should we expect to find?

Figure 5.1 (with some qualifications noted in figure 5.3) presents expectations based on theory and/or empirical generalizations from earlier studies. All of the relations given in these figures have some grounding in theory and I shall treat them as predictions. That is, I expect these relations to appear unless other factors intervene. Such interventions are likely.

Suppose – it happens not to be true – that projection is used frequently by lower-class males. This might be true for a variety of reasons. Suppose further that these males tend to get high scores on projection whether their family situations are or are not the ones expected to be associated with projection in figure 5.1: are or are not work groups in which parents do not permit direct expressions of deviance. Suppose, finally, that the remaining subjects in my sample are significantly more likely to employ projection under the conditions given in figure 5.1. I would take that to be support for the prediction in the figure with the qualification that other factors (sex and socio-economic status) also prove important.

There are no strong grounds for predicting the relative importance of the variables in figures 5.1 or 5.3 – as compared with variables *not* presented in these figures – in occasioning the appearance of a particular defense. One can say from present theory that variables in figures 5.1 and 5.3 should relate to defenses in the ways predicted, but their influence may be qualified by other variables and even overpowered. On the other hand, it would be a contradiction of expectations in figures 5.1 and 5.3 to find a particular defense significantly related to variables in that figure other than the ones it indicates.

As already indicated, I systematically examined the relations between unique scores on defenses and all of the variables itemized in figures 5.1 and 5.3

Figure 5.3. *Defenses by rows and columns in figure 5.1 expected to be associated with high unique scores.*

		Columns			
		Impulse expressed directly toward target?			
		No		Yes	
		Some expression authorized?			
Rows	Levels of social complexity	A. Yes	B. No	C. Yes	D. No
Defense					
Intellectualization	V.Constitutional order			+	+
Isolation	IV.Work group			+	
Projection	IV.Work group				+
Rationalization	IV.Work group				+
Displacement	III.Charismatic center	+	+		
Repression	II.Social interdependence	+	+		
Reaction formation	II, V.Social interdependence	+			
	Constitutional order		+		
Denial	II.Social interdependence			+	+
Doubt and indecision	I.Interdependence		+		
Regression	I.Interdependence			+	+

and additional variables (*e.g.*, sex, family size) given in chapters 3 and 4. I report any significant results, but I take as relevant only the ones concerning the independent variables in figures 5.1 and 5.3 when evaluating the theory which these figures embody. As we shall see, the data provide considerable support for that theory.

Level V. Constitutional order: intellectualization

1. Clinical descriptions

(Bibring and others, 1961: 68) based on thinking as a special and limited variety of doing: the control of affects and impulses through thinking them instead of experiencing them. Intellectualization is a systematic overdoing of thinking, deprived of its affect, in order to defend against anxiety attributable to an unacceptable impulse. It is the thinking process, defensively directed against and replacing emotion and impulse. In that thinking has been in one sense defined as experimental action in small and contained degree, intellectualization restricts the individual to the realm of testing.

(Freud, 1936: 161–2) the point at issue is how to relate the instinctual side of human nature to the rest of life, how to decide between putting sexual impulses into practice and renouncing them, between liberty and restraint, between revolt against and submission to authority . . . The *thinking over* of the instinctual conflict – its intellectualization – would seem to be a suitable means (of surmounting the danger) . . . But this merely takes place in thought; it is an intellectual process . . .

(Haan, 1974: 150) Retreat from the world of impulse and affect to a world principally of words and abstractions. Pedantry. S[ubject] thinks and talks on a level of abstraction not quite appropriate to the situation, uses jargon, is unable to be specific where this would be called for. Or S[ubject] is pedantically over-detailed and over-precise. Pseudo-intellectuality.

2. Interpretation

An appropriate defense against charges at this level of social relations will be founded on meticulous attention to the group's broad purpose and setting. At this level of social relations, people are empowered with a wide discretion and required to use it creatively to serve the group. Care and wholeheartedness are signs that they take seriously the charge given them. Skillful execution demonstrates that they deserve the high position they hold.

Two of the ten ego defenses in my series are obvious candidates for justifications of this sort. They are intellectualization and complex forms of reaction formation.

In figure 5.1, intellectualization is related to strains in families at level V (constitutional order). Strains at this level are indexed by a family's being organized as a constitutional order rather than as a work group and by its being a hierarchical association or an egalitarian social system.

The clinical descriptions of intellectualization cover a wide range but have much in common with one another. Thus Bibring and her collaborators treat intellectualization as a form of isolation in which inner conflicts are thought about but in which their seriousness is not consciously recognized. In these circumstances, the person can work on his problems, and analyze them, as if they were devoid of personal meaning. His obsession with these problems belies his claim that his deviant tendencies should not be taken seriously. Anna Freud gives even greater stress to the person's "thinking over of the instinctual conflict" and gives, as examples, adolescents and young adults who deal with their personal conflicts in a remote and highly abstract manner: their treatment, perhaps, of a difficult personal conflict as if it were an abstract problem in metaphysics, religion, or political theory. In Haan's description, there is less stress on the presence in intellectualization of analytic thinking and there is the contrary suggestion that we have in this defense the inappropriate use of words and abstractions by someone who wants to appear reflective but does not bring it off. "Pseudo-intellectuality" is Haan's word for it.

All of these problems show us a person who is able to express and handle a personal problem as long as he can regard it as being not quite his own. That achieved, he can address it calmly and deliberately. He is no longer overwhelmed by a sense of urgency or shame or guilt. On the other hand, he is likely to be so obsessed with the problem that he is not able to do some other important things.

In all definitions, intellectualization involves at least the trappings of analytic thought. That being so, it comes as no surprise to find in my own sample that unique scores on this defense are positively correlated ($r(118) = 0.25$, $p < 0.01$) with what Haan calls "total coping scores," these being the sum of a subject's standardized scores on the ten coping mechanisms listed in chapter 1 and figure 1.1 (and described in figure 5.2). For all analyses in this chapter, I have used unique scores on intellectualization as standardized for the subjects' scores on total coping.

Does intellectualization involve high levels of analytic thought? Not necessarily. The person who intellectualizes tries to place his possibly deviant desires in the context of all relevant considerations. He makes a great effort to take account of every detail, and of the broad character of a social relationship, in determining the behavior that is and is not desirable. But all of this activity may tend more toward rumination than analytic precision. There may, as Haan stresses, be more of the trappings of analysis than of a highly abstract dissection of problems.

If there is disagreement among observers about the quality of analyses made in intellectualization, there is none about the magnitude of the efforts these involve. Intellectualizing is hard work. It involves sustained and thorough efforts and there are no obvious guidelines to use in deciding when one has done enough. This suggests the employment of the kind of discretion, commitment, and contribution demanded by social relations at level V. As we have seen, social relations at lower levels of complexity are more likely to provide, and even impose, clear guidelines for action (levels II and IV) or to lack a social framework that supports sustained effort (levels I through III). A constitutional order provides all of these conditions that seem necessary for intellectualization to appear.

In which column of figure 5.1 should this defense be placed? Cases cited in the clinical literature, including those of Anna Freud, play up the extent to which intellectualization permits some expression of deviant impulses: even a fairly direct expression. That suggests a placement in column C or D of the figure. But, in which of these columns? That is not clear. Some discussions, Anna Freud's among them, suggest that intellectualization can be used if the impulse is expressed in a socially acceptable form. (Because hers is the "classical" discussion, I placed this defense where her portrayal would seem to indicate: at the intersection of level V and column C in figure 5.1.) Two conditions were given in figure 5.1 as conducive to socially acceptable expressions: parental permission of children's direct expressions of possibly deviant desires (will accept the child even if his behavior does not fit standards the parents prefer) or their support for such expressions (facilitate children's acting on their needs and desires). But, in other examples of intellectualization, there is a quite direct and "tactless" expression of prohibited desires (figure 5.1, column D) accompanied by explanations that resemble rationalization (except that a higher degree of intellectual complexity is apparent). (The conditions suggested in the figure as generating these tactless expressions are the opposite of those for column C.) None of the clinical descriptions we have examined seems to preclude either of these possibilities. Final placement (as in figure 5.3): row V and columns C or D.

3. Findings

Abstract intellectual activity is more common among only and first-born children (Zajonc and Markus, 1976). Unique scores on intellectualization are higher for first-born and only children than for other ($r(118) = 0.30$, $p < 0.01$). As table 5.2 shows, they are also higher among adolescents whose families do not support a direct expression of members' needs and desires or that are organized as constitutional orders. (In this table, the direct relationship with birth rank is significant ($r(86)=0.40$, $p<0.01$) as is the multiple correlation ($R(7,78)=0.46$, $p<0.01$).) If the effect of birth rank is partialled out, adolescents from the less supportive families that are also organized as constitutional orders are significantly more likely than others to exhibit intellectualization (see table 5.2 for the specification of this comparison): partial $r=0.22$, $p<0.05$.

Eighty-three per cent of the first-born and only children from the less supportive families have high scores on intellectualization. Seventy-six per cent of the later-born children from the more supportive families have low scores. Adolescents who are not in these two categories have higher scores on intellectualization if they come from families, whether work groups or constitutional orders, that are organized as hierarchical associations or as egalitarian social systems (families, therefore, that encourage and also prohibit their members' pursuit of both personal and common interests): $r(45)=0.41$, $p<0.01$.

Unique scores on intellectualization are not related significantly to any of the other indices of familial relations that define the rows and columns of figure 5.1. They do correlate significantly with one other variable used in this study, fathers' scores on intellectualization: $r(104)=0.21$, $p<0.05$. As indicated earlier in this chapter, this association does not add to, or eliminate, intellectualization's associations with other variables as just reported.

4. Discussion

Perhaps the general meaning of the findings is that high unique scores on intellectualization are consistent with a style of defending that is characteristic of first-born and only children. With that taken into account, scores are higher, as expected, among adolescents from families organized as constitutional orders. The expectation that scores on this defense will be associated with parents' responses to direct expressions of possibly deviant desires is also confirmed. But that correlation is the reverse of the one implied by Anna Freud's discussion and recorded in figure 5.1: adolescents with higher scores on intellectualization are more likely in column D (their parents do not support direct expressions of such desires) rather than column C. Possible grounds for such a finding were discussed in the section on interpretation.

Level IV. Work groups: isolation

1. Clinical descriptions

(Bibring and others, 1961: 68) the intrapsychic separation of affect from content. Isolation is a *splitting off* process followed by three possibilities: (1) the idea is repressed,

Table 5.2. *Intellectualization: by birth rank, parental support for direct expression of desires, and constitutional order:* N = 86

Birth rank	Parental support for direct expression of deviant desires	Constitutional order	N	Mean unique score
First or only	High	Present*	1	76
		Absent*	4	50
	Low	Present	11	67
		Absent*	19	63
Later born	High	Present#	7	39
		Absent#	7	31
	Low	Present	15	52
		Absent#	22	44

*, #Combined in computing the partial correlation reported in the text.

(2) the affect is repressed, (3) neither the idea nor the affect is repressed, but, once separated, the affect is displaced to a different or substitute thought. Isolation refers to the "loss" of affect . . .

(Fenichel, 1945: 155) here the patient has not forgotten his pathogenic traumata, but has lost trace of their connections and their emotional significance.

(Haan, 1974: 149) In part it is a matter of the affect's not being related to the idea. This is in the direction of inappropriate affect. Subjects high on this can't generalize, synthesize or integrate meaningfully because they keep apart the ideas and concomitant affects that belong together . . . Isolated affect may occur . . . with some delay or diffuseness but is unfocused on the real causation. Ideas that are logically related and depend upon each other are not put together.

(Symonds, 1946: 476–7) Isolation may be defined as the tendency to eliminate feeling from behavior and thereby relieve the individual from suffering anxiety at the open expression of his unconscious impulses . . . depends on overdevelopment of intellectual traits. The individual substitutes intellectual formulations, theorizing, and problem-solving for the working out of his emotional problems . . . Repression blots an impulse from consciousness and prevents any recognition of its symptomatic nature. Isolation recognizes the symptom but fails to grasp its significance because it has been separated from its emotional and affectional component . . .

2. Interpretation
Isolation is a defense that may cut across the columns of figure 5.1. But no one thinks it is a simple defense.

I begin with an example. Suppose that a boy who is angry with his mother wants to hurt her but feels that such an act, or the desire to perform it, is personally and socially unacceptable. If he defends by means of isolation, he can acknowledge one or another aspect of his motivation, but not all of it, as truly his own. Perhaps he constantly snaps at his mother. In this way he shows his anger and the target toward which it is directed but not his desire to hurt. Indeed, there seems "no reason" for his behavior and he may excuse it through rationalizations. Again, the boy may frequently have a dream in which his mother is injured in an accident and may ask himself, and perhaps his mother, what this could mean. The dream makes visible the target of his feelings and the outcome of his desire but not his feelings or desire as such.

To put the case more generally, the person who isolates wants to do something he finds unacceptable but he does find it acceptable to think, or do, some part of what he desires if it need not be seen as the outcome of that unacceptable desire. It is the full course of thought or overt action that is unacceptable. Taken by themselves the component parts of that course are harmless and no one should be concerned by their presence.

These components make it difficult to place isolation in the columns of figure 5.1. It can involve overt behavior that expresses a deviant impulse and, in some instances, the expression is fairly direct. In other cases, the expression seems indirect. In still others, this expression is so divorced from the impulse itself that it can be argued that the impulse, as such, goes unexpressed. It is true, however, that the classical definitions of isolation (note, for example, those of Fenichel and Symonds) entail a person's acting rather directly on a deviant desire but doing it in such a way as to make it acceptable to others. That was the basis for my placing isolation in column C.

In what row of figure 5.1 does it belong? I have linked it in that figure to strains in families at level IV (work group). Strains at this level are indexed by a family's being organized as a work group rather than as a constitutional order and by its being a hierarchical association or an egalitarian social system.

In isolation, the person seems to make use of his character and general repute as the basis for justifying questionable thoughts or deeds. He says, in effect, that what he does, or seems to do, need not be taken seriously because it is unrepresentative of his real commitments: it would be "out of character" for him to be, or to do, that of which he is accused. A defense of this sort must rest upon a record of routine contributions to the group and that consideration suggests it will be found in social relations organized at the level of a work group – or higher.

To "have character" is to have durable and wholehearted commitments that underpin our stability and, even more, our faithfulness in our relations with other people (Allport, 1924: 124; Dewey, 1922: 38-43; Dewey and Tufts, 1908: 255; Gerth and Mills, 1953: 22; Peck and Havighurst, 1960: 1). We are people of "good character" if we have such commitments and if they lead us to be supportive and steadfast in social relations.

There are several reasons for thinking that defenses based on a claim of good character might be associated with strains in work groups. First of all, a claim of good character can be established only for social relations that endure. One has to build up a record of faithful performance across many situations. It is against that record that a desire or act that appears deviant can be judged exceptional or judged as not being what it seems. Work groups enable, and require, a person's faithful performance of socially sustaining activities over a substantial period of time. These conditions are not as likely to be met in social relations confined to the narrower or more fleeting contacts found at levels I through III in figure 5.1.

Second, good character concerns broad commitments and the general nature of conduct over a wide variety of specific acts. As I suggested in chapter 4, each person in a work group is responsible for the performance of particular roles in a division of labor and this requires, and facilitates, his steady meeting of broad requirements – his being steadfast and industrious. And his performance can be taken as showing the extent to which his broad personal interests foster the broad interests of the group (Swanson, 1970: 136). A person cannot perform well in one or more specialized roles unless he understands how they fit together to serve broader collective purposes and unless he can modify what he does the better to promote the whole enterprise.

Third, certain strains are endemic in work groups, thus guaranteeing the members' need to defend. We found in chapter 4 that even people who have the best of intentions are almost certain to do things while pursuing their particular roles that give those roles more weight, or less, than the group's current needs will justify. These people will therefore wonder, as will others, whether their motives and skills and commitments are what they should be. We also saw that role specialists develop a basis for questioning the judgments of charismatic leaders and that, within the terms of organization of a work group, this implies an attack on the group's solidarity and, at the same time, an effort to promote the group's interests. In this situation, sustained efforts to promote collective interests can be seen as a sign of good character and a justifiable basis for acts, such as criticizing the leader, that would otherwise be unacceptable.

When a person is accused of unacceptable conduct, the structure of a work group affords some specific resources for a defense. It not only provides possible grounds for a claim of good character but, given the acceptance of that claim, it makes the accuser into someone who has unnecessarily jeopardized social solidarity. This is so because conduct that only "seems" bad should be excused in a person of good character; a person who has proven his commitment and his worth. What is more, it can often be argued that a judgment of conduct as good or bad is premature and is therefore unjustified and a threat to the relationship. This can be grounded in the fact, already discussed, that people who carry out roles in a division of labor are usually empowered to exercise discretion and to do what is necessary for their specialized work, providing only that their activities promote, and do not disrupt, the group's total effort. We have seen that this authorization contains inescapable ambiguities. Given this authorization and these ambiguities, an accused person can always say that the special rights associated with his role are being attacked and, with them, essential foundations for solidarity in a division of labor.

Might isolation be associated with social relations at level V, that of a constitutional order? The usual clinical descriptions say that one defense at that level, intellectualization, is a form of isolation and that the two are sometimes difficult to separate, but they also tend to describe isolation as a less creative and analytic means of asserting solidarity and that implies less of a requirement than in intellectualization to exercise a wide-ranging but highly responsible discretion in formulating one's behavior. Again, intellectualization is usually so defined that the person justifies himself through some creative contribution to the group. Isolation rests on a record of social contributions and, although these could be creative, the typical definition does not suggest it. In summary, isolation could be associated with social relations at level V, but this seems less likely than in the case of intellectualization.

3. Findings

First-born and only children tend to have high scores on intellectualization. If they are male and from families in which the breadwinner has an entrepreneurial occupation, they are likely to have high scores on isolation (91% of the 11 cases). Other adolescents in my sample tend to have high scores (table 5.3) if reared in families organized as work groups, especially if their parents either permit or support the direct expression of possible deviant desires. The main effect for being reared in a work group is significant ($r(79) = 0.36, p < 0.01$) as are the trends for the table as a whole ($R = 0.39, p < 0.01$). All trends in the table are in expected directions.

Unique scores on isolation correlate significantly with a few of the other variables examined in this study: the fathers' MMPI scores on undercontrol ($r(88) = 0.22, p < 0.05$), the fathers' CPI scores on self-control ($-0.25, p < 0.05$) and good impression ($-0.24, p < 0.02$) and the mothers' CPI scores on socialization ($0.21, p < 0.05$) and flexibility ($0.21, p < 0.02$). The mothers' scores on the CPI suggest a restless, excitable, assertive person, and one who is self-centered.

Table 5.3. *Isolation: by parental permission of, or support for, direct expression of desires and work group:* N = 79

Parents permit or support direct expression of deviant desires	Work group	N	Mean unique score
Yes	Present	34	60
	Absent	24	39
No	Present	11	48
	Absent	10	37

4. Discussion

Isolation seems to occur among adolescents whose parents have some tolerance for their children's direct expression of possibly deviant desires – providing it does not get out of hand – and who do not press youngsters to show the great care and thoughtfulness found in intellectualization. As we have seen, isolation is one of the defenses that Miller and Swanson (1960) found associated in adolescents with their fathers' having an entrepreneurial occupation, an occupation they saw as requiring initiative and risk-taking and a strong self-control. This relationship appears in the present sample, but only for males who are also first-born or only children. The remaining relationships uncovered in this sample are the ones anticipated and summarized in figure 5.1.

Level IV. Work group: projection

1. Clinical descriptions

(Bibring and others, 1961: 69) the perceiving and treating of certain unacceptable inner impulses and their derivatives as if they were outside the self. The impulses may arise in the id, or activity of the superego may be so reflected, as, for example, in a hallucinated recrimination.

(Haan, 1974: 152) A process by which an objectionable, internal tendency is unrealistically attributed to another person or persons in the environment instead of being recognized as a part of one's self . . . Manifestations: suspicious about what . . . [others know] about them and about . . . [their] intentions . . ., feeling of being victimized by one's boss or fellow workers, perception of the world as a jungle and feeling that one needs to be constantly on guard. Readiness to see in personal interactions (either his own or those of others) the possibility of being made a sucker. These concerns may be used to justify retaliatory measures.

(Shapiro, 1965: 68, 70) the attribution to external figures of motivations, drives, or other tensions that are repudiated and intolerable in oneself . . .

Projection . . . does not involve a breakdown of cognition and a withdrawal of attention from the external world . . . projection is generally faithful to and does not distort apparent reality, nor does it usually include perceptual distortion. Projection distorts the significance of apparent reality.

(Symonds, 1946: 296) Projection has two principal meanings. As most commonly used, projection is a reference of impulses, thoughts, feelings, and wishes originating in the person himself to persons and objects in the outside world . . .

The second meaning . . . he attempts to influence and control another person through whom he lives out his own needs.

Projection may be thought of as a form of displacement.

2. Interpretation

A person who projects thinks that he is accused, or is likely to be accused, of having directly violated his commitments to other people and that, if it occurred, such conduct on his part is unacceptable. That places projection with the defenses in column D of figure 5.1. In my sample that would mean that an adolescent's parents would not accept him unless his behavior fitted their standards and/or would not facilitate his acting on needs and interests that have the possibility of being deviant.

Projection also seems to belong at level IV in that figure. Like isolation, it involves a person's claiming that it would be "out of character" for him to be, or to do, that of which he is accused.

In projection, the person stands accused of bad conduct. He replies that he is obviously of good character and that his accuser must therefore be malicious, be making reckless charges, or be trying to provoke or seduce him. Or he says that other people – acceptable people – are like he is and that he, too, is therefore acceptable (Holmes, 1978). It follows that his accuser is the one who is destroying the social compact. What seems to be bad conduct by the defendant – suspiciousness, perhaps, or anger – is really the act of a person defending his rights and exercising them (Campbell and others, 1964: 5–6).

Projections seem rarely to be inventions. Research on psychiatric patients and on clinically normal people supports Fenichel's (1945: 147) conclusion that

projections . . . are not performed at random but are directed toward some point in reality where they are met halfway. The paranoid person is sensitized, as it were, to perceive the unconscious of others, wherever this perception can be utilized to rationalize his own tendencies toward projection . . .

Heilbrun's (1973: 238–46) findings, and Weinstock's (1967a: 71), are typical in showing that the use of projection is associated with a person's being reared by a mother who is brutal, highly controlling, low in nurturance: a person about whom the child must be wary and with whom his relations are strained.

Table 5.4. *Projection: by parental permission of, and support for, direct expression of desires, work group, and association:* N = 87

Parents permit and support direct expression of deviant desires	Work group that is also an association	*N*	Mean unique score
Yes	Present	2	24
	Absent	9	24
No	Present	12	67
	Absent	64	47

Could projection be associated with social relations at the level of a constitutional order? This seems unlikely because projection does not involve the claim that one's conduct is justified by virtue of one's creative and positive contributions to the relationship.

3. Findings

As table 5.4 shows, the findings for my sample of adolescents are consistent with these expectations and with the placement given this defense in figure 5.1. They are, in some ways, a mirror image of those for isolation. Unique scores on projection are higher if the parents neither permit nor support direct expressions of possibly deviant desires ($r(87) = 0.34$, $p < 0.01$). They are also higher for adolescents reared in families organized as work groups – providing (a discovery not anticipated in figure 5.1) they are also organized as associations ($r = 0.23$, $p < 0.05$). For the table as a whole, $R = 0.41$, $p < 0.01$.

In this sample, projection is also correlated with other variables, but none remains important when the variables already discussed are taken into account. High scores on projection are correlated positively with fathers' MMPI-based scores on lying ($r(88) = 0.22$, $p < 0.05$) and negatively with their CPI scores on self-acceptance (-0.28, $p < 0.05$). They correlate negatively with two of the mothers' scores on the MMPI: depression ($r(103) = -0.21$, $p < 0.05$) and psychasthenia (-0.25, $p < 0.02$). Finally, scores on projection correlate positively with the fathers' ratings on intellectualization ($r(104) = 0.23$, $p < 0.02$).

4. Discussion

In this study, as in many others, projection is associated with prohibitions on the direct expression of desires. The findings also suggest that it is especially likely when those prohibitions are accompanied by the person's having rights to pursue personal interests. Groups organized as associations specifically provide such rights. Thus, in a family organized in this way, a child is able to counter accusations against his conduct by pointing to his right to pursue personal preferences and to accuse his accusers of trying to deprive him of rights that are properly his.

Level IV. Work group: rationalization

1. Clinical descriptions

(Bibring and others, 1961: 69) attitudes, beliefs, or behavior which might otherwise be unacceptable may be justified by the incorrect application of a truth, or the invention of a convincing fallacy.

(Fenichel, 1945: 485–6) [A person] finds one reason or another why he has to behave in this way or that, and thus avoids becoming aware that he actually is driven by an instinctual impulse. Aggressive behavior often becomes sanctioned on condition that it is viewed as "good"; a like situation holds for sexual attitudes. The ego, afraid of its impulses, tries to vindicate them, and is able to yield to them as long as it believes in their justification.

Probably various types of rationalization exist; one of them could be called idealization. The realization that an ideal requirement is going to be fulfilled brings to the ego an increase in self-esteem. This may delude it into ignoring the fact that through the idealized actions there is an expression of instincts that ordinarily would have to be repressed . . . In this state of elation the ego relaxes its ordinary testing of reality and of impulses so that instinctual impulses may emerge relatively uncensored. Reality, therefore, is much more readily misapprehended in states of elation, intoxication, or self-satisfaction . . .

(Haan, 1974: 150) [A person] offers apparently plausible causal context to explain behavior and/or intention, which allows impulse *sub rosa* gratification to escape attention, but omits crucial aspects of situation, or is otherwise inexact. He needs to offer causal explanations but they do not hold water, needs to justify himself in terms of fortuitous circumstances; fate just came out that way.

(Symonds, 1946: 454) may be defined as faulty thinking which serves to disguise or hide the unconscious motives of behavior and feeling . . . a selection of facts that can be used . . . in order to justify certain conclusions already reached . . .

2. Interpretation

If a person defends by rationalizing, he has wanted something, or done something, that is unacceptable. If he has done something and his conduct is clearly unacceptable – and that is how rationalization is pictured in most illustrations – then this defense belongs with projection and the others in column D of figure 5.1.

The person who rationalizes tries to explain how he could have wanted what he wanted, or behaved as he has, despite his desire to do what is right. The heart of his defense is that he did not intend to do or desire anything that is wrong. He also does not blame himself or other people for the things that happened. He attributes his deviance to happenstance or to conditions beyond his control. What happened was accidental or incidental. He is not to blame nor is anyone else. If sincere, this argument affirms the person's solidarity with others and implies that he is not likely to deviate in the future.

Is rationalization a simple defense or is it complex? Elkind (1976: 178, 182) says that it is simple and is used by very young children. What he seems to mean is that young children excuse themselves by saying, "I didn't mean it." Berndt and Berndt (1975), Keasey (1977), and other investigators have shown that children as young as age four can distinguish between harming someone by accident and harming him by intent and have shown that, at that age, children may excuse their own "deviance" as unintended.

There is, however, another meaning for rationalization and investigators who adopt it will consider rationalization to be a complex defense. In this meaning, a person rationalizes if he shows that what he really intended was quite different from what he seemed to do or desire and if he proceeds to show that his behavior can be given this different, and favorable, interpretation. Chandler, Paget, and Koch (1978), who think that rationalization involves such reinterpretations of the meaning of behavior, also find that children who are high in analytical ability (they have in mind Piaget's portrayal of "formal operations") are better able to perceive this form of rationalization in the behavior of others.

The simple form of rationalization cannot be used too often or used with regard to sustained relationships. No one will believe that accidents and happenstance occur so often. To be plausible for sustained relationships, the person must be able to establish the real nature of his commitments; to show that he has acted on them again and again; to show that something that no one intended and that is beyond his control has affected his behavior for some time and has led to the false impression that he has deviant desires. The defenses coded for my sample of adolescents tend to refer to such sustained social relationships and, in that context, rationalization is likely to be a complex defense.

As we have seen, the social relations in a work group make it possible for a person to demonstrate his commitments in sustained contributions. They would, therefore, be sufficient to undergird a complex form of rationalization. The social relations in a constitutional order could also serve for this purpose, but seem to demand more in a successful defense than rationalization provides.

Specifically, they demand evidence of the person's taking initiatives and going beyond the call of duty in supporting the group's life and work. Rationalization requires only the demonstration of good and faithful service. For that reason it seems most appropriate to place it at level IV in figure 5.1: work group.

A comparison of these findings for rationalization with those for projection is of interest. Both defenses are associated with variables that define level IV (work group) and column D in figure 5.1 but they differ in the basis for their placement in that column. Projection is placed there because it is associated with parents' insisting that children conform overtly to standards of conduct that parents approve. Rationalization is placed there because it is associated with parents' not trying always to support their children's pursuit of their interests and the satisfying of what the children define as their needs. In short, projection is associated with direct pressures on children to adopt standards other than they might whereas rationalization tends to be used if parents question the lines of action their children take.

3. Findings

My findings on rationalization are consistent with these expectations. As table 5.5 shows, rationalization is more likely if parents do not support the direct expression of deviant desires – providing the family is organized as a work group – $(r(100) = 0.23, p < 0.05)$. The findings also show that scores on rationalization are higher if the family's organization embodies the structural incompatibilities found in hierarchical associations and egalitarian social systems ($r = 0.20, p < 0.05$). For the table as a whole, $R = 0.29, p < 0.05$.

Scores on rationalization correlate significantly with only a few of the other independent variables used in this study and none of them seems to account for variance additional to that accounted for by independent variables already presented. These remaining correlations are between rationalization and the mothers' MMPI-based scores on overcontrol ($0.22, p < 0.05$) and their CPI-based scores on dominance ($-0.21, p < 0.05$).

4. Discussion

In this sample, rationalization seems like intellectualization in its correlation with a lack of parental support for direct expressions of possibly deviant desires and with pressures to take account of the structural complexities, temptations, and cross-pressures embodied in hierarchical associations and egalitarian social systems. It is different in being associated with the lesser demands for intellectual and personal effort associated with groups organized as work groups rather than as constitutional orders.

Table 5.5. *Rationalization: by parental support for direct expression of desires, work group, and certain structural incompatibilities in their families:* N = *100*

Parents do not support direct expression of deviant desires and family is work group	Family has structural incompatibilities*	N	Mean unique scores
Yes	Yes	24	59
	No	17	49
No	Yes	26	46
	No	33	38

*Family is a hierarchical association or egalitarian social system.

Level III. Charismatic center: displacement

1. Clinical descriptions

(Bibring and others, 1961: 66) a purposeful unconscious shifting from one object to another in the interest of solving a conflict. Although the object is changed, the instinctual nature of the impulse and its aim remain the same.

(Haan, 1974: 154) Subject temporarily and unsuccessfully attempts to control unacceptable impulses or affects in relation to their original objects or situations, and then expresses them in a situation of greater internal or external tolerance. Situational displacement may occur as a temporal displacement (*e.g.*, carrying frustrations home from office) or as an object displacement (*e.g.*, repressed resentment towards parents or authorities is expressed in hostility towards weaker or defenseless persons, children, subordinates, or members of minority groups). Sexualizes neutral situations, but inhibited or hostile in the actual situation. Wishes for dependence or succorance, etc., in relationship [to] historically significant figures are readily transferred to present figures.

(Symonds, 1946: 252) Displacement may be defined as a shift of emotion, wish, idea, or fantasy from a person or object toward which it was originally directed to another person or object . . . a shift of feelings or attitudes rather than an actual shift of behavior, but a shift in behavior may be the form in which it is outwardly observed . . .

2. Interpretation

Displacement is a kind of substitution. A person wants something. His feelings – anger, perhaps, or sexual desire – are not themselves objectionable. Their direction is (Atkinson, 1969: 118). The person blames himself for feeling as he does toward some person or group. In displacing, he finds an alternative target for the feelings aroused by the object toward which they are unacceptable. This enables him to behave as he thinks he should while expressing his impulse.

Displacement seems to belong among the defenses in which a desire is not expressed directly toward its target. Should it be grouped, in figure 5.1, with the defenses in column A or in column B? In column A for my sample: the parents approve (or are tolerant) of individuated interests in children (e.g., trust children, encourage them to pursue personal interests); in column B, they do not.

The problem lies in the differing fates in this defense of two components of desire. The impulse is expressed. That suggests that displacement belongs in column A where indirect expressions are tolerated. On the other hand, it is not expressed, even indirectly, toward its true target. That suggests a placement with the defenses in column B where even indirect expressions are forbidden. The answer is not clear.

In what row in figure 5.1 should this defense be placed? I have proposed a connection with familial strains at level III, charismatic center. These strains are indexed in figure 5.1 by the parents' personalities not being appropriate for their roles.

Displacement requires that a person be able to distinguish between those targets in a relationship that cannot be the object of certain feelings without destroying solidarity and those targets which can. This sort of distinction is possible in relations organized around a charismatic center and, perhaps, in more complex relations as well. The presence of a charismatic center limits a person's obligations in a relationship. Collective actions and interests are supported by the charismatic leader, and by the independent enactors. They are also to be supported by all members and the ability of the charismatic leader to serve as leader must be sustained. In other matters, people are free to exercise their own discretion. If strains arise from the actions of the charismatic leader, the resultant feelings are acceptable if they do not upset the solidarity of this collectivity. They may, of course, put a strain on relations outside the collectivity.

Displacement could be used at higher levels of social organization, but it seems unlikely as a principal defense at those levels because it does not, of itself, make the full justification that such levels require. It is not based upon a record of sustained contributions – of character – required in relations organized as work groups and does not, in itself, entail the exercise of a wide-ranging discretion on the group's behalf that is required at the level of a constitutional order. On the other hand, social relations at these higher levels of organization do afford a specified, and therefore limited, basis upon which solidary relations rest and that makes it possible for a person to protect those relations

Table 5.6. *Displacement: by parental approval of individuated interests and role appropriateness of father's personality:* N = 76

Parental approval of individuated interests: standard scores*	Is father's personality role appropriate?	N	Mean unique score
40–59	Yes	32	47
	No	23	60
Below 40 or above 59	Yes	15	38
	No	6	41

*Mean set at 50, standard deviation at 10.

while venting his feelings on other targets. This suggests that displacement might be an ancillary defense at these levels or that aspects of displacement might be a part of defenses appropriate at these levels. The latter is, in fact, true by definition. Something of displacement is, by definition, a part of intellectualization, isolation, projection, and of the more complex forms of reaction formation.

Displacement seems less likely in relations simpler than organization under a charismatic center. Relations of interdependence are so diffuse, and relations in networks of social interdependence are so personalized and intertwined, that people will find it hard to specify with confidence what might or might not upset the relationship.

3. Findings

In my sample of adolescents, displacement has a curvilinear relationship to the parents' scores on approval of individuated interests. Table 5.6 shows that parents who are highly approving, or who give little approval, (scores more than one standard deviation above or below the mean) tend to have children who do not exhibit displacement as much as the rest of the sample ($r(76) = 0.23$, $p < 0.05$). (Perhaps if parental approval is very low, displacement is not possible and, if approval is very high, displacement is less necessary.) Scores on displacement are also higher for adolescents whose fathers' personalities are not role appropriate (in this case, they do not have as high scores as their wives' on the CPI based index on task leadership: ($r = 0.23$, $p < 0.05$)). For the table as a whole, the value of R is 0.31, $p < 0.05$. There are no relations of displacement with the role appropriateness of the mothers' personalities or with the parents' absolute CPI scores on task or social-emotional leadership. I will discuss this further in connection with related findings that are described later in this chapter.

In my sample, unique scores on displacement have scattered relations with other variables but none of these remains significant when one controls for the variables already considered. There are, for example, correlations with two of the fathers' scores on defenses (but with none of the mothers!): with the fathers' scores on isolation ($r=0.22$, $p<0.05$) and on rationalization ($r=0.20$, $p<0.05$). Displacement is related positively to the mothers' scores on undercontrol ($r(103)=0.20, p<0.05$). Displacement correlates negatively with the fathers' MMPI scores on depression ($r(88)=-0.20$, $p<0.05$) and femininity (-0.25, $p<0.02$) and the mothers' MMPI scores on lie (-0.22, $p<0.05$). It is also related to one of the fathers' scores on the CPI (that for communality: $r=0.20$, $p<0.05$) and to three of the mothers' scores on this index: self-acceptance ($r=-0.21$, $p<0.05$), socialization ($r=-0.22$, $p<0.05$), and communality ($r=-0.22$, $p<0.05$). These maternal scores are mainly ones that are regarded as measures of socialization, maturity, and responsibility and suggest that the mothers of adolescents scoring high on displacement tend to be immature, defensive, wary, and impulsive. Were our measure of displacement, and these measures for other key variables, more sensitive, we might find displacement related to these measures of maternal deficiency when the effects of displacement as a response to paternal role incompetence are removed. In the present sample, no such relationship appears.

4. Discussion

As anticipated, unique scores on displacement are associated with parents' disapproval of individuated interests (rather than with their feelings about direct expressions of deviant desires). The relationship is curvilinear and therefore consistent with theoretical uncertainties about a placement in column A of figure 5.1 as against column B. Displacement also shows the expected correlation with a father's personality that is not role appropriate.

Levels III to V: Review of findings on five complex defenses

Before turning to simpler defenses, it may be useful to review the fit between the findings reported thus far and the expectations summarized in figures 5.1 and 5.3. Four of these five complex defenses (intellectualization, isolation, projection, and rationalization) were expected to be related to a family's organization for taking collective action: its organization as a work group or constitutional order. Each is, and significantly so. Intellectualization was expected to be more likely in families organized as constitutional orders and the other three in those organized as work groups. These expectations are confirmed, but, where parents have intermediate scores on tolerance for individuated interests, intellectualization is also associated with strains in work groups. In addition, two defenses, intellectualization and rationalization, are associated with the presence of structural incompatibilities (*i.e.*, a hierarchical association or an egalitarian social system) in families' organization for collective action.

Displacement, a somewhat simpler defense, was expected to relate to strains in a family's organization around a charismatic center, this as indicated by the role inappropriateness of the father's or mother's personality. A significant effect of that sort is present with regard to fathers.

One of these defenses, displacement, was expected to be associated with parents' feelings about their children's pursuit of individuated interests; the other four with parents' permission of, or support for, the children's direct expression of possibly deviant desires. Trends of this sort occur in each case and are statistically significant in all cases except that of isolation. (But, in the case of rationalization, it is the *combination* of lack of support for a direct expression of desires with organization as a work group that relates to the variance in the scores.)

There seemed no clear grounds for expecting displacement to be related to parental approval as against parental disapproval of individuated interests and scores prove, in fact, to have a curvilinear relationship to this variable. Two defenses, intellectualization and isolation, were expected to be higher if parents permitted or supported direct expressions of desires. That is so for isolation and reversed for intellectualization. Both projection and rationalization were thought more likely if parents tended not to permit and/or support such direct expressions and these are the relations that appear.

Some variables that I had thought might be related to defenses at levels III through V are not: in addition to the role appropriateness of the mothers' personalities, these are the parents' absolute scores on the role-related CPI factors, their educations, and the family's socio-economic status as indexed by Hollingshead's method. On the other hand, with regard to level of social relations, these complex defenses relate significantly only to variables chosen to represent strains at the level at which each defense was expected to occur.

There is, then, considerable support in these data for the expectations summarized in figures 5.1 and 5.3. The principal exception is the placement of intellectualization only in column D and not in column C as well.

Level II. Social interdependence: repression

1. Clinical descriptions

(Bibring and others, 1961: 69–70) uniquely related to, and predominately directed against, specific instinctual impulses.

(Fenichel, 1945: 148) an unconsciously purposeful forgetting or not becoming aware of internal impulses or external events which, as a rule, represent possible temptations or punishments for, or mere allusions to, objectionable instinctual demands . . .

(Haan, 1974: 156) Unconsciously purposeful forgetting. Gaps in recall of the past. Just can't remember or elaborate. Constriction of thinking not due to low I.Q., manifested as a naive, oblivious, unthinking attitude. Distinguished from denial and blocking due to doubt or slowness in starting, in relation to the interviews. Evidence of various symptoms which imply theoretically the presence of widely repressive measures.

(Symonds, 1946: 225) By repression will be meant the exclusion from consciousness of thoughts, feelings and wishes. Inhibition will be used to mean the blocking of impulses from motor expression . . .

2. Interpretation

In defending against strains on solidarity in social interdependence, a person must show that he has met his obligations to people with whom he is linked in a network of specific rights and duties. Three defenses, repression, reaction formation, and denial, seem suitable for this purpose. As we shall see, each requires, at minimum, that a person has a reasonably clear understanding of what he should and should not do. That sort of clarity is available in social interdependence but not in relations at level I, interdependence.

Two of these three defenses, repression and reaction formation, are pictured in the clinical literature as relatively simple (the more common designation) or as quite complex (Gedo and Goldberg, 1973). We must consider both forms of each defense. Denial seems always to be treated as a relatively simple defense.

The person who represses will not allow himself to think about his deviant desires or to act upon them. He accomplishes this by focusing upon socially proper standards. By that means, he shows that he is committed to solidarity with other people.

All of the standard definitions of repression make criterial this effort to prevent an unacceptable impulse from influencing one's behavior. This suggests that a child's use of repression should be related to his parents' tolerance for possibly deviant desires – their tolerance for individuated interests – and therefore to columns A and B in figure 5.1. But to which one?

One argument predicts that repression will occur if the parents are intolerant. A corollary predicts that this will be especially likely to the extent children are subordinated to their parents rather than possessed of important independent rights and powers.

Sears, Maccoby, and Levin (1957: 362–93) popularized an alternative account. Repression can be seen as a thoroughgoing form of conscientiousness, and conscientiousness, they tell us, can be produced if parents are tolerant of a child's possible deviance, are warm and supportive, allow the child a wide area of discretionary action, and, all the while, are pressing him to become responsible for his own good conduct. Their own study of the socialization of conscience supported this conclusion and, as we shall find in chapter 6, reviews by Hoffman and others report many corroborative studies.

The two arguments are not necessarily incompatible (a point recognized by Sears, Maccoby, and Levin, 1957: 364). For our purposes, they suggest that repression is more likely to be associated with the conditions in columns A or B than with those in C or D.

At what level in figure 5.1 does this defense belong? In figure 5.1, I have linked repression to familial strains at level II, social interdependence, and have listed three possible indices for these strains: the low socio-economic status of the breadwinner, high parental scores on defensiveness, and the family's having a hierarchical organization.

I have suggested that repression requires a clarity about social relations that is not available at level I and therefore requires a higher placement. Anna Freud notes that, although usually treated as a simple defense, repression is not the very simplest in cognitive composition (1936: 51).

Repression consists in the withholding or expulsion of an idea or affect from the conscious ego. It is meaningless to speak of repression where the ego is still merged with the id . . .

On the other hand, if repression is not among the very simplest defenses it can be among the most distorting and, in that sense, among the very simplest mechanisms. The usual argument is that repression can be used effectively on only a limited front because it is all too effective and that a person who tries to repress more than a small segment of his desires will make himself a behavioral cripple. Anna Freud (1936: 49–50) underscores the distinctive power and danger of repression as compared with other defenses:

from the point of view of efficacy it occupies a unique position in comparison with the rest. In terms of quantity it accomplishes more than they; that is to say, it is capable of mastering powerful instinctual impulses, in face of which the other defensive measures are quite ineffective. It acts once only, though the anticathexis, effected to secure the repression, is a permanent institution demanding a constant expenditure of energy. The other mechanisms, on the contrary, have to be brought into operation again whenever

Table 5.7. *Repression: by parental approval of individuated interests and egalitarian family structure: adolescents aged 16 years and older:* N = 50

Parents' score on approval of individuated interests is two or more standard deviations below mean	Family has egalitarian structure	N	Mean unique score
Yes	Yes	3	76
	No	16	60
No	Yes	4	50
	No	27	39

there is an accession of instinctual energy. But repression is not only the most efficacious, it is also the most dangerous mechanism. The dissociation from the ego entailed by the withdrawal of consciousness from whole tracts of instinctual and affective life may destroy the integrity of the personality for good and all . . .

That argument suggests that people will use repression to deal with strains in social relations that involve narrowly defined social rules to which no exceptions are permitted. Because relations organized in terms of social interdependence turn on the performance of relatively narrow and specific duties, a placement at level II seems plausible (but see Smith and Danielsson, 1982). Relations at higher levels involve more diffuse obligations and also require that further special requirements be met to demonstrate solidarity.

3. Findings

In my sample of adolescents, the correlates of repression prove to depend upon age. For those 16 years and older (table 5.7), repression is more likely if the family is egalitarian and if the parents are exceptionally low (two or more standard deviations below the mean) in tolerance of individuated interests. (In table 5.7, the main effect for egalitarian structure is significant ($r(50) = 0.40$, $p < 0.01$) as is the overall R: 0.44, $p < 0.05$.)

Among adolescents aged 15 years and younger, the picture is different. Those from homes having all of three characteristics have higher scores on repression: the families are hierarchical, the parents are not exceptionally low in tolerance of individuated interests, and the fathers are defensive ($r(43) = 0.36$, $p < 0.05$).

Certain of the parents' scores on measures of personality are also related to their children's unique scores on repression. On the CPI, there is a negative correlation between repression and the fathers' scores on sense of well-being ($r = -0.22$, $p < 0.05$) and the mothers' scores on responsibility ($r = -0.18$,

$p < 0.04$). Scores on repression are also related to several of the fathers' scores on the MMPI: depression (0.23, $p < 0.05$), psychopathic deviate (0.20, $p < 0.05$), paranoia (0.21, $p < 0.05$), psychasthenia (0.30, $p < 0.01$), and schizophrenia (0.27, $p < 0.02$). (A stepwise multiple correlation shows that the removal of the correlation with psychasthenia renders all of the others insignificant.) Adolescents were also more likely to have high scores on repression if their fathers had high scores on the scales for psychoneurotic tendencies that Block derived from the MMPI ($r = 0.25$, $p < 0.02$).

The correlations with psychasthenia and psychoneurotic tendencies are of special interest because Block (1965: 112) regards these as good substitute measures for his scale of ego resilience and, as we saw in chapter 4, he treats persons with low scores on ego resilience as having "small adaptive margins and consequently to react to their stresses in rigidified or chaotic ways," to be "unable to respond effectively to the dynamic requirements of their situation." That kind of parental unadaptiveness may indeed be one source of repression in children.

There were, however, no significant direct relations or interactions between the parents' personality scores and repression when familial egalitarianism, parental tolerance of individuated interests, and fathers' defensiveness were taken into account and these latter conditions retained their relations with repression when the parental scores on personality were controlled.

4. Discussion

The uses and meanings of repression are diverse. So are these findings. Of the variables operationalizing the rows of figure 5.1, those for level II – father's defensiveness and a hierarchical family network – are linked to unique scores on repression, but only for younger adolescents from families in which the parents are at least somewhat tolerant of individuated interests. Among older adolescents, high unique scores on repression are more likely if the family's network is egalitarian and the parents are quite intolerant of individuated interests.

In both cases, then, it is the parents' feelings about individuated interests that are important and not their views on the direct expression of desires. Variables expected to be related to defenses at level II are also important. But the direction of the relationships varies by age of subject. The picture for younger adolescents associates repression with strong strains in social interdependence but at least some support for individuated interests. Perhaps what we have are parents who have some tolerance for a child's having desires that are "different," but who are rather arbitrary when declaring some of his desires out of bounds. The association among older adolescents between repression and an egalitarian network suggests that the parents are not likely to be capricious or despotic and the connection with high intolerance of individuated interests suggests that they think certain interests are desirable and others not and press their children to pursue what is "right." These patterns do not have a perfect fit with explanations that are frequently offered for repression, but the first resembles arguments that stress the role of strong and arbitrary parental demands; the second, arguments like those of Sears, Maccoby, and Levin that see repression as the effect of combinations of support and reasonableness with pressure for good conduct. And, perhaps, the conditions that lead to repression tend generally to vary with the age of the child. But that will need to be explored in other studies.

The finding of a correlation between repression and low scores of fathers on ego resilience may also prove important. These scores suggest rigidity and lack of adaptiveness. Perhaps, like defensiveness, low ego resilience generates the high levels of tension concerning rights and duties that make for strains on social interdependence. Perhaps such rigidities have the meaning I suggested for high defensiveness in chapter 4: when a person is highly defensive, "his demands on himself and, at least indirectly, on others are extensive, and so constant, as to press on the limits of what is reasonable or justifiable." If so, these correlations are consistent with the placement of repression at level II in figure 5.1.

A special note. What relationship there is in my sample between repression and parental defensiveness is to the father's defensiveness. (And it is the fathers' scores on ego resilience that correlate significantly with defensiveness.) We found that it was the role inappropriateness of the father's personality that was related to displacement. We shall find further evidence for the importance of fathers' characteristics as we turn to the social correlates of reaction formation and denial.

Level II. Social interdependence: reaction formation

1. Clinical descriptions

(Bibring and others, 1961: 69) the management of unacceptable impulses by permitting the expression of the impulse in an exactly antithetical form; in effect the expression of the unacceptable impulse in the negative . . .

(Fenichel, 1945: 151) reaction formations represent ... a consequence and reassurance of an established repression ... The person ... has changed his personality structure ... so that he may be ready whenever the danger occurs.

(Haan, 1974: 155–6) A personality change involving unconsciously determined transformations of impulses and affects into their opposites, resulting in an alteration of behavior which may occasionally break down so that the original impulse is in evidence. A very clean and orderly man with the secret, messy top drawer. S[ubject] is excessively or brittlely kind, altruistic, or submissive as a defense against hostile impulses (or is excessively clean and orderly, self-sufficient, tough and masculine, feminine, and so on) . . .

Highs "protest too much" against the impulse (excessive talk about cleanliness) and the spotty, brittle employment of the defense can be rated.

Lows may admit all kinds of impulses (*e.g.*, a wish to submit totally to drugs) or may not seem to have impulse problems because of other, more salubrious provisions for impulse such as sublimation, effective suppression or substitution.

(Symonds, 1946: 424) the adoption of behavior and feelings which are quite the opposite of those which would normally result from the uninhibited expression of impulses and wishes . . . doing the opposite of what one really feels like doing . . .

2. Interpretation

Some clinicians treat reaction formation as an extreme form of repression (Fenichel, 1945: 151), some as a form of displacement (Miller and Swanson, 1960: 107–9). There are, however, differences between reaction formation and these other defenses. First, in repression, "good" behavior is achieved through the blocking of deviant thoughts and actions, whereas, in reaction formation, it is actively pursued. (Thus, in one of Haan's examples, the man with tendencies to be messy and disorganized is, instead, clean and orderly.) Second, in repression, a deviant desire is blocked from expression even in thought. In reaction formation it is expressed, although indirectly. Third, in displacement, a desire is redirected: turned from a forbidden target toward one that is acceptable. In reaction formation, a person substitutes an acceptable desire for one he considers destructive of social solidarity.

Is this a complex defense or one of the simplest? There are strong arguments for both positions and it may be that we need to think of two or three forms of reaction formation rather than one.

The argument for high complexity pictures a person as making spontaneous and perhaps creative contributions to a social relationship, contributions of the sort associated with level V in figure 5.1, and as making several interrelated discriminations in order to develop a new pattern of action. As this argument would have it, the person moves beyond the negative goodness involved in repression and goes on to positive actions. He goes beyond the minimum that duty requires and makes a contribution. He shows that, whatever his deviant desires, he cares deeply about his relations with others, actively nurturing and enhancing those relations. And he tries to analyze himself and his situation in order to do what is appropriate. Thus, in the example from Haan, he discriminates between behavior that is, and is not, acceptable and between behavior that is acceptable and behavior that is so patently creditable that he and other people will dismiss from their minds any doubts about his commitment. He then organizes his life in such a way that it embodies these creditable standards. All of this implies a high degree of social and intellectual understanding.

These complex discriminations may be associated with commitments to social solidarity that are freely given. Or with an anxious scrupulosity (note Haan's repeated use of "excessive" in describing this defense) – a scrupulosity fueled, perhaps, by fears that deviant impulses may get out of hand. Or, as is most likely, by some mixture of the two. In any case, a placement at level V would be indicated.

The usual argument for simplicity builds upon the assumption that reaction formation is used when repression is insufficient; when the conditions that lead to repression are present but the defender is required to display good behavior and not just the absence of bad behavior. Perhaps he feels that his thoughts, as well as his behavior, are closely monitored and that the penalties for deviant thoughts are severe. He then concludes that he dares show no sign, however slight, of having unacceptable interests or desires. In order to ward off any such suspicions, he goes beyond repression and becomes actively "good." By that argument, reaction formation is produced by a parental intolerance of individuated interests (column B of figure 5.1) even more severe than that associated with repression but, otherwise, by conditions from which repression would grow: the conditions associated with level II (social interdependence) in figure 5.1.

It may be unlikely that one would find much evidence for reaction formation in this simple form in clinically normal populations. Its appearance may imply intense and sustained social pressures; pressures of the sort more likely to be found in the backgrounds of psychotic patients (Frosch, 1983). That being so, a complex form of reaction formation would be the one that would appear in my sample. In that form, reaction formation would belong at level V in figure 5.1.

In what columns of figure 5.1 should reaction formation be placed? We already have the answer (column B) for the case in which this defense is seen as one of the simplest. Given that the person using reaction formation does not express deviant desires directly, columns C and D are presumably inappropriate. This leaves column A as a possibility and that is the placement which seems implied in interpretations that picture reaction formation as a moderately complex or highly complex defense. Such interpretations seem to assume that reaction formation grows when parents accept a child who has deviant wishes but only if these are incidental to his growing toward more acceptable orientations. The parents ask that he behave well and, in that context, pass over a great many signs of deviance. The child can have many deviant tendencies if it seems, on balance, that his conduct and commitments are strongly supportive of social solidarity: if he often goes beyond the call of duty in promoting the common life.

3. Findings

The actual findings for my sample of adolescents are consistent with the placement of reaction formation among the defenses in column A. Adolescents whose parents are tolerant of individuated interests in their children are more likely to have high unique scores on reaction formation: $r(114) = 0.39$, $p < 0.001$. Among adolescents whose parents are a standard deviation or more above the mean on tolerance of individuated interests ($N = 18$), 78% have scores above the mean on reaction formation. Among those whose parents are a standard deviation or more below the mean on tolerance of individuated interests ($N = 21$), 81% have scores below the mean on reaction formation. Thus, in these groups, there is little variance in reaction formation that is left to explain.

The second major finding is that reaction formation is especially likely among adolescents if their parents tolerate individuated interests *and* their fathers' personalities are not role appropriate ($r(79) = 0.26$, $p < 0.05$). This suggests a placement of reaction formation at level III, charismatic center, in figure 5.1.

Among the adolescents I have studied, scores on reaction formation also correlate significantly with other indices. High scores are associated with the fathers' being undercontrolled ($r = 0.23$, $p < 0.05$) on the MMPI indices, and being high on the CPI scale for communality ($r = 0.30$, $p < 0.01$). Reaction formation is related positively to the fathers' MMPI scores on schizophrenia (0.21, $p < 0.05$). The adolescents' scores on reaction formation correlate positively with their own scores on tests of intelligence ($r(118) = 0.19, p < 0.05$). None of these associations between reaction formation and psychological tests seems to affect the relations found with parental approval of individuated interests and the role of appropriateness of the fathers' personalities or to survive the control of these other variables.

4. Discussion

There are ambiguities about the level of relations for which reaction formation is likely to be suitable as a defense. In this sample, reaction formation is correlated with an indicator for a level, level III, between those usually discussed. (And, one notes, once again, that it is a characteristic of fathers rather than mothers that correlates with a pattern of defense.) Is the unanticipated placement at level III in some sense "correct"? Or is it due to the mixing in the raters' minds of images of reaction formation as both a simple and a complex defense? We cannot tell from these data. Studies of this defense should distinguish operationally among its simple, intermediate, and complex forms (Rapaport, 1951) and look for separate sources for each.

By contrast, the data are strongly consistent with the idea that parental tolerance of individuated interests fosters adolescents' use of reaction formation.

Level II. Social interdependence: denial

1. Clinical descriptions

(Bibring and others, 1961: 65) Denial accomplishes the negation of awareness in conscious terms of existing perceptions of inner or outer stimuli. Literally seeing but refusing to acknowledge what one sees or hearing and negating what is actually heard are expressions of denial . . . It is to be distinguished from avoidance which is manifested, for example, by the actual closing of the eyes or the refusal to look . . . In contrast to repression, which is immediately concerned with drive discharge, denial is closer to the perceptual system, whether it operates with regard to the external world, the environment, or the internal world, the self.

(Fenichel, 1945: 144–5) The ability to deny unpleasant parts of reality is the counterpart of the "hallucinatory wish fulfillment." Anna Freud has called this type of refusal to acknowledge displeasure in general "pre-stages of defense." The gradual development of reality testing makes such wholesale falsification of reality impossible . . . As long as the ego is weak, the tendency toward denial may remain relatively superior; in later childhood, the characteristic solution is that the objectionable truth is denied effectively in play and fantasy, whereas simultaneously the reasonable part of the ego recognizes the truth and the playful or fantastic character of the denial. Some of this "denial in fantasy" remains in the normal adult who, knowing an unpleasant truth, nevertheless (or, rather, therefore) may enjoy daydreams that deny this truth . . . Only in . . . psychoses . . . do serious and important denials remain victorious in adults . . .

(Haan, 1974: 152) Denial of facts and feelings that would be painful to acknowledge and focusing on the benign or the pleasant. Basic formula: there is no pain, no anticipation of pain, no danger, no conflict. As applied to the past, the formula is: it did not happen that painfully at all. Pollyanna attitude. Every cloud has a silver lining.

2. Interpretation

The person who denies is acting as if the world really is as he wants it to be and as if everything will turn out according to his wishes (Bennett and Holmes,

1975). He says, in effect, that limitations, weaknesses, dangers, or moral faults that other people see in his behavior are really of no consequence.

This course of action need not be defensive. It may be simply naive, as when a young child tries to kill someone by wishing him dead. It may, as in some psychoses, indicate that a person's desires have overwhelmed his judgment. It may result from the person's judging correctly that he is right and others are wrong.

The person who defends himself by denying affirms his solidarity with others. He subscribes to the social standards that would ordinarily apply to his behavior and he is committed to change his behavior if it can be shown that he has violated those standards. He regrets upsetting other people and he himself may have some doubts about the wisdom of his own behavior. But he says, in the end, that, if proper standards are properly applied, his behavior is justifiable; that the charges made against him will prove excessive; that he will do no real harm and that much good may result if he goes on as he has; that all his obligations will be met and that he will not have required too much from others.

This interpretation seems to hold even in extreme cases. The patient who announces just after his legs have been amputated that he plans a career as a ballet dancer may, or may not, be denying. If he is, he is rejecting a claim that he and others are making, the claim that he should plan a sedentary, limited life. He is saying that standards – standards which he accepts – are being applied in too limited or too broad a fashion; that he can and will do good and worthwhile things providing excessive limits and demands are not laid upon him.

Denial is, as Lewin (1950) suggests, an optimistic defense. The person assumes that there are grounds for thinking that his relations with others are dependable and supportive; that the requirements for social solidarity are reasonable if properly applied. These assumptions are compatible with what little data we have on social situations correlated with denial: for example, with Weinstock's (1967a: 69) finding that men who use denial were reared in families in which both parents were satisfied with their circumstances in life and in which the fathers were even-tempered, relaxed, and friendly in dealing with their children.

I have suggested in figure 5.3 that denial be placed at the juncture of column C and level II (social interdependence) to indicate a social setting embodying conditions of the sort that denial seems to manage. Like other defenses in column C, denial involves the direct expression of a deviant wish but an expression that avoids abrasiveness. Rebellion, aggressiveness, or negativism are not present or are played down. Denial also seems to belong in column C because this defense makes sense if the person can expect that other people will accept his expressed needs; if they are willing to allow and facilitate that expression in so far as this proves possible.

It must be admitted, however, that this placement is contrary to that suggested by much of the clinical literature. Denial is frequently seen as an act of desperation and defiance: an acting out of desires when impulses are strong and prohibitions and threats are great. The person is understood as feeling that he has about as much to gain by expressing his desires as he has to lose by doing so. He does, however, try to justify his actions by claiming that, if properly evaluated, it will be seen that his behavior is not so objectionable after all. This line of argument leads to a placement in column D of figure 5.3 (and 5.1) and, although I find it less plausible, I have placed it there as well as in column C.

Why place denial at level II? As an optimistic defense, it is unlikely to involve problems of basic trust, as at level I, and it does imply at least the dependable, supportive relations of level II. It also implies that there are some reasonably clear and limited rights and duties to which the person subscribes and the possibility of judging whether excessive demands are being made or unwarranted limits are being set. The strains on solidarity that I have associated with level II – the defensiveness of the parents in the family – also seem appropriate to denial. As we have seen, these strains necessarily set greater limits and demands for the behavior of the children than are warranted by the specific rights and duties involved in exchange and yet these strains are not incompatible with the parents' being reasonably dependable and supportive.

Why not place denial at a higher level in figure 5.1? The two highest levels require features in defenses that denial lacks: creative and wide-ranging contributions to a social relationship or a history of competent and faithful service in a specialized role. Level III requires of a defense that the expression of deviance not undermine the charismatic center. There is nothing in denial that deals specifically with that problem.

3. Findings
In my sample of adolescents, unique scores on denial are likely to be high if *all* of three conditions are met: the family is egalitarian, the parents support and not merely permit the direct expression of desires, and the father is defensive ($r(79) = 0.42$, $p < 0.001$). Denial also correlates negatively with the mothers' MMPI scores on depression (-0.24, $p < 0.02$) and psychasthenia (-0.32, $p < 0.01$). Neither of these indices has a significant relation with denial once the relevant familial conditions are controlled and none destroys the relations of denial with those conditions.

4. Discussion
The findings are consistent with an interpretation of denial as a defense against strains in social interdependence (level II) and as an "optimistic" defense (the

latter indicating a placement in column C). As with repression, the other defense expected to be at level II, denial exhibits correlations with the degree to which the family is hierarchical or egalitarian and with the fathers' defensiveness. And, here again, it is a characteristic of fathers that relates to adolescents' defenses.

Level I. Interdependence: doubt and indecision

1. Clinical descriptions

(Fenichel, 1945: 297) Doubt is the instinctual conflict displaced to the intellectual field . . .

(Haan, 1974: 151) Inability to resolve ambiguity. S[ubject] doubts the validity of his own perceptions or judgments, unable to make up his mind, and is unable to commit himself to a course of action or presentation of incidents. He hopes that problems will solve themselves or that someone will solve them for him. States problem then qualifies it to death. Some manifestations: uncertainty whether one has answered the questions right; uncertainty about handling others the way they should be. Evidence of strenuous efforts to avoid uncertain situations implies an awareness on S[ubject]'s part that he can become stalemated by doubt.

2. Interpretation

As a defense, doubt and indecision involves more than uncertainty and more than a vacillation of judgment and action when facing ambiguity. The uncertainties in this defense are moral and the person has grounds for accusing himself of being faithless. He wants something and thinks he may have a right to it. He also thinks that he may not have that right and that others may reject him if he asserts it. He blames himself for wanting something that might undermine solidarity, but he does not abandon his desires.

In doubt and indecision, a person does not act on his desires, directly or indirectly. By being indecisive, he affirms his commitment to social solidarity and also keeps alive the possibility of getting what he wants if it proves justifiable. In extreme and prolonged cases of doubt, people constantly "think rather than act, . . . prepare constantly for the future and never experience the present" (Fenichel, 1945: 298).

In placing doubt at the intersection of column B and level I of figure 5.1, I indicate a situation in which a defense with these characteristics could arise. Doubt and indecision seems to belong in column B because the person does not act on his possibly deviant desires. An adolescent might avoid acting on such desires if, as in column B, his parents have little tolerance for different and deviant wishes in children.

Level I, interdependence, provides a social relationship that might lead a person to be uncertain about the justifiability of his desires: really not to know whether they threaten solidarity. In figure 5.1, I have proposed four possible indices of strains at this level for families in my sample: parental instability, lack of parental acceptance of the child, an unhappy marriage, and absence of close, supportive ties within the family.

In social relations at this level, people need one another and are therefore drawn together. But their relations do not entail specific rights and duties. They lack clear rules and roles and agreed-upon limits. It is understood in these relations that participants have the right to *seek* gratification from others but it is not certain which of their attempts will prove acceptable or which would destroy the relationship. Given this ambiguous context, we might expect that low levels of closeness, warmth, and stability in interdependence would make people especially cautious; would increase the likelihood of their defending by means of doubt and indecision.

The meaning I am giving to doubt and indecision is not the same as the one found in Erikson's discussion of "autonomy *vs.* shame and doubt," the second of his stages of personal development. (In appendix 3, I associate Erikson's description of doubt with the second level of collective development, that of social interdependence.) In my description of doubt, I picture a person who feels justified in having certain desires and also as thinking that there are strong grounds for rejecting those desires in order to meet his social commitments. He is conflicted and therefore uncertain. Rather than taking a chance on jeopardizing solidarity and his self-regard, he takes no action at all.

By contrast, Erikson has in mind the situation in which a person feels incompetent to meet minimal standards in social relations, relations that he is committed to sustain. He is expected to proceed but does not know what to do or how to do it. The uncertainty is not over the rights and wrongs of his desires but over the action he should take given his incompetence.

3. *Findings*

Among adolescents in my sample, doubt and indecision are likely among those whose families have two characteristics: the parents are not tolerant of individuated interests and relations in the family are not close ($r(91) = 0.32$, $p < 0.01$). There are also some significant correlaions between scores on this defense and the parents', especially the fathers', scores on the CPI and MMPI. Fathers of high scorers on doubt and indecision are more likely to have low scores on the good impression scale of the CPI ($r = -0.29$, $p < 0.01$). (By contrast, mothers of high scorers tend to have high scores on the CPI scale for flexibility ($r = 0.28$, $p < 0.02$).) The relations between doubt and indecision and the fathers' scores on the MMPI are as follows: K (the correction score which indicates high ego strength among clinically normal adults): $r = -0.25$, $p < 0.02$; depression: $r = 0.23$, $p < 0.05$; paranoia: $r = 0.19$, $p < 0.03$; and psychasthenia: $r = 0.18$, $p < 0.05$. Block's scales based on the MMPI are also related to doubt and indecision. The fathers' scores have the clearest relations: the correlation with the fathers' scores on undercontrol being 0.31 ($p < 0.01$) and that with their scores on psychoneuroticism being 0.22 ($p < 0.05$). There is a negative relation between the mothers' scores on overcontrol and their children's scores on doubt and indecision: $r = -0.25$, $p < 0.02$.

Adolescents' scores on doubt and indecision are also related to their fathers' scores on the same defense ($r = 0.25$, $p < 0.02$) and on regression ($r = 0.24$, $p < 0.05$). There is a significant and negative correlation with the mothers' scores on repression ($-r = 0.20$, $p < 0.05$).

A stepwise multiple correlation shows that the relations of these parental defenses and of the parents' scores on the CPI and MMPI with doubt and indecision all drop to insignificance when the effect of Block's scores on undercontrol are taken into account. An analysis of variance indicates that both fathers' undercontrol ($p < 0.002$) and a low rating of closeness in the family (combined with low parental approval of individuated interests) ($p < 0.04$) contribute to the explanation of variance in doubt and indecision but that there is not a significant interaction ($p < 0.21$) in their relations with this defense. For the table (not shown) as a whole, $F(3,81) = 4.48$, $R = 0.31$, $p < 0.01$.

4. Discussion

The several findings on familial relations and on parental personalities suggest that doubt and indecision is more likely when relations with the family are not close and dependable (recall that Block's measure of undercontrol catches an impulsive "acting up"). This is consistent with the placing of this defense at level I in figure 3.1. The findings also show that doubt and indecision are especially likely if parents show the intolerance of indivuated interests in their children indicated by column B of figure 5.1.

Level I. Interdependence: regression

1. Clinical descriptions

(Bibring and others, 1961: 69) a return to a previous stage of functioning to avoid the anxieties and hostilities involved in later stages; a reestablishment of an earlier stage where conflict is less. As a purposive way of handling a specific conflictual situation, regression is a defense and an ego mechanism. It is a "way out" and, as it were, flight into earlier modes of adjustment.

Haan, 1974: 153) The person resorts to evasive, wistful, demanding, dependent, ingratiating, non-age-appropriate behavior to avoid responsibility, aggression and generally unpleasant demands from others and self, and to permit and encourage concomitant indulgence from others. Non-productive fantasy would be part of this, where the fantasy is an end in itself or used defensively against action, effort and real accomplishment. The fantasy would temporarily reduce tension.

(Symonds, 1946: 204) Regression . . . has two distinct meanings. In its first meaning, regression is used to refer by reversion to a pattern of behavior which was the individual's at an earlier age. This might better be called retrogression . . . In the second meaning (regression proper) a person may not be repeating his own earlier patterns of behavior . . . This meaning . . . refers to a surrender of sublimation in favor of a more primitive and natural form of expression . . . to any kind of immature behavior . . .

2. Interpretation

Regression is not always a defense. It can be "a return to earlier points of fixation" as "an outcome of a breakdown of equilibrium at a later phase of development" (Bibring and others, 1961: 69). It can also be a purposeful tactic, one in which a person seeks, in more "primitive" or undifferentiated modes of action, some better solution to his current problems. This is what Kris (1952) had in mind in his famous description of "regression in the service of the ego."

When it is a defense, regression is a cry to be accepted despite one's having expressed deviant impulses in a direct fashion and it is an affirmation of solidarity with others. (That brings us to columns C and D of figure 5.1.) It is a cry to be accepted not in this role or that but as a whole person who has many needs that must be met through social relations. (That brings us to level I in the figure.)

The person who regresses has done something that he thinks may have threatened solidarity; something that raises questions about his real commitments. This places regression among the defenses used to deal with people's direct, overt deviance.

Has this defense any characteristics which suggest whether the person finds that his deviance is at least partially acceptable to others? The usual description of regression suggests that the person expects considerable opposition. Haan is typical in using words like "demanding," "evasive," "aggressive," and "unpleasant." Given that stress in the clinical literature, and the fact that I am depending upon Haan's code, I have placed regression in column D of figure 5.1 rather than column C. I should note, however, that there is another side to the matter. The essence of regression is that the person becomes childish and dependent in order to assert what he thinks are his rights and also to affirm his need for others and his desire for solidary relations with them. He may do this

Table 5.8. *Regression: mean unique scores by parental permission of direct expression of desires and closeness:* N = 88

Parents permit direct expression of desires	Closeness	N	Mean unique score
Both	High	28	48
	Low	10	66
One or neither	High	26	36
	Low	24	57

in a manner that is aggressive and demanding or in one that is more appealing and open. Some of Haan's description indicates these latter features: an approach that is ingratiating and wistful and that seeks indulgence. Were these latter features the more prominent, they would suggest a person who thought that other people would accept him and be helpful despite his deviant conduct and we would put regression in column C.

Regression does seem a defense appropriate for strains in interdependence, hence its placement at level I. The individual feels that he has some right to be accepted as a person who needs others and who is needed by them. He does not claim some specific right or the prerogatives of some particular role but asks for consideration as a person whom others claim to want and to need as such. That seems the meaning of his demands and childishness. At the same time, he displays his helplessness to proceed without acceptance and support from others and in that way he demonstrates his commitment to his relations with them. These appeals for basic acceptance as a person, and to rights as a person, suggest that the individual is dealing with strains in interdependence rather than with problems in some more specialized relationship.

3. Findings

As table 5.8 shows, regression tends to be associated positively with parents' permitting direct expressions of desires, and with familial relations that are not close. The direct effect for relations that are not close is significant ($r(88) = 0.32$, $p < 0.01$).

Regression correlates significantly with certain personality characteristics of the fathers. A high score on regression is associated with the father's use of doubt and indecision ($r = 0.28$, $p < 0.01$) and regression ($r = 0.23$, $p < 0.05$) as defenses and with the father's having a low score on the scale for sense of well-being ($r = -0.27$, $p < 0.02$) on the California Personality Inventory. The fathers of high scorers are also likely to have high scores on some scales of the MMPI: hypochondriasis (0.21, $p < 0.05$); psychasthenia (0.22, $p < 0.05$), and schizophrenia (0.28, $p < 0.04$).

For the adolescents whose parents came from the original Oakland Growth Study, there are tantalizing relations between regression and scores on Haan's index of skill in interpersonal morality. The correlation between the children's own scores on Haan's index and their scores on regression are -0.35 ($p < 0.03$). Their scores on regression correlate at -0.55 ($p < 0.001$) with their fathers' Haan scores and at -0.34 ($p < 0.03$) with their mothers'. Unfortunately, the Haan index was not available for parents and children coming from the Berkeley Guidance Study.

None of these parental characteristics has a significant relation to regression among female adolescents when closeness and parental permission of direct expression of desires are controlled or, among males, once birth order is controlled. The relations of closeness, tolerance of deviant conduct, and birth order to regression are little affected by controls for any one of these other variables.

4. Discussion

It seems that, in this sample, regression, like denial, tends to belong in column C rather than in column D of figure 5.1. As expected, it is related to strains in interdependence: the families lack close, interpersonally productive relations and the fathers tend to use primitive defenses and to lack poise, ascendency, and self-assurance.[2] (The parents of adolescents in this sample who get high scores on the other simpler defenses – doubt, repression, and denial – seem worried and defensive but do not show such sharp signs of incapacity in interpersonal relations as do the fathers of high scorers on regression.) Families in which regression is high seem to foster direct acts of deviance but provide little in the way of resources for reconciling people to themselves or one another. The deviant acts threaten an already unstable relationship. Perhaps the only way in which the deviant person can remain within the group and express his solidarity and regret, and his hope for the reconstruction of relations, is through regression.

[2] The findings for familial relations and for the personalities of fathers are consistent with Weinstock's (1967a). He reports that adult males who tended to regress grew up in homes in which relations with the parents were strained, and in which the father was a worrier, highly restrictive of his children, and unable to behave steadily and supportively in times of interpersonal conflict. The mothers of these regressors seem more assertive and impulsive than those in my sample. Weinstock describes them as irritable, psychologically unstable, brutal and unwise as disciplinarians, and as playing favorites among their children.

Levels I and II: review of findings on five simpler defenses

The meaning of several of these defenses is not as precise as were those for more complex defenses and that sometimes led to less certainty about their placement in figure 5.1. Doubt and indecision seemed the clearest of the set and the findings show that it is indeed most likely to appear under the expected circumstance; level I, column B. The expectations for regression and denial were relatively clear as to level and both were thought to vary with parental permission or support for direct expressions of desires. There were, however, grounds for uncertainty as to whether it would be the presence or absence of such permission or support that would correlate with high scores on these defenses. The findings show that these defenses do correlate with events at the levels at which each is placed in figure 5.1 and that they are more likely when parents tolerate direct expressions of possibly deviant desires. The placement of reaction formation in the columns of figure 5.1 seemed clear: column A. This proves correct: this defense is strongly and positively correlated with parental tolerance of individuated desires. On the other hand, there was great ambiguity as to whether, given both conceptual and operational definitions, it belonged at level II or at level IV or higher. In the event, it correlates with signs of strain at level III. The expectations for repression were clear as to level but uncertain as between columns A and B. The findings confirm a placement at level II and in columns A or B rather than C or D.

These simple defenses are not associated with certain variables that I had thought possible as indices of strains at levels I and II: at level I, the parents' personal stability, their acceptance of this particular child, and the strength of the marital bond; at level II, the mothers' defensiveness. A possible reason is suggested by findings described in chapter 6 and I will hold any further discussion until they are before us.

Levels I–V: review of findings on all defenses

Were the independent variables contained in the rows and columns of figure 5.1 the only ones that prove important, I could summarize the findings in this chapter by showing the mean score on each defense for each cell of that figure. In actual fact, and as one would expect, one or more additional variables are often important. That makes impossible so convenient a tabulation. Rather, an overview must catch main tendencies that are present in the midst of the complications that "real life" provides. That is the kind of summary I will try to develop as I look at the several findings when taken together.

The findings for the simpler defenses are not as strongly supportive of the expectations embodied in figure 5.1 as were those for the more complex defenses but are generally in expected directions. Combining both sets of findings, we see that, of the nine defenses for which a prediction concerning level seemed possible (all but reaction formation), eight (all but intellectualization) were found related to the conditions associated in the figure with the anticipated level and not to conditions linked to other levels. Intellectualization is linked to the level expected and, depending on parental tolerance of individuated interests, with the adjacent level as well. Reaction formation is not associated with conditions at the one level precluded by existing conceptualizations: level I.

Displacement, repression, reaction formation, and doubt and indecision were expected to be related to parental tolerance for individuated interests. All are and, for all except repression, the relationship is statistically significant. None is related to parents' views on their children's direct expressions of desires. Reaction formation and doubt and indecision are found most likely in the column of figure 5.1 (A or B) that was anticipated.

The other defenses were expected to vary with parents' feelings about children's direct expressions of desires. That is the observed trend for all of them and the significant trend for all but isolation and regression. (None is related to parents' approval or disapproval of individuated interests in children.) On the other hand, only projection and isolation are associated with the specific column (C or D) in this group that was indicated in figure 5.1.

To summarize: there is considerable support in these findings for the expectations embodied in the rows of figure 5.1 (and 5.3), and in the groupings by columns A and B as against C and D. But regression, denial, repression, displacement, and intellectualization are not associated with the specific column anticipated within these groupings.

It seems important that the variables which have significant and independent relations with unique scores on defenses tend to be those which, like the defenses themselves, reflect the temptations to deviate and the styles of justification that arise *within* the interpersonal and organizational relations *inside* the family. Thus, in this sample, it is more often birth rank, a position in the intra-familial organization, and not age, a position in a role system of the broader society, that correlates independently with unique scores on defenses. On the California Personality Inventory, it is fathers' scores on attributes related to task leadership – when these are taken as higher or lower than those of their spouses – that correlate independently with defenses.[3] Taken

---

[3] But see the renewed appreciation of the father's importance in Earls (1976), Lamb (1976), Lynn (1974), Oshman and Manosevitz (1976), and Parsons (1954).

separately, the fathers' scores, and the mothers', do not show such correlations when indices of familial organizations are controlled. Again, it is an index of interpersonal closeness which reflects the whole network of attachments among the parents and children, and not the feelings of orientations of the fathers or of the mothers toward their children generally, or toward a particular child, that correlates with the children's efforts to justify themselves. It is, thus, as an organizational theory of the family would have it: the characteristics of the parents in their relevance for familial functioning are what is salient in predicting the unique defense scores of adolescent children. Likewise, an important intra-familial property like family size which, of itself, has no implication for the members' temptations to deviate, or for their mode of self-justification, is not related to defenses. And important properties of personal functioning as indicated by adolescents' and parents' scores on tests of intelligence or parents' scores on tests of personality are either unrelated to adolescents' unique scores on defenses or (with the exception of adolescent unique scores on doubt and indecision) have associations that disappear when variables specified in figure 5.1 are controlled.

In sum, the findings in the present chapter support the continued exploration of certain constellations of social relations as conditions consistent with the use of certain defenses. They also point to work that needs to be done in future studies. One obvious step in future research is to get separate codes for the main variants of defenses that seem heterogeneous. Another is to improve the reliability, and the divergent, as well as the convergent, validity of all the codes. A third is to add codes for defenses that are commonly observed but that are not contained in Haan's present scheme: undoing, for example, restriction of the ego, or turning against the self (see appendix 5). Fourth, and concerning independent variables, there needs to be a search for additional and systematic conditions that lead people to defend. Defenses may be ubiquitous and inevitable in human affairs, but individuals differ in the frequency and urgency with which they defend. Some conditions leading to defense, a weak charismatic center, for example, are caught in the operational definitions of the rows of figure 5.1. These must, however, be only a sample of the ones that are commonly present and we need to develop rational grounds for identifying and sampling the others. Finally, as in all studies of socialization, only longitudinal designs hold the possibility of conclusive results. The theory with which I have worked is causal and longitudinal but, in most cases, the data are only cross-sectional. We shall need to observe families as they first form and then see the consequences for the children's defenses of differences in the way in which different families get organized.

Why are characteristics of fathers especially important?

As we have seen, displacement is related to the role appropriateness of fathers' personalities but not of mothers'. Repression and denial correlate with fathers' defensiveness, not mothers'. Doubt and indecision and regression are associated with the closeness of familial relations and the index of closeness turns on the ties of the mother and children to the father (as well as to each other) – rather, say, than on the father's ties to the mother and children or of all family members to one another equally or of the children to the parents equally. And, for most defenses, it is "negative" properties of the fathers' personalities, rather than of the mothers', that show the greatest number of connections. (This is true for seven defenses: "disturbed" features in both parents' personalities have some relations with adolescents' use of displacement, neither relates to their use of denial, and negative features only of mothers' personalities relate to adolescents' use of rationalization.)

The reasons for the salience of fathers' characteristics are not obvious, but I would like to suggest some possibilities:

- First, a negative point: it is not that mothers are less variable in the relevant personal characteristics. In my sample, at least, the parents do not differ in this respect.
- Second, it is likely that most parents in this sample are "traditional" with respect to their familial roles. That may mean that fathers tend to have more connections, interests, and resources outside the family and therefore that they are more likely than mothers to be drawn from the family, thus becoming a source of marital and familial instability. Were that so, strained familial relations might turn especially on the fathers' attachments and role competence.
- Third, strains in a group's operations depend heavily upon the competence with which authority is exercised and the degree to which it is found acceptable. If, in traditional families, fathers tend to have somewhat greater authority, at least in extreme situations, then strained relations might depend especially upon their commitment and social competence.

Predicting "raw" scores

The patterns of independent variables employed in this chapter to predict unique scores on each defense were also used to predict the original "raw" scores. The relations are statistically significant in two cases: closeness of familial relations is again related negatively to doubt and indecision ($r(114) = -0.22, p < 0.02$) and, among males, first-born and only children tend to have lower scores on regression ($r(57) = -0.26, p < 0.05$). Thus the patterns

associated with the unique scores are not usually associated with raw scores
embodying high degrees of defensiveness.

Toward wider issues

What is the meaning of the findings in this chapter for some of the more general
questions of theory and method that one encounters when studying defenses?
And especially for the understanding of combinations of defenses? I devote
chapter 6 to issues of that sort.

6 Extensions, explorations, and conclusions

In chapter 5 I took up one defense and then another, looking for conditions in which each would be appropriate. In this chapter, I move in the same way but focus on profiles of defenses. Then I link the results to what has gone before.

Most people use more than one defense at a time. Why does a person use one of these *combinations* of defenses rather than another?

The ideas built into the rows and columns of figure 5.1 can help in answering that question but they will not be sufficient. Defensive profiles combine defenses from several of those rows and columns. This suggests that the distinctions in figure 5.1 will prove too fine-grained and that it will be combinations of the independent variables given in the figure that correlate with profiles of defenses. If that is so, it will allow us to *extend* earlier theory from single defenses to combinations of defenses. We may need something more.

To get at the systematics of defenses, we needed to compare the distinctive features of each defense with all of the others and that implied the use of unique scores. Combinations of defenses, even if each is represented by a unique score, are more likely to embody defensiveness as well. This is so because, if other things are equal, a person employing several defenses is more likely to be preoccupied with justifying himself than is a person employing only one. Combinations of independent variables from figure 5.1 may help to account for that increased preoccupation, but it is possible that additional and unsuspected considerations come into play. We need to give them an opportunity to do so. That is why I will analyze profiles and their correlates by means of the method for "automatic interaction detection" (AID) developed by Sonquist, Baker, and Morgan (1974) and suited for *explorations* in which several independent variables are to be related to a single dependent variable.

I will use AID with two sets of defensive profiles. The first set is based upon the unique scores used in chapter 5. The matrix of correlations among the adolescents' *profiles* of unique scores was subjected to a varimax factor analysis in order to identify youngsters having similar profiles of unique scores across the ten defenses.

138

The second set of profiles is based upon scores obtained from a varimax factor analysis of the raw scores on defenses. An inverse factor analysis using these scores identifies clusters of adolescents having similar profiles.

To anticipate the results of these analyses:

- The placement of defenses by rows and columns in figure 5.1 continues to be useful in these new analyses.
- The varimax factors based upon the raw scores provide a kind of unique score for *groups* of defenses. Their correlates resemble those for unique scores on individual defenses as reported in chapter 5.
- The correlates of profiles of defenses, whether those profiles are based upon the unique scores for individual defenses or upon scores for varimax factors derived from the raw scores, include many features of the mothers' personalities, the mothers' defensiveness, and signs that one or both parents do not accept the adolescent being studied and/or are dissatisfied with their marriages. These correlates are most likely to accompany profiles of relatively simple and highly distorting defenses. I offer suggestions as to why this might be so.

The profiles of defenses in these two sets are the combinations that are the most common in my sample. There are, however, other combinations of defenses that have been identified as important in clinical practice. Each of these combinations is interpreted as composed of defenses that complement one another as methods for dealing with particular forms of strain in social relations. (Indeed, the profiles associated with certain anxiety syndromes have paradigmatic status in the theorizing about defenses.) The last set of profiles considered in this chapter are the ones linked with three of these syndromes: obsession, hysteria, and phobia.

In psychoanalytic interpretations, each anxiety syndrome has been centered in strains in social relations that seem to be at one, or adjacent, levels in figure 5.1. The defenses employed include some that are appropriate to that level and also "related" defenses at other levels. That seems roughly what one finds in data from my sample of adolescents.

The findings on the social settings of these three sets of profiles emerge from extensions of ideas presented in earlier chapters and include discoveries that open wider prospects for research. I close this chapter by reviewing the findings from earlier chapters, linking them with the findings in this chapter, and offering some general conclusions.

Individuals' profiles of unique scores on defenses

To identify clusters of adolescents having similar profiles of unique scores across the ten defenses, the matrix of correlations among the adolescents' profiles of unique scores was subjected to a varimax factor analysis. Nine

Table 6.1. *Grouping of subjects by similarity in profiles of unique scores on ten defenses: varimax factor analysis*

Profile factor	Eigen-value	Cumulative percentage of communality accounted for:	Profile of scores distinguished by:
I	19.28	16.3	High scores on regression and rationalization and low scores on displacement
II	17.09	30.8	High scores on intellectualization, rationalization, and projection and low scores on doubt and regression
III	16.92	45.1	High scores on isolation and doubt and low score on denial
IV	14.13	57.1	High scores on isolation, denial, reaction formation, and repression
V	13.33	68.4	High scores on isolation and doubt and low scores on projection and regression
VI	10.28	77.1	High scores on doubt, rationalization, and repression and low score on projection
VII	19.83	84.3	High score on intellectualization and low scores on rationalization, denial, and projection.

Figure 6.1. *Classification of profiles of unique scores*

Level of cognitive complexity of most defenses profile	Expression of deviant desires		
	Prohibited	Permitted if high, specific standards are met	Permitted if general standards are met
V			VII IV
II–IV		I II V	III
I	VI		

significant factors emerged, the first seven being clear enough to be interpreted. (These are described in table 6.1.) I then used the roster of independent variables listed in chapters 3, 4, and 5 to predict individual's scores on each of the seven master profiles identified by the factor analysis. As already stated, the method used in this analysis was that for "automatic interaction detection" (AID).

The seven profile factors (Q factors) can be distributed as were the unique scores for individual defenses in chapter 5: distributed, that is, by the cognitive complexity of their component defenses and by the extent to which they allow for the (controlled) expression of deviant desires. That ordering is given in figure 6.1 and I shall use it as a help in describing the findings.

A word about the arrangement of defense profiles in figure 6.1. This is a modified version of figure 5.1. Each defense profile contains several defenses and these are usually at different, though adjacent, levels of complexity (the *rows* of the figure). An examination of the profiles also suggests that the distinctions among the sources of threat embodied in the *columns* of figure 5.1 are not always maintained. One can see that although some profiles consist of defenses in which little or no expression of deviant conduct is probably available (profile VI), others are made up of defenses in which such expression is possible and even approved but within rather definite boundaries (profiles I, II, and V), and still others consist of defenses in which expression is possible and within a wider zone of discretion (profiles III, IV, and VII). All of this suggests that we must use grosser distinctions of threat and complexity than were found in figure 5.1. With that qualification, we can make use of the considerations familiar from that figure. By working across the figure from left to right and bottom to top, we can tie new findings to those already in hand. My discussion begins, therefore, with the profile factor in the lower-left of the figure, factor VI, and moves upward and to the right. Proceeding in that way, I describe profiles VI, I, and II in this chapter and, with these as illustrations, characterize the correlates of all seven profiles. Details on the other profiles are given in appendix 6.

Profile factor VI. High on doubt, rationalization, and
repression; low on projection

As we saw in chapter 5, doubt, rationalization, and repression can each be a relatively simple defense and can represent a fear of an active, overt expression of deviant desires; a passive or highly controlled approach as a basis for self-justification. When the three occur together, these features are more likely. The low score on projection reinforces the judgment that the stance is passive and controlled. In sum, the profile suggests a person who is indecisive and doubting, one who is not willing to be assertive and who is unsure about the proper limits for the expression of his desires.

Before performing an AID analysis on this and other profiles, I asked Norma Haan to examine each profile and to say what each meant to her. Dr Haan looked at the profiles as if they were comprised of raw scores on defenses rather than unique scores, that being the form in which she is accustomed to evaluating these materials. Nonetheless, her comments underscore many of the same themes given in my own analysis, always with the difference that, given her assumption of raw scores, she interprets profiles as having a more defensive meaning than I do. Thus she said of profile factor VI:

Indecisive and vacillating, interpersonally involved but needing to make excuses, to justify himself. Not particularly aware of others but needs others. Can't hazard hostility or assertiveness that would upset . . . interpersonal involvements.

Table 6.2 shows the statistically significant results from the AID analyses of this profile factor. Three analyses are presented. The first uses the fathers' scores on the CPI and MMPI as the independent variables in predicting the correlation of adolescents' profiles of unique scores with the profile of factor VI. The second uses the mothers' scores on these tests to make such predictions, and the third uses the remaining independent variables that are listed in chapters 3, 4, and 5.

Using an option in the AID computer program, all independent variables were treated as if they were nominal. The program allows each nominal independent variable to be examined for any dichotomous grouping of its components that will produce a statistically significant difference in the means of the two groups on a particular dependent variable. The largest such difference is then recorded. Thus, as shown in the first series of analyses in table 6.2, the fathers' scores on the CPI and MMPI scales were reviewed for their usefulness in predicting the adolescents' scores on profile factor VI. One possible dichotomization of a scale on the CPI, self-acceptance, proved to have the strongest relation to the adolescents' scores and the total sample was so dichotomized ($t(86) = 2.93$, $p < 0.01$). The program then repeats the process of reviewing all independent variables for the strongest predictor of variance in each of the two groups in this new dichotomy, in this case group 3 containing 11 adolescents whose fathers were high on self-acceptance and group 2 containing the 77 adolescents whose fathers had lower scores. In this particular instance, no review was made in connection with group 3 – the group of 11 – because I had set 20 as the minimum number of adolescents required to be in a group before it could be matched against independent variables. The review of group 2 found that the variance in these adolescents' scores on profile factor VI

Table 6.2. *AID analysis of profile factor VI*

Group to be dichotomized	Dichotomize on	To form groups	N	Mean	t	p <
	Fathers' scores on the CPI and MMPI					
Total sample	Self-acceptance	3. High	11	0.10	2.93	0.01
		2. Low	77	−0.07		
2	Hypochondriasis	5. High	38	0.02	2.29	0.05
		4. Low	39	−0.15		
5	Sense of well-being	7. High	22	−0.11	3.11	0.01
		6. Low	16	0.19		
	Mothers' scores on the CPI and MMPI					
Total sample	Depression	3. High	31	0.15	4.27	0.001
		2. Low	69	−0.11		
2	Socialization	5. High	30	0.02	3.02	0.01
		4. Low	39	−0.20		
5	Good impression	7. High	20	−0.08	2.24	0.05
		6. Low	10	0.20		
4	Hypomania	9. High	25	−0.12	2.63	0.02
		8. Low	14	−0.34		
3	Psychasthenia	11. High	16	0.28	2.96	0.01
		10. Low	15	0.01		
	Other independent variables					
Total sample	Mother's acceptance of child	3. High	61	−0.07	2.61	0.02
		2. Low	54	0.09		
2	Entrepreneurial–bureaucratic	5. High	22	−0.06	3.05	0.01
		4. Low	25	0.24		
3	Mother's ego control	7. High	42	−0.14	3.60	0.001
		6. Low	15	0.15		
4	Mother's acceptance of child	9. High	14	0.10	2.60	0.02
		8. Low	11	−0.26		
7	Role appropriateness of fathers' personalities	11. High	19	−0.23	2.00	0.05
		10. Low	13	−0.01		

was most strongly related to their fathers' scores on a scale of the MMPI, that for hypochondriasis. This division of group 2 produces groups 4 and 5 and the computer reviews the ability of all independent variables to predict the variance in each of these groups. No independent variable had such a relation to the variance in group 4 but a scale on the CPI, sense of well-being, has such a relation to the variance in group 5 ($t(36) = 3.11$, $p < 0.01$). Group 5 was dichotomized into groups 6 and 7. Group 6 has fewer than 20 adolescents in it and was not considered further. Group 7 was reviewed but no independent variable proved to have a significant relation to variance in this group in profile factor VI and the analysis ended.

Based on standard interpretations of the measures of personality and the other indicators that appear in table 6.2, we can conclude that adolescents having high scores on profile factor VI are likely to deal with mothers who are active and effective but who are cold, cautious, and defensive and who are also undependable and demanding. The fathers tend not to be effective or steady and well-balanced. They do not have confidence in themselves or others; they are likely to be apathetic, defensive, awkward, dull. To top it off, the mothers tend not to accept this child. (It is not clear to me why, among mothers whose acceptance is low, those in families in which the breadwinner works under bureaucratic rather than entrepreneurial conditions have children with the highest scores on factor VI.)

Given what we found in chapter 5, the flavor of the results is not unexpected. Relatively simple defenses are found associated with a situation in which there are strong grounds for mistrust, many assaults on a person's rights, and much questioning of the rightfulness of his conduct. Defenses that can entail little or no expression of deviant desires or conduct are employed in a relationship that leaves the person little leeway for the exercise of discretion and little support for initiatives or explorations. What is less expected is the relative importance of the mothers' views and characteristics (as combined with the fathers' inadequacies). We shall find related outcomes on other defense profiles and I will discuss the underlying question after all the other findings have been examined.

Profile factor I. High on regression and rationalization; low on displacement and projection

As we found in chapter 5, regression and rationalization tend to be associated with different levels in the complexity of the social relations with which they deal. They have in common the implication that the person has given direct expression to a deviant desire and that, while defending against the desire or the consequences of its expression, he has yet fully to relinquish the thought that his desire is, in some sense, justified. The use of either defense thus implies that the defender expects some understanding and support when his distress is made known. When the two defenses occur together, it suggests that the defender is dealing with relations that are not clearly dependable or close but that do contain some sources of support. The low score on displacement in this profile suggests a lack of opportunities for indirect but adequate outlets for deviant feelings.

After examining this profile, Dr Haan wrote:

This . . . appears to me . . . an anxious, oversocialized, other-directed, interpersonally embroiled . . . person who needs most of all to maintain relations with others and would not hazard self-assertiveness.

Table 6.3 contains the findings from the AID analyses. An adolescent's high scores on this factor are associated with his mother's being immature, changeable, and impulsive and with his father's being cheerful, balanced, and dependable. They are also associated with the use of rational forms of discipline. The adolescent therefore has grounds for mistrust occasioned by his mother's behavior but has, in his father, a source of strength and support. The father, and also the use of a rational form of discipline, should provide the child with some distance from the problems he encounters in the family and some objectivity in his dealings with them.

Profile factor II. High scores on intellectualization, rationalization, and projection; low scores on doubt and regression

The three defenses on which this person has high scores can be complex, and two of them, projection and intellectualization, always have that meaning. The two scores on which he has low scores are among the simplest. The two high scores on defenses that are clearly complex also concern defenses in which a person gives some expression to deviant desires or conduct and in which he tries to take control of his relations with others and himself and to use intellectual resources for that purpose. This suggests an active, confident approach in the management of self-justification. The defenses that are not used suggest a relatively unassertive and dependent style in interpersonal relations and in self-justification, thus underscoring the interpretation given to those that are actually employed.

Dr Haan commented on this profile as follows:

. . . a rigid, self-justifying person; always in control and always certain . . . would not be able to relax, experience pleasure, be passive, be "a student." Vigilant about situations where he might find himself one down. Interpersonally involved but guarded.

Table 6.3. *AID analysis of profile factor I*

Group to be dichotomized	Dichotomize on	To form groups	N	Mean	t	p<
		Father's scores on the CPI and MMPI				
Total sample	Masculinity–femininity (MMPI)	3. High	72	0.04	1.70	0.10
		2. Low	16	−0.13		
3	Hypomania	5. High	10	−0.20	2.66	0.01
		4. Low	62	0.08		
4	Paranoia	7. High	14	−0.10	2.64	0.02
		6. Low	48	0.13		
6	Depression	9. High	32	0.06	2.30	0.05
		8. Low	16	0.26		
		Mothers' scores on the CPI and MMPI				
Total sample	Communality	3. High	70	−0.06	2.94	0.01
		2. Low	33	0.16		
3	Sociability	5. High	58	−0.11	2.80	0.01
		4. Low	12	0.19		
5	Tolerance	7. High	44	−0.04	3.10	0.01
		6. Low	14	−0.34		
7	Sociability	9. Very high	21	−0.14	2.08	0.05
		8. High	23	0.04		
2	Responsibility	11. High	15	0.03	2.14	0.05
		10. Low	18	0.27		
9	Femininity (CPI)	13. High	10	0.01	2.28	0.05
		12. Low	11	−0.27		
8	Flexibility	15. High	10	0.18	2.34	0.05
		14. Low	13	−0.05		
		Other independent variables				
Total sample	Rational discipline	3. High	26	0.15	2.76	0.01
		2. Low	48	−0.10		
2	Mothers' total score on three defense factors	5. High	30	−0.13	2.41	0.05
		4. Low	17	−0.26		

Table 6.3 (*cont.*)

Group to be dichotomized	Dichotomize on	To form groups	N	Mean	t	p<
5	Fathers' total score on three defense factors	7. High	16	−0.13	2.12	0.05
		6. Low	12	0.15		
3	Mother's ego control	9. High	16	0.05	2.12	0.05
		8. Low	10	0.22		

The results of analyses given in table 6.4 show that high scores on this factor are found for adolescents whose mothers are well-organized, deliberate, active, energetic, and outgoing. These mothers have high standards for others and themselves and they tend to be somewhat emotional and high strung and rather rigid, formal, and cautious. The fathers, by contrast, are likely to be balanced, self-controlled, warm, wise, efficient and capable. The fathers in these families are attached to the mothers, but the mothers are impatient with the children and press them to change their behavior. In sum, high scores are associated with familial situations in which there is a reasonably solid marital relationship and in which both parents, by precept or example, set high standards for conduct and problem-solving. The parents are effective, energetic, and outgoing people. The mother is, however, rather rigid and demanding and, unlike the father, is rather nervous and of sensitive temperament. There are, then, grounds in this family for an adolescent's trusting others and feeling that he can rightfully take initiatives and exercise complex forms of discretion but there are also, what must seem to him, rather irrational constraints. This is a pattern of social relations that seems plausibly to belong at a level of figure 6.1 above the lowest – the problems encountered are not centrally those of basic mistrust or of basic attacks on participants' rights – and to afford the exercise of some discretion, but not a wide discretion in expressing desires or experimenting with conduct.

Overview of these profile factors

The four remaining profile factors are described in appendix 6, but the correlates of those already presented are typical and we can turn to the general results for all seven profiles. They are rather different from those for unique scores taken singly.

The AID program permits the computation of coefficients of multiple

148 *Extensions, explorations, and conclusions*

Table 6.4. *AID analysis of profile factor II*

Group to be dichotomized	Dichotomize on	To form groups	N	Mean	t	p<
		Father's scores on the CPI and MMPI				
Total sample	Psychasthenia	3. High	74	0.08	2.03	0.05
		2. Low	14	0.25		
3	Depression	5. High	22	−0.15	2.32	0.05
		4. Low	52	0.06		
4	Self-control	7. High	13	0.32	3.21	0.01
		6. Low	39	−0.02		
		Mothers' scores on the CPI and MMPI				
Total sample	Flexibility	3. High	27	−0.10	2.86	0.01
		2. Low	76	0.10		
2	Good impression	5. High	50	0.18	2.63	0.02
		4. Low	26	−0.05		
5	Hysteria	7. High	28	0.28	2.14	0.05
		6. Low	21	0.05		
6	Capacity for status	9. High	10	−0.19	3.01	0.01
		8. Low	11	0.27		
7	Schizophrenia	11. High	18	0.18	2.10	0.05
		10. Low	10	0.45		
4	Depression	13. High	13	0.11	2.71	0.02
		12. Low	12	−0.17		
		Other independent variables				
Total sample	Strength of father's marital bond	3. High	83	0.06	2.41	0.02
		2. Low	25	−0.13		
3	Mothers' acceptance of child	5. High	72	0.02	2.61	0.02
		4. Low	11	0.33		
5	Positive discipline	7. High	20	0.12	2.19	0.05
		6. Low	26	−0.10		
2	Child's age	9. 16 or older	13	0.02	2.34	0.05
		8. 15 or younger	12	−0.29		

Table 6.5. *AID analysis: coefficients of multiple correlation (R) between Q factors and the combinations of independent variables in tables 6.2 through 6.4 and A6.1 through A.6.4.*

Profile factors	Fathers' scores on the CPI and MMPI	Mothers' scores on the CPI and MMPI	Other independent variables
I	0.36	0.55	0.39
II	0.39	0.56	0.41
III	0.39	0.28	0.39
IV	0.42	0.42	0.57
V	0.42	0.42	0.51
VI	0.42	0.56	0.55
VII	0.52	0.46	0.41

correlation (*R*) between each profile factor and the set of independent variables significantly related to it. (There is, however, uncertainty about the degrees of freedom associated with these coefficients and, therefore, about the limits of confidence to be assigned them.) Table 6.5 presents the coefficients.

This table, and our review of each profile factor, underscores certain contrasts between the correlates of these profiles and the correlates of the unique scores for the several defenses as described in chapter 5. First, certain independent variables are frequently related to the profile factors yet, with other variables controlled, they are rarely or never related to the unique scores for single defenses. These include the measures on the family's social status and occupational setting, the parents' personalities, the parents' acceptance of the child under study, the strength of the marital bond, and the methods the parents used in disciplining their children. Second, certain independent variables that had important relations with the unique scores of individual defenses are unrelated to scores on the profile factors, or are related in only a minor way. These are the following variables employed to define the existence of problems at particular levels of complexity in social relations: closeness, the fathers' defensiveness, the role appropriateness of the parents' personalities, the indices for the presence of a work group or a constitutional order, and indices for other properties of the family as a decision-making group. Third, profile factors at lower levels of cognitive complexity and/or implying less freedom for the expression of deviant desires seem more likely than others to be correlated with signs that the mother is disturbed or functioning inadequately (*e.g.*, profile factors I, II, V, and VI).

What do these findings mean? It will take some new and appropriately designed studies to find out. The following is but one possible interpretation.

The defenses in most profile factors cross-cut two or more levels of cognitive complexity (profiles I–V) and three or more columns of figure 5.1 (profiles III–VI). Therefore, independent variables referring only to one such level or column will not be significantly related to the profile scores. Independent variables catching rougher distinctions in complexity and threat (such variables, perhaps, as the combinations of parental personalities that AID uncovers) may therefore be more effective. That is what we find here. With that qualification, the findings for profile scores correspond to the general ordering of figure 6.1, an ordering which follows, in a broad fashion, that of figure 5.1.

But the profile factors have an additional property. Each combines unique scores on several defenses. In that way it brings back some of the defensiveness that was removed when the unique scores were calculated for individual defenses. With defensiveness may come a higher and more generalized anxiety. Each profile factor could then be seen as representing a type of justification common to the component defenses and also a considerable defensiveness and anxiety in their use. Perhaps that is why indicators of the family's socio-economic status and occupational setting, of the adequacy or inadequacy in the parents' personalities, and the parents' methods of discipline relate to the profile scores but, with other variables controlled, tend not to correlate significantly with the unique scores on individual defenses.

Toward profiles as based upon raw defense scores

Unique scores on defenses have not previously been the subject of research. Neither have profiles of such scores. Earlier studies have dealt with measures of defense more like those contained in the raw scores from which the unique scores were derived. The scattering of findings that have been published on defensive profiles depended on similar measures. As we shall see, the correlates of raw scores on defenses, and of profiles of such scores, resemble both the ones uncovered in previous research and, in important ways, those I have described for unique scores and for combinations of unique scores.

The defenses as indexed in Haan's raw scores are not independent of one another. Each overlaps with some of the others in contents and in defensiveness. To examine the social settings within which particular profiles of these defenses are likely to appear, we need first to perform a factor analysis that will bring together defenses that are strongly intercorrelated and that will distinguish these groupings from one another. The scores on the factors from that analysis can then be the basis for defining profiles of defenses as based upon raw scores.

Table 6.6. *Factor analysis of children's defense scores*

Defenses	Factor loadings		
	I	II	III
Isolation	31	56	54
Intellectualization	49	05	25
Rationalization	70	26	11
Doubt and indecision	01	54	15
Denial	56	54	10
Projection	66	22	16
Regression	48	66	00
Displacement	60	20	45
Reaction formation	18	15	66
Repression	32	56	25
Eigen-value	4.6	1.1	1.0
Cumulative percentage of variance	46	57	67

Factors among defenses as estimated from the raw scores

Varimax factor analyses were performed separately for the original defense scores of boys and girls. The patterns for the two sexes were essentially the same and are combined in this report. Table 6.6 gives the results.

Three significant factors appear. Factor I is defined by high and similar loadings of five defenses: intellectualization, rationalization, denial, projection, regression, and displacement.

This factor consists primarily of defenses in which a person expresses a forbidden desire directly but perhaps in a socially acceptable manner (five of the six defenses). Most of the defenses in this group can serve as defenses against objective anxiety (four of the six), and most (four of the six) can be relatively complex. Factor I is distinguished most clearly from the other factors by high loadings of two mechanisms that can serve as complex defenses against objective anxiety: rationalization and projection.

Factor II has especially high loadings from isolation, doubt, denial, regression, and repression. These are primarily defenses of low cognitive complexity (four of the five listed) and include all four of what seem the simplest defenses. This factor is especially distinguished from the others by the high loadings of doubt and indecision and repression and the low loadings of intellectualization and displacement.

Three defenses have relatively high loadings on factor III. They are isolation, reaction formation, and displacement. All of these are useful as defenses against conscience and all are relatively complex. The properties of this factor that most distinguish it from the others are the high loading of reaction formation and the low loading of denial and regression.

To summarize, one of the children's factors, factor II, consists of the simplest defenses, and the other two factors consist of defenses of greater complexity. One of the two, factor I, contains primarily defenses against objective anxiety and the other, factor III, defenses against conscience.

Social correlates

Scores based upon these varimax factors are, of course, a kind of unique score. As we saw in chapter 5 and table 5.1, the original score on each of the defenses correlates significantly with the original score on each of the others. This must be due in part to the fact that all of the original scores estimate defensiveness as well as features of defenses distinctive of one or a few defenses. Each factor identified by a varimax factor analysis is a variable common to the defenses having high loadings on that factor; a variable distinctive to that set of defenses: unique to that set. This means that any variance common to all of the original scores is removed. In the present instance, it means that defensiveness is removed from the scores for factors.

The nature of scores on these factors helps us anticipate the nature of their correlates. Because the scores catch patterns of defense broader than that unique to any component defense, it is likely that they are fostered by a broader spectrum of social relations but of relations found important in analyses of unique scores in chapter 5.

Analyses of the social correlates of these factors are fully presented in appendix 6. In this chapter I only summarize those results. I begin with factor II, the cluster of defenses that are regarded as the least complex and the most distorting.

The defenses with the highest loadings on this factor are doubt and indecision, repression, regression, and denial. Two of these, doubt and indecision and repression, are often considered to be defenses against conscience; the other two are thought to be defenses against objective anxiety. Thus the factor cuts across the distinction between threats from conscience as against objective anxiety and focuses on the low complexity and/or high distortiveness of these defenses. This suggests that high scores on this factor will be related to strains at levels I and II (interdependence and social interdependence) in the families from which these adolescents come.

Scores on this factor are not significantly related to the children's age, sex, or birth rank or the size or socio-economic status of the family from which they come. They are related to certain strains within those families, especially strains specified in figure 5.1 as located at levels I and II. To summarize detailed findings from appendix 6, children who use simple, highly distorting defenses tend to be reared by parents, especially by fathers, who tend themselves to be anxious, neurotic, and defensive (level II) and who are not close to their children (level I). The parents tend also to lack skills of interpersonal moral reasoning, to disapprove of their children's having individuated interests, and *not* to discipline children by appealing to positive values. That picture is roughly consistent with suggestions in the clinical literature that "primitive" defenses are used when social relations are greatly and pervasively disturbed, with Hedegard's (1968) finding that they are more likely in situations of high anxiety, with Weinstock's (1967a) report that, in children, regression and doubt and indecision are associated with neurotic symptoms in their parents, particularly their fathers, and with Miller and Swanson's (1960: 213–30) discovery that, among adolescent boys, denial was related to the children's having lower scores on intelligence, to their mothers' use of power assertion as a method of discipline (in their research only mothers were studied), and to their mothers' giving only occasional rewards in disciplining their children.

The two remaining defense factors for children, factors I and III, are not associated with indices of parental stress and disturbance. Both factors involve more complex and less distorting defenses than those in factor II.

The defenses that load most heavily on factor I are intellectualization, rationalization, denial, projection, and displacement. In four of the five a person can justify his direct expression of an undesired impulse and in three of these defenses the expression has not been acceptable to others. The theory and findings in chapter 5 suggest that high scores on such a profile will *not* be associated with strains at the simpler levels of relations (levels I and II in figure 5.1) and that they will be associated with parents' disapproving direct expressions of deviant desires (figure 5.1, column D).

The findings reported in appendix 6 are generally consistent with those expectations. Children are likely to have high scores on factor I if their parents, especially their fathers, are relatively stable and adequate persons and if the parents set a particular style of life – of interests and conduct – which they press their children to adopt. The parents tend to disapprove children's having individuated interests or their directly expressing any "deviant" desires. As I argued in chapter 2, people always have deviant interests and deviant lines of conduct. The expectable result is that they will have to justify their expression of these tendencies if it threatens their solidarity with people with whom they are interdependent (Berkowitz, 1973; Miller and Swanson, 1960: 315–36). The parents in the families of children with high scores on factor I define such expressions as a threat. A negative relation of scores on this factor to an entrepreneurial middle-class status is consistent with Miller and Swanson's (1960) findings reviewed in chapter 3.

The third of the children's defense factors, factor III, has high loadings from three defenses often regarded as defenses against conscience: isolation, reaction formation, and displacement. All can be relatively complex and all involve a socially acceptable expression of a desire or a line of conduct. Once again, one would *not* expect high scores on such a factor to be associated with strains at the simpler levels of familial relations. On the other hand, the parents should permit at least indirect expressions of deviant desires.

The detailed findings in appendix 6 show that scores on this factor are related to only a few predictors. The children themselves tend to have *low* scores on one of Block's indices of personal stress: undercontrol ($r = -0.24$, $p < 0.05$). On the other hand, the fathers tend to be undercontrolled according to Block's index (0.21, $p < 0.05$) and, contrary to an expectation just stated, to have high scores on an indicator of strain at a simple level of familial relations: high scores on many defense factors ($F(2,101) = 3.51$, $R = 0.26$, $p < 0.03$).

These few findings for factor III do not reveal any definite pattern of social relations in which these complex defenses against conscience are likely to emerge. Perhaps what is most significant is the relative *absence* of indications that the parents or children are under pervasive personal stress or that the parents strongly oppose the children's pursuit of desires or conduct that is possibly deviant.

Individuals' profiles as based on factors from raw defense scores

As we have seen, the factor scores derived from raw scores are a kind of unique score. Where there are an appreciable number of significant correlations with independent variables, the relations obtained strongly resemble those reported in chapter 5 and anticipated in figure 5.1 except that we deal now with clusters of defenses. As we turn now to profiles of scores on these three factors, we must expect what we found when dealing with profiles of unique scores: the emergence of profiles that cross-cut the rows and columns of figure 5.1 and the greater likelihood that defensiveness will be involved as we combine a form of unique scores from which it was largely removed. Indeed, the amount of cross-cutting of rows and columns will be much greater than before because the score on each factor already embodies such combinations of defenses.

In developing profiles based on the three factor scores, scores on each defense factor were dichotomized at the median. The seven profiles of dichotomized scores (high-high-high, high-high-low, . . ., low-low-low) were then made the dependent variables in a discriminant function analysis. All of the predictors that had been found related to any one of the three original defense factors were employed as independent variables. No significant results appeared.

In a second analysis, each of the seven profiles of scores was treated as a dummy variable to be predicted from the array of independent variables by means of an AID analysis. Only the extreme patterns of defense factors (high-high-high; low-low-low) prove to be significantly related to variables in this array of predictors. (Because as many adolescents, or more, exhibited certain of the other patterns, these findings are not the result of a lack of subjects having less extreme patterns.)

The AID results strongly resemble those we have examined for profiles of defenses based on unique scores. For simplicity, I present only the main trends from the AID analysis and for subjects having high scores on all three defense factors. (This means subjects high on defensiveness and, probably, on anxiety.) The fathers are likely to be defensive and the mothers are not self-accepting or socially comfortable. Both parents are dissatisfied with their marriage. Relations in the family are not close. The parents do not discipline through appeals to positive values and they tend to be intolerant of the child's individuated interests and also of his direct expressions of deviant impulses. From the perspective of figure 5.1, these are families with powerful strains at level I and II. The mother as well as the father is a source of tensions and dissatisfactions and the parents oppose direct or indirect expressions of possibly deviant desires by children (columns B and D of figure 5.1).

The AID results thus resemble those obtained for profiles based on unique scores. First, they correlate with "independent" variables that cut across the rows and columns of figure 5.1. Second, there are important relations with maternal as well as paternal variables. The general points made in discussing the AID analyses based on unique scores seem appropriate here as well.

Individuals' profiles of defenses in three anxiety syndromes

To this point, we have found that variables given in the rows and columns of figure 5.1 help us to predict adolescents' scores on profiles of defense, whether those profiles are based on a factoring of raw scores or on unique scores. They also help in predicting adolescents' factor scores as derived from raw defenses scores. Although characteristics of the mothers' personalities are not generally related to the unique scores or factor scores, they are strongly associated with both types of profile scores. I have offered suggestions to explain these several findings. As we turn to the third and last set of profile scores to be examined – those associated with obsessions, hysteria, and phobias – we will find that the ideas and findings associated with figure 5.1 are directly relevant.

In Sigmund Freud's (1926) thinking, and in that of subsequent analysts, each of these anxiety syndromes is associated with a characteristic pattern of defenses. In the terms of figure 5.1, the defenses in each pattern spread across rows and/or columns in the figure. On the other hand, analysts regard each syndrome as *centered* in strains in familial relations that are characteristic of *just one* of the rows in this figure. Defenses in the syndrome that are assigned other levels in figure 5.1 are seen as augmenting or buttressing defensive activity at the level at which the focal strains are located.

Consider first the case of obsessions. Obsessions are associated with desperate but failing efforts at repression and with the person's trying to cope with the behaviors that escape repressive control by using such defenses as isolation and doubt and indecision. Obsessions are seen, however, as unlikely to entail the use of denial.

In this interpretation, obsessions and the defenses associated with them involve constant attention to the way one expresses deviant impulses while not giving up entirely on such expressions. The exception, and it is the key to the whole pattern, is the effort at repression. It is the person's lack of success in repressing that leads to the "spill-over" of possibly deviant desires and behaviors, a spill-over that he cannot control and must defend against by other means.

Freud saw all of the anxiety syndromes as related to children's struggles with the structure of authority and affection they found in relations with, and between, their parents, struggles focused on a challenge to the authority and prerogatives of the father. Within that framework, he saw obsessive symptoms and the associated defenses as focused on what he called "anal" concerns: for example, concerns about being subjected to undue demands or failing to perform as one should. (See appendix 3 for systematic connections with Freud's and Erikson's developmental stages.) In the conceptualization of figure 5.1, that suggests a focus on the strains around particular rights and duties that we associated with strains in level II, social interdependence.

Are obsessive symptoms and defenses among adolescents in my sample related to strains at level II, social interdependence? Some data were available on that subject.

Sixty-seven of the adolescents in my sample had completed the CPI. By means I describe elsewhere (Swanson, 1986a), I derived a score for number of obsessive symptoms from the CPI items. As I indicate in appendix 3, one of the profile factors based on the unique scores on defenses (profile factor III) proved to consist in the obsessive profile of defenses.

As I report in the original description of the findings, neither the score on obsessive symptoms nor that for profile factor III relates to independent variables specified in figure 5.1, but there are such relations when adolescents having scores above the mean on *both* symptoms and defenses are compared with others. These high scorers are significantly more likely to have highly defensive fathers (an indicator of familial strains at level II in figure 5.1) and fathers who have entrepreneurial occupations. Thus there is evidence that this syndrome is focused on strains at level II in 5.1. But defenses usually seen as connected to the syndrome are linked in figure 5.1 to strains at other levels in familial relations. An account of the appearance of this total syndrome thus takes us well beyond ideas now in hand while finding that those ideas are of some use.

Similar points can be made concerning findings on hysteria and phobias. I take up each in turn.

The profile of defenses thought characteristic of hysteria, social phobias, and agoraphobias has high scores on repression, displacement, and, possibly, denial, and a low score on regression. But phobias are regarded as being at a higher level of cognitive complexity than is hysteria.

From early on, hysteria has been seen as well embodied in the relevant profile of defenses. Other symptoms (*e.g.*, conversions or theatricality) have been understood as superficial (Krohn, 1978). This profile of defenses has been seen as focused on concerns that are identified in figure 5.1 as being at level III, organization under a charismatic center. In that context, the profile is seen as indicating an effort to show the essential innocence of one's desires, to show that they will not challenge the parents in their "official" roles, especially the parent who serves as charismatic center. One of the defenses in the profile, displacement, is at level III in figure 5.1; two others, denial and repression, are at the next lower level; repression and displacement are both related to parents' feelings about children's expressions of individuated interests (figure 5.1, columns A and B). In sum, the defenses in this profile are relatively localized in the rows and columns of figure 5.1.

I identified adolescents having the relevant profile of defenses and those having scores above the sample mean on the MMPI Hysteria Scale (as derived from the CPI). Those having either characteristic are more likely than others to have parents who do not support individuated interests in their children (column B in figure 5.1) and also to have fathers whose personalities are not role appropriate (an index of strain at level III, organization under a charismatic center). Thus the relations with independent variables in figure 5.1 that are found for the profile of defenses or of symptoms characteristic of this syndrome are close to what would be expected on theoretical grounds.

Several studies show that defenses like those in hysteria are found in social phobias and agoraphobias but suggest the presence of one or more of the more complex defenses against conscience (reaction formation, isolation, intellectualization) as well. Evidence from experimental as well as clinical studies (reviewed in Swanson, 1986a) also suggests that these phobias are more complex cognitively than is hysteria. They also involve a more conforming, less challenging stance than hysteria, the phobic symptoms being offered as evidence of the person's vulnerability, his need for others, and the improbability, despite appearances to the contrary, that he will directly challenge existing structures of authority. They testify to his being secure and comfortable within the social relationships but wary of the disrupting effects of external contacts and influences.

In addition to the relevant profile of defenses, I had scores on the number of social phobias that adolescents checked on the CPI. (Social phobias were the only form of phobia represented by a sufficient number of items on the CPI from which to derive a sensible score.) The more of these indicators of phobic pattern an adolescent had, the more likely he was to have parents who support individuated interests in children (column A, figure 5.1), to have a father whose personality was role appropriate (level III), and to come from a family embodying the conflicts inherent in hierarchical associations and egalitarian social systems (level IV or V). These relations are therefore consistent with expectations from theory.

To summarize, there are profiles of defenses that have some spread across the rows and columns of figure 5.1 but, because they tend to accompany particular anxiety syndromes, and because those syndromes are related to specific sectors of the rows and/or columns of the figure, the profiles show similar associations. The ideas embodied in figure 5.1 help us to predict these correlations.

Some general conclusions

The question set out in chapter 1 was this: Why do individuals use some ego defenses and not others? In moving from that point to this one, we have uncovered some parts of an answer and some additional questions. I want now to bring these findings together.

1. I argued that it would help in answering the original question if we first clarified the nature of ego defenses. In chapters 1 and 2, I proposed that we think of these defenses as justifications that people make to themselves and others – justifications so designed that the defender, and not just other people, can accept them. What is justified, I proposed, are an individual's tendencies to undermine his ties to others: ties that he wants, in part, to keep. The defenses offer proof that, however things may seem, the individual's fundamental commitment is to the preservation of these ties: he wants and needs them and will play his part in maintaining them.

2. I also proposed that individuals will always find it necessary to use some defenses because they will never find themselves completely at one in any social relationship. They will always have reason to want to get more from the relationship than it offers or to contribute less to it. They will always have desires that can be met through other and competitive relationships. Defenses will therefore be an inevitable and ubiquitous part of people's participation in social life.

3. These arguments resemble some other accounts of defenses, but are different – at least in emphasis. They picture defenses as social in origin and reference. They suggest that defenses are aspects of the individual's activity as a social participant – as a self or person – and that they therefore are a form of self process. My arguments do not exclude the possibility that defenses may operate "unconsciously" or be in some sense "irrational," "inadequate," "self-deceptive," or highly "defensive," but they do not treat such properties as necessary or defining features of defenses. Indeed, the arguments imply that defenses must meet at least some of the ordinary criteria of evidence and logic if they are to be successful as justifications that seem satisfactory and "true" to the defender as well as to other people.

4. These general arguments were the basis for a new look at two grounds on which defenses have been classified: their classification according to the nature of the threat concerned and their ordering by level of cognitive complexity (or distortingness). I suggested that Anna Freud's classification of defenses by sources of threat is helpful but in need of clarification. Rather than distinguishing simply (and ambiguously) between defenses against conscience and defenses against objective anxiety, I proposed a four-fold classification.

Some defenses seem to turn on whether a person's possibly deviant desires can be expressed indirectly or in socially acceptable ways. Displacement and reaction formation, for example, consist in such expressions; repression blocks them. Other defenses turn on whether possibly deviant desires can be expressed directly, providing that the expression is qualified or restrained enough to make it acceptable. A defense like isolation seems to embody such a direct but restrained expression; defenses like projection and regression embody less qualified or acceptable expressions. What Anna Freud calls defenses against objective anxiety seem to fall in the very last of these categories; all of the other categories meet her criteria for defenses against conscience. I closed this particular discussion by suggesting that other people's acceptance, or lack of acceptance, of direct or indirect expressions of possibly deviant desires will influence the defenses that participants use. People tend, I argued, to use defenses (justifications) that fit the social circumstances in which they find themselves, in this case the social acceptability or unacceptability of some degree of social deviance. Since these ideas were to be applied to adolescent children in relations with their families, I described measures of such acceptance, or lack of acceptance, by parents.

5. Defenses have also been classified as varying in degree of cognitive complexity. I proposed that more complex defenses are likely to be used to deal with strains in more complex social relations; that the more complex a strained social relationship, the more considerations there are that must be taken into account in an adequate defense. Focusing on adolescents and families, I suggested that in families (as in any group) there are levels of social relations and that these differ in organizational complexity. I identified these levels as the ones that appear in the main stages of group growth and development, relations at earlier levels continuing to exist at later stages but becoming organized within more complex arrangements. I proposed operational definitions for strains focused at each of five such levels of social relations as found in families and I suggested, in a preliminary way, how particular defenses might be especially appropriate in dealing with tensions and strains at particular levels. (Appendix 3 uses this material for an interpretation of what are usually taken to be steps and stages in the psychological development of individuals and for a specification of the cross-societal meaning of age role systems.)

6. The developments given in steps 4 and 5 above resulted in a cross-classification (figure 5.1) of strains on social solidarity against which a person might have to defend: from step 4, strains entailed in lack of social acceptance of direct or of indirect expressions of possibly deviant desires and strains entailed in a qualified acceptance of such expressions; from step 5, strains at

various levels of social relations, these varying in organizational complexity. Particular defenses were located in this cross-classification as especially appropriate for coping with the combination of strains at that intersection of types of strain. Chapter 5 presented the results of applying these ideas and the accompanying methods to defenses displayed by a sample of adolescents, the defenses focusing primarily on the subjects' relations in their families.

Both the strains identified in step 4 and those from step 5 prove generally related to adolescents' defenses in the ways expected, the relation between the cognitive complexity of defenses and the organizational complexity of the levels of social relations within a family at which strain occurs being especially strong. These findings, and those in chapter 6, make it clear that defenses are "rational," at least in the sense of being "tailored" to fit the nature of the social relationship that they help to maintain.

An important incidental finding: knowing that a family shows strains at a particular level of social relations does not enable one to predict whether it will show strains at other levels or, if it does, at which other levels. Thus, contrary to some theorists, families that have strained relations at simpler levels do not necessarily exhibit strains at higher levels of organization.

7. Chapter 5 took up defenses one by one, associating each with distinctive social circumstances. Chapter 6 has done the same for profiles of defenses. The findings in chapter 6 are in part an extension and application of ideas and findings from chapter 5, but there are some important differences.

(a) The classification of strains embodied in figure 5.1 helps greatly in identifying conditions in which adolescents get high unique scores on defenses: in chapter 5 on any given defense and, in chapter 6, on groupings of defenses obtained from a varimax factor analysis of the raw scores for ten defenses. (Because these latter groupings contain defenses from more than one row or column in figure 5.1, it is combinations of the sources of strain in that figure which relate to factor scores.)

(b) In chapters 5 and 6, adolescents' unique scores – on individual defenses or on factor scores for clusters of defenses – relate especially to features of their fathers' performance in familial roles. When we look at the social correlates of the profiles of defenses that are the most common in my sample of adolescents, we find that features of their mothers' performance and outlook are of equal or greater importance. Why should this occur? My suggestion turns on the fact that, whereas the unique scores are purged of defensiveness, the profile scores bring defensiveness back into the picture. The suggestion is that an adolescent's difficulties in dealing with his mother may be vital for his defensiveness. Defensiveness means preoccupation with justifying oneself. It might be argued that mothers tend to be more important in these matters because they are usually the principal source of love, understanding, and personal acceptance: the chief controllers of affective resources. They are also "there" more of the time and are the persons most likely to be putting limits on affectivity.

But all of that is debatable and, in any case, does not explain why it is the fathers' performances that relate more strongly to adolescents' unique scores on defenses. Is it that the things that fathers do and feel tend to be especially important for a family's organization as a group or collectivity, mothers' behaviors being more important for interpersonal relations? (For a discussion of this distinction, see Swanson, 1970.) Is it related to fathers' having more connections outside the home? Are fathers therefore a more likely source of marital instability? Whatever the answer, and unless my findings are just a chance occurrence or one peculiar to my sample, the prominence they give in one case to fathers and in another to mothers is obviously important. And their meaning remains to be determined.

(c) It is the case, however, that "personality" characteristics of both parents, although not of great importance as correlates of unique scores, are more likely to be important as correlates of scores on the profiles of defenses most common in this sample. These defensive profiles cut across rows and columns of figure 5.1 and therefore catch broad defensive styles (*e.g.*, direct or indirect expressions of impulses together with justifications thereof; cautious expressions of desires in ways that are not confrontational; a general lack of expression of possibly deviant impulses). This may be why the profiles tend to correlate with combinations of "personality" characteristics of the parents, characteristics which, when taken together, constitute broad approaches in supporting and directing children (*e.g.*, strong and helpful but sets high standards; warm and pleasant but vacillating). Perhaps these combinations of parental characteristics are a useful operational definition for *combinations* of the independent variables in figure 5.1 that are required for predictions of children's defensive profiles. Unique scores on individual defenses, and discriminations like those in figure 5.1, seem necessary for studies of the *systematics* of defenses and their sources. As we come to *profiles* of defenses, broader "chunkings" of independent variables become necessary.

(d) The profiles of defenses associated with obsessions, hysteria, and phobia introduce further complexities. Each profile has been thought to be focused on certain strains in social solidarity and the ideas and methods embodied in figure 5.1 enabled us successfully to predict the level of social relations with which each syndrome would be associated in this sample. On the other hand, the existence of such syndromes of defenses and symptoms must have added to the "error" in analyses in chapters 5 and 6. This is so because the defenses in each syndrome come from more than one level of social status in figure 5.1 and do so in a special way. One or two are "at" the level which is taken in clinical accounts to be focal for the syndrome. The rest are at other, usually lower, levels. They primarily buttress the defenses at the focal level. My finding on these syndromes is that there are strains in familial relations at the focal level but not at others.

To eliminate this source of error in future research, we shall need a basis for predicting when it is that defenses serve primarily to augment others rather than themselves being directly responsive to strains in social relations. And a basis for saying which defenses will be used in such buttressing roles.

8. There are, of course, many other, and narrower, findings that need debate (*e.g.*, those for the social correlates of each defense) and many, many questions about the indices I have used for independent variables. I want, however, to close with reflections on three questions encountered in most studies of defenses (if only at the point at which their larger meaning is addressed): (a) Do the measures used actually capture variance in defenses? (b) Should one assume that the defenses as studied here will be stable? (c) What of sources of anxiety and danger not considered in this study and of the defenses that might be appropriate for dealing with them?

(a) On methods of observing defenses

In this study, I relied upon a code for defenses that was developed by Norma Haan. To apply this code, clinical psychologists were asked to read the transcripts of tape-recorded interviews and to note defenses as they appeared in these records. Does this procedure get at ego defenses in the ordinary meaning of that term?

A defense involves relations among several components. Ideal evidence for the existence of a defense would show that every required component was in place and in its proper relationship to each of the others. Thus one would want evidence for the existence of a particular impulse, for the individual's judgment that this impulse was unacceptable, for his judgment that he was unacceptable to himself by virtue of having this impulse, for his conclusion that there are grounds for his being unacceptable to himself – despite his having this impulse and for his coming to justify himself, to himself, on the basis of these considerations. To say that a particular course of action is an aspect of an ego defense, we should, ideally, be able to situate it in the context of this set of components and relations. One cannot say that a person is projecting simply from knowing that he blames others for faults that are his as well as theirs. He may be telling a lie and know it. He may be trying to deflect blame from himself. He may be honestly mistaken.

No method has been found that produces full and objective evidence for the existence of all of the aspects of any defense. There are several methods, Haan's among them, that have some face validity and that have been shown to produce results which, in turn, correlate with other variables in the way that valid results should. Some of these methods are objective and quasi-experimental; some are objective and naturalistic.

Miller and Swanson (1960) and Aronfreed (1964) tried to create experimental situations that would occasion defenses in children. In their studies, children completed projective stories before and after encountering a threat. The threats were varied in order to occasion defenses against conscience or defenses against objective anxiety. These investigators found an increase, after appropriate threat, of themes and events in projective stories that they interpreted as defenses. What is more, the defenses that increased were of the sort that seemed appropriate to the nature of the threat.

In designs of this kind, there is evidence for the presence of a threat and for a predicted change in behavior following that threat. There is no direct evidence, however, that the subjects perceived an impulse within themselves which they found unacceptable, or evidence that they felt unacceptable because they had such an impulse, or evidence that they changed their behavior in order to reinstate themselves in their own eyes. All of these events are inferred.

A second method of observing defenses is found in Blum's (1956) Defense Preference Inventory and Gleser and Ihilevich's (1969) Defense Mechanism Inventory. Subjects are shown projective pictures (Blum) or given stories to read (Gleser and Ihilevich). The pictures or stories depict characters who have inner conflicts that are supposedly common (*e.g.*, sibling rivalry, Oedipal strivings, problems of sexual identity or of independence from authorities) and the subjects are asked to choose one sentence, from a set provided, that is representative of their reaction. The several sentences present different defensive responses – or so they do if one assumes the presence in the stories of the whole context of components that defines a defense. That context is only inferred. There is no direct evidence that the subject himself has comparable inner conflicts or impulses nor is there evidence that he would spontaneously employ any of the defensive behaviors provided. There is also no evidence that the subject feels any need to defend when he encounters impulses like those exhibited by characters in the plots.

Relative to these other procedures, that of Haan has some possible advantages. It is possible that a clinician who reads a long interview about a person's intimate social relations will sense the subject's desires, will correctly identify his feelings about those desires, will see the points at which the subject feels that he needs to justify himself in his own eyes, and will detect the method of justification employed.

But there are problems. The clinician cannot usually point to clear and specific evidence for his judgments on each of these points. A subject who, in fact, defends, may be sufficiently relaxed in the situation of the interview – sufficiently removed from the pressures he encounters in real life – so that his defenses are not visible. Or the defenses he exhibits may concern the fact of his being interviewed rather than the relations he is discussing in the interview. And so on.

We can, I think, conclude that none of the procedures for studying defenses gets at all of the evidence one would need for a confident judgment that some course of action is defensive. We can also conclude that none is clearly superior to the others. At the same time, all of these procedures provide results that correlate in sensible ways with other variables. The results can therefore be considered useful although provisional.

(b) On the stability of styles of defense

Most older children and adults are probably able to employ any of the common ego defenses. The form of defense they actually employ is, at least in part, a function of the source of the threats they encounter and of the specific problems of social integration that they are pressed to resolve. This implies that the likelihood of such a person's using a particular defense is determined by the presence and persistence of particular sources of threat and particular problems of social integration.

Such information as there is on the subject is consistent with that conclusion. Miller and Swanson (1960) and Aronfreed (1964) were able in a matter of minutes to change the defenses that children employed by changing the kind of threats that those children had to handle or changing the alternatives available to those children for resolving their difficulties. On the other hand, these and other investigators (Lazarus, 1966: 242–5) have found a person's style of defense to be related to such enduring characteristics of the individual as the social class of the family in which he was reared or to his intelligence or to measures of his personality characteristics. Gleser and Ihilevich (1969: 55) report that scores for particular defenses on their Defense Mechanisms Inventory have an average test–retest reliability of 0.89 across an interval of one week and of 0.76 across a period of three months. Blum (1956) found that a significant minority of subjects tended to use the same defense or defenses across all of the projective pictures that he presented to them. Further research

(Blum, 1956: 34) disclosed that such subjects are "more maladjusted" than are those who vary their defenses as their situation varies. In sum, both the theory I have presented and the findings from existing research make a place for persistence in the form of defense that a person uses and a place for change in his defenses. This is consistent with studies of wider ranges of cognitive and motivational styles (Bem and Allen, 1974).

(c) On other sources of anxiety and danger

The columns of figure 5.1 were derived from Anna Freud's (1936: 54–65) discussion of defenses that arise from two sources of anxiety and danger: defenses against conscience and defenses against objective anxiety. But Freud lists two other sources of the threats against which ego defenses are used. One is any sudden accession "of instinctual energy" as at puberty or the climacteric. The other is the breakdown within the ego of "harmony between its impulses." These latter dangers may be accompanied by feelings of guilt and shame or they may not.

Unlike the threats catalogued in figure 5.1, the problem posed by these further dangers is not so much one of the person's justifying himself as it is of his restoring his powers, empowerment (Swanson, 1973), and integrity as a person. This is a great theme of Erikson's (1959, 1968) discussions of crises of identity, crises which seem to recur, at least in complex societies, throughout adulthood (Levinson and others, 1978).

Many of the familiar defenses can be brought into play in this situation, repression, for example, or intellectualization or isolation, but new and more specific strategies are also used to ward off the threats. Erikson describes one of these in his sketch of the "psychosocial moratorium," the procedure of putting all final decisions on one's course of action in abeyance while exploring alternatives and developing new commitments around which to organize one's life. There seem to be many others (Levinson and others, 1978; Vaillant, 1977). (The most detailed evidence from longitudinal studies (Block and Haan, 1971) indicates that major crises due to these threats to ego integrity are not common and shows that, when they do occur, they can be triggered by adventitious events or by systematic changes in social relations.) A full account of methods by which people protect themselves as persons must include defenses appropriate to these problems. This account has yet to be developed.

Appendix 1. Supplementary tables

Table A1.1. *Significant intercorrelations among independent variables**

Variable**	N	2	3	4	5	6	7	8	9	10	11	12	13	14	15	16	17	18	19	20	21	22	23	24
1# Age	118																							
2# Sex	118	—				21								20				-19						
3 Birth rank	118		—	32				20													-20			
4# Size of sibship	118			—					-28													-28		
5 Socio-economic status	118				—							-22									-20			
6# Entrepreneurial status	108					—																		
7# Strength of marital bond: father	108						—									26						-28		29
8# Strength of marital bond: mother	115							—								40			27			-26		20
9# Role appropriateness of father's personality	82								—														-36	
10# Complexity of familial decision-making pattern: constitutional order	100									—														
11# Parents approve individuated interests	114										—	-21				31	19					-31		-29

Table A1.1 (*cont*).

Variable**	N	2	3	4	5	6	7	8	9	10	11	12	13	14	15	16	17	18	19	20	21	22	23	24
12# Parents permit direct expression of desires	94											—		-21	-21								19	19
13# Family supports direct expression of desires	111												—	-25	-24	-22								
14# Father accepts child	108													—										
15# Mother accepts child	115														—									
16# Closeness	114															—							-28	
17# Discipline: reasoning	74																—							
18# Discipline: power assertion	74																	—		-23	-20			
19# Discipline: positive appeals	74																		—					
20# Father's personal stability	108																			—		-27		-18
21# Mother's personal stability	115																				—			
22 No. of high scores on three defense factors: father	104																					—		
23 No. of such scores for mother	104																						—	
24# Hierarchical network	100																							—

*All correlations are significant at the 0.05 level or beyond.

**Variables marked with a cross-hatch (#) were dichotomized. Scores, from low to high, ran as follows: 1: 15 years and younger to 16 years and higher; 2: male to female; 3: first born, middle-born, last-born; 4: 3 or fewer to 4 or more; 5: upper working to upper middle and up; 6: bureaucratic to entrepreneurial; 9: father has lower score than mother on "task leadership" *vs.* all other patterns; 10: simple to complex; 12: no. of parents accepting is: none, one, two; 22 and 23: no. of scores above the median on each of three defense factors is none, one, two or more. Scores on all other cross-hatched variables were dichotomized: below median score *vs.* scores at or above the median.

Table A1.2. Correlations of fathers' CPI and K-corrected MMPI scores*
with variables from table A1.1

CPI and MMPI dimensions	Variables from table A1.1																							
	1	2	3	4	5	6	7	8	9	10	11	12	13	14	15	16	17	18	19	20	21	22	23	24
Dominance							21									21								
Capacity for status										23							34							
Sociability										25						21	21							
Social presence									−23							32	23					−27		
Self-acceptance																22								
Sense of well-being																28	21	29		21	30			
Responsibility				22						26										25				
Socialization								24									23	28						
Self-control											−27	24		−24						34	25			
Tolerance				28						32							26			22				
Good impression																	23		30	30				
Communality																	−43							
Achievement: conformity														−22	25					24				
Achievement: independence				22						27							24			29				
Intellectual efficiency										23						22	26							
Psychological-mindedness																	26						−20	
Flexibility												22	−21				39							
Femininity										−30														
Overcontrol																−22								

Table A1.2 (*cont.*)

CPI and MMPI dimensions	1	2	3	4	5	6	7	8	9	10	11	12	13	14	15	16	17	18	19	20	21	22	23	24
																				Variables from table A1.1				
Undercontrol																	−30		−26					
Neurotic tendencies																−30			−27					
Lie																	34		25					
Frequency											22									−23	−31			
Correction																			29					
Hypochondriasis																		−22				−21		
Depression					21											−27								
Hysteria																	33							
Psychopathic deviate								−24												−22	−21			
Masculinity − femininity																	23							
Paranoia										23												24		
Psychasthenia																					−21			
Schizophrenia							−22								−24					−22	−32			
Hypomania																								
Social introversion										−23														

*Scores were available for 88 fathers.

Table A1.3. *Correlations of mothers' CPI and K-corrected MMPI scores* with variables from table A1.1*

CPI and MMPI dimensions	Variables from table A1.1																							
	1	2	3	4	5	6	7	8	9	10	11	12	13	14	15	16	17	18	19	20	21	22	23	24
Dominance	22								33	22		21		21										
Capacity for status					20				21							34								
Sociability									30					22										
Social presence						21											21							
Self-acceptance																								
Sense of well-being															22			32			30			
Responsibility				21								29												
Socialization			24																30					
Self-control																			46					
Tolerance																	23							
Good impression												20					24	36			30			
Communality			20					−30									−29							
Achievement: conformity																	23		33					
Achievement: independence																	24							
Intellectual efficiency																			22					
Psychological-mindedness					21											28								
Flexibility					20												37							
Femininity															−20									
Overcontrol									−33															
Undercontrol																		−31						

Table A1.3 (*cont.*)

CPI and MMPI dimensions	Variables from table A1.1																							
	1	2	3	4	5	6	7	8	9	10	11	12	13	14	15	16	17	18	19	20	21	22	23	24
Neurotic tendencies																		−28						
Lie					−20					−21							21		26					
Frequency								−29										−40	−20	−31				
Correction													−23	26		.			37					
Hypochondriasis																								
Depression											−22									−20				
Hysteria																								
Psychopathic deviate							−21	−36										−25		−21	21			
Masculinity–femininity																28								
Paranoia					22	−34	−41								29									
Psychasthenia																		−20		−21				
Schizophrenia																				−32				
Hypomania									23															
Social introversion														−27	−21									

*Scores were available for 103 mothers.

Table A1.4. Correlations of cognitive and moral indices* with variables from table A1.1

Population and index	N	Variables from table A1.1																						
		2	3	4	5	6	7	8	9	10	11	12	13	14	15	16	17	18	19	20	21	22	23	24
Fathers																								
WAIS intelligence	100											−21												
Piaget pendulum	25				51								46	43										
Piaget correlations	25																				57			
Piaget composite	22																							
Formal morality	29	40														38						37		
Interpersonal morality	29	52		37												38			−35			−37		
Defense factor I	118				−22																	54		
Defense factor II	118				−22																	59		
Defense factor III	118				−22																	32		
Mothers																								
WAIS intelligence	114				28							33						35						
Piaget pendulum	27																							
Piaget correlations	27									−38														
Piaget composite	24																							
Formal morality	31								42									−34				32		
Interpersonal morality	31								32			45						−37						
Defense factor I	118																							
Defense factor II	118																							
Defense factor III	118																							

Table A1.4 (*cont.*)

Population and index	N															Variables from table A1.1								
		2	3	4	5	6	7	8	9	10	11	12	13	14	15	16	17	18	19	20	21	22	23	24
Children																								
WAIS or WISC intelligence	108		−23		21				24		29					27								
Piaget pendulum	26																							
Piaget correlations	24																							
Piaget composite	23																							
Formal morality	31																				31			
Interpersonal morality	30															33								

*Piagetian and moral scores for Oakland sample only.

Table A1.5. *Spearman-Brown reliability coefficients for the ratings of defenses*

Ego processes	Subjects		Spouses		Children	
	Male	Female	Male	Female	Male	Female
Isolation	0.24	0.56	0.59	0.35	0.32	0.39
Intellectualization	0.65	0.58	0.79	0.51	0.38	0.48
Rationalization	0.77	0.62	0.46	0.65	0.51	0.66
Doubt	0.79	0.71	0.69	0.70	0.54	0.51
Denial	0.84	0.83	0.57	0.61	0.69	0.52
Projection	0.59	0.71	0.77	0.70	0.65	0.71
Regression	0.76	0.68	0.81	0.58	0.42	0.49
Displacement	0.78	0.67	0.67	0.63	0.49	0.71
Reaction formation	0.67	0.53	0.64	0.61	0.51	0.48
Repression	0.71	0.79	0.71	0.73	0.41	0.49
N	105	129	92	95	72	93
Range of coefficients	0.24–0.84	0.53–0.83	0.46–81	0.35–0.73	0.32–0.69	0.39–0.71
Median coefficient	0.74	0.68	0.68	0.62	0.50	0.50

Appendix 2. Development of scores on disciplinary practices

In 1968–70, subjects and spouses were asked to fill in a questionnaire. Two of the questions were concerned with methods of disciplining children. These appear in figure A2.1.

For the present study, I wanted to identify the parents' typical methods of disciplining their children. I did not want those methods to be weighted by the frequency with which parents employed discipline in general. This required the transformation of the parents' responses to question 47 from absolute to ipsative scores. To make that transformation, I calculated each parent's mean frequency on all nine disciplinary practices and then subtracted that mean frequency from each of the nine discipline scores to produce nine discipline deviation scores – each deviation score thus indicating the amount by which the use of a given practice differed from a parent's average frequency of exercising discipline.

The next step was to conduct a factor analysis of these deviation scores. Before that could be done, it was necessary to remove at least one item from the set in order to eliminate the singularity that would otherwise be built into a correlation matrix of ipsative scores. It happened that one item among the nine, item 5 ("tell them of the examples of good people"), correlated poorly with all the others. It could be removed from the matrix without losing crucial information. The factor analysis of the remaining eight deviation scores is reported in chapter 3. (The initial analysis was performed for mothers and fathers separately. When it was evident that the two factor solutions were similar, the process was repeated for the combined sample. The three factors given in chapter 3 are those for mothers and fathers taken together.)

Figure A2.1. *Disciplinary items from the parents' questionnaire*

47. Indicate in one of the columns from (1) to (5) the frequency of your various responses (now or when they were younger) to your children's intending (or doing) something wrong:

	(1) Almost never	(2) Sometimes	(3) Moderately	(4) Most of the time	(5) Always	Most and least typical
Stop them, control them						
Tell them about the bad things that could happen to them						
Point out the way other people could be affected						
Discuss and examine the various aspects of the issue with them						
Tell them of the examples of good people						
Attempt to teach them what's right and wrong						

Figure A2.1 (cont.)

47. Indicate in one of the columns from (1) to (5) the frequency of your various responses (now or when they were younger) to your children's intending (or doing) something wrong:

	(1) Almost never	(2) Sometimes	(3) Moderately	(4) Most of the time	(5) Always	Most and least typical
Tell them how pleased I'll be if they do right						
Tell them how angry I'll be if they do wrong						
Let them know how disappointed I'd be in them						

48. NOW IN THE RIGHT-HAND COLUMN ABOVE, "Most and least typical," please check (√) the two you're *most* likely to do, and (×) the two you are *least* likely to do.

Appendix 3. Social foundations of personal development

The analysis in chapter 4 makes use of an observation from the studies of developing groups: the finding of a similarity between the sequence of social relations and personal adjustments that appear in developing groups and the sequence of psychosocial stages that Erikson sees in the development of individuals as persons. The psychosocial problems that Erikson thinks are salient at the beginning of personal development, problems of basic trust and mistrust, are said also to preoccupy people at interdependence, the first stage of group development. Similarly, questions of autonomy and of shame and doubt are said to be important at the second stage of group development, social interdependence, and, by Erikson's account at the second stage in personal development. In chapter 4 these connections were made for the first five stages in the two sequences of development, personal and collective.

Several students of collective development have noticed these similarities (Kaplan and Roman, 1963) and have seen in them (Gibbard, Hartman, and Mann, 1974: 85):

the ready and appealing possibility that individual development is replicated in the development of the group as a whole. The sequence of collective development then becomes the transition from childhood (dependence) to adulthood (intimacy).

By this interpretation, individuals in developing groups find themselves having social relations like the ones they had early in life, drawing upon skills acquired earlier, and experiencing a reactivation of perceptions or feelings which date from infancy or childhood or some later period of development. This may well be true, but it cannot be the whole story or even the main part of it. The adult in the new or evolving group is not simply reliving or reintegrating his past. He is finding his way into a new relationship, one in which he begins as a dependent and must move toward the status of a participant who contributes to collective life as a member of a work group, a constitutional order, or an even more complex form of collective effort. The sequence of relations intrinsic to collective development poses for participants the same sequence of psychosocial problems that they encountered in the course of their personal development.

179

If that is correct, we may have a basis for overcoming difficulties in Erikson's account of personal development and in Piaget's (Kohlberg and Armon, 1984). These accounts have two problems in common. Both of them describe stages in personal development but neither accounts in systematic terms for the number, the ordering, or the contents of these stages and neither explains how an individual comes to move from one stage to another. I think that these problems can be solved if we conceive of personal development as a process in which an individual learns to become a participant in organized collective life – at whatever age that may occur or recur.

A great deal depends, of course, upon what is meant by "development" and by "personal." The sequence of stages that Erikson proposes is developmental in the sense that new stages replace old ones through a process of differentiation and reintegration. In such a process, skills and orientations developed at earlier stages are not lost but are transcended and brought within a new, more generalized integration at later stages. This is true of Piaget's stages as well.

Erikson's stages concern an individual's growth as a person. So do Piaget's. This means that both writers deal with the steps through which an individual becomes acquainted with his own behavioral processes and organization: the steps through which he gains a progressively more differentiated knowledge of his own impulses, affects, capacities, expectations, priorities, potentialities, and the like; the steps through which he attains an ever more generalized perspective from which to guide and integrate his own actions and to interpret the action of others. By contrast, neither Erikson's stages, nor Piaget's, are based primarily upon the individual's growth as an organism or upon merely quantitative increases in his stock of knowledge.

Erikson's own studies, and Piaget's, have often dealt with personal development in one or another of the periods of an individual's life: infancy, childhood, adolescence, and so on. Both writers describe several of these periods. This does not mean, however, that the sequence of stages which either describes should be associated only with an individual's early years of life or with his movement from birth through old age. There is a great deal of evidence that people can go through many, perhaps all, of these same stages at any point in life if they find that they must be "born again": must relate to others deeply and as whole persons in what is, for them, a novel collective enterprise. Thus stages which seem identical in sequence and contents to those given by Erikson have been found to characterize the careers of patients in psychotherapy, of new members of monasteries and convents, of inductees into elite military organizations, of some people who are imprisoned for long periods, of students in residential schools, and of participants in self-developing groups (Curle, 1947; Curle and Trist, 1947; Dunphy, 1966; Gibbard, Hartman, and

Mann, 1974; Goffman, 1962; Parsons, 1951: 428–79; Swanson, 1965b; Van Maanen, 1976; Wanous, 1977).[1] Stages which strongly resemble the cognitive and the moral series of Piaget have been observed among people who are involved in the growth of large collective movements and of small groups (Swanson, 1971, 1974; Tuckman, 1965).

These findings suggest that at least some of the main stages observed in personal development across the life career are not necessarily associated with an individual's being of a certain age. Rather they are aspects of his being socialized: of his gradually becoming a full participant in the life of some group, at whatever age that may occur; of his becoming acquainted with the social arrangements that collective acts entail and of his developing the commitments to a particular social relationship which participation in its activities requires.

In group growth and development, people move together through stages in an emerging relationship. They participate, in sequence, in forms of association that grow from their attempts to benefit from one another and from a common life. When an individual of any age enters an existing group, he joins people who already have the several types of association – interdependence, social interdependence, solidarity around a charismatic center, and so forth – sketched in chapter 4. To the extent that this group differs from others he has known, and to the extent it requires that he participate as a whole person (therefore with diffuse and wholehearted commitment to his fellows and to the group as a whole) he cannot participate until he has been "born again."

This new member, be it a baby in a family or a postulant in a religious order or any other novice, has much to learn. He is far from being able to take part in the group's work and farther from being able to represent its interests.

To older members, the newcomer is a promise and a charge. He is a sign of their potency to perpetuate themselves and the life they value but they must bear the expense of his upbringing.

Interdependence is a fact from the beginning. The newcomer depends on the group for much or all of his nurture and the group depends on him for its future. One or more members must be assigned special responsibility for his care and early upbringing. To lighten their work and advance his training, they must transform the relationship to one of social interdependence and do so as quickly as possible. This means that the novice must learn to help with his own immediate nurture, to order his demands to the schedule of his caretakers and, in so far as he can, to assist in the process. Thus the familiar practices of teaching the young child to dress himself, to eat, sleep, and defecate at

---

[1] These phenomena seem more likely to occur in organizations which exercise what Etzioni (1975) calls "normative" controls rather than "utilitarian" or "coercive" controls.

appointed times and places, to keep his toys "where they belong," to share in simple tasks, and to avoid disrupting his parents in essential work. When he can do these things dependably, and appreciates something of the social arrangements through which the group operates, he can be moved to a wider empowerment and wider responsibilities.

The main stages of socialization have, therefore, the same contents as the main stages of group development. In both cases, there is a process of acquainting people with the arrangements that collective acts entail and of fostering in people the commitments which those acts require. As I see it, personal development as treated by Erikson and Piaget consists in the individual's acquisition, in series, of these varieties of knowledge and commitment.

What I am suggesting is testable but untested. It can be summarized by recasting the well-known formula inspired by August Comte (1830; Baldwin, 1895) and disseminated by Granville Stanley Hall (1904): personal development is, in one sense, a recapitulation of collective development.[2] I will examine Erikson's stages from this perspective, then Piaget's. I close with a deeper grounding of development, personal and collective, in analyses sketched by Parsons (1955) and by Parsons and Olds (1955). Figure A3.1 provides the framework for this discussion.

Erikson's psychosocial stages

Erikson's treatment of personal development elaborates and extends that of Freud (Gouin Decarie, 1965; Wolff, 1960) and each stage in Erikson's sequence consists in an orientation of an individual toward others and himself, specifically in a set of terms on which an individual believes other people will gratify and, simultaneously, threaten him. Another way to conceive of these terms is to think of them as setting out specific grounds of social solidarity and as fostering specific forms of deviance. These conceptions helped us link levels of social complexity to defenses in chapter 4 and are noted in the rows of figure A3.1.

Stage I: *basic trust* vs. *basic mistrust*

Erikson associates the first stage of development (figure A3.1, column C, stage I) with the period from birth through the first year or two of life (columns G

---

[2] I should add two qualifications that distinguish my suggestion from Comte's or Hall's. First, I do not take the growth of the organism to be an intrinsic part of personal development. Second, I associate collective development with the growth of any collectivity, whether large or small, that is capable of taking corporate action. Unlike Comte and Hall, I do not limit this development to advances in the complexity of human civilization.

Figure A3.1. *Stages of development*

A. Stage	B. Collective development	C. Erikson's psychosocial stages	D. Piaget's cognitive stages	E. Piaget's moral stages	F. Kohlberg's moral orientations	G. Chronological age	H. Age roles
I	Interdependence	Trust vs. mistrust	Sensory-motor		Obedience and punishment	0–1	Infancy
II	Social inter-dependence	Autonomy vs. shame and doubt	Pre-operational	Morality of constraint	Naively egoistic: instrumental	2–3	Early childhood
III	Charismatic center	Initiative vs. guilt			Good boy	4–5	Pre-school
IV	Work group	Industry vs. inferiority	Concrete operations	Morality of cooperation	Authority and social order	6–10	Childhood
V	Constitutional order	Identity vs. identity diffusion	Formal operations		Contractual-legalistic	11–15	Adolescence
VI	Political community	Intimacy vs. isolation operations	Consolidated formal		Conscience or principle	16–20	Youth
VII	Regime	Generativity vs. stagnation				21–44	Young adulthood
VIII	Administrative system	Integrity vs. disgust, despair				45 and over	Maturity

and H). The critical facts, he reminds us, are that the infant needs things and, although active, cannot care for himself. He encounters people who are also in need and also active. In most cases, the things he does for them, and they for him, gratify all concerned.

He and they are interdependent and he learns to adapt to that situation. He learns to depend on them. He also learns that they are not always dependable. He learns to receive and accept, to be accepted in his state of need, to signal others, and to expect that his immediate needs will be gratified when they are displayed. And he learns that the costs of getting gratifications will not be too high. It is not that the infant is self-consciously aware of these conditions of his life. Rather these are the conditions under which he lives and to which he adapts.

Erikson goes on to some facets of these same conditions that are not as benign. Even the most loving and faithful parents will sometimes fail the infant. They cannot come to him at once or do not know what will satisfy him. And no parent is always loving and faithful and no infant can understand why he is sometimes gratified and, at other times, is not. He comes to associate other people with both gratification and a lack of gratification: in this sense both to trust and to distrust them.

There are, then, several similarities between the relations of people at the origin of a self-developing group and the relations between an infant and his parents. In both cases, people find themselves in need and learn that the activities of others provide gratifications and entail costs and risks. In both cases, people are interdependent because they are drawn to one another by gratifications and because the gratifications outweigh the costs and risks. In both situations, trust and mistrust – tendencies toward solidarity and social disruption – are highly salient. In neither situation are people able, at this point, to engage in collective action.

Stage II: *autonomy* vs. *shame and doubt*

Erikson says that this stage is typically found at ages two and three. By that time, most children can walk and talk. They and their parents make claims on one another and the parents begin to honor some of the child's claims only if he honors some of theirs. In this way, the child is introduced to a system of rights and duties.

He also encounters difficulties. He is certain to want some things that conflict with his relations with others. He is also a newcomer to life in a system of mutual claims and frequently makes mistakes. Coming fresh from interdependence, and accustomed to being accepted simply for what he is, he is distressed at being pressed to make himself acceptable by what he does.

We saw earlier that social interdependence, when a stage of collective development, refers to people's making claims upon one another and negotiating a network of complementary claims (these including claims on the collectivity as a whole). Taken together, these claims comprise a "plan" or "agreement." Some participants come to play an especially facilitative role in these developments and thus to serve as foci for collective action. At this stage, however, the participants are not organized to take joint actions that require a centralized control or coordination.

Compare this with the situation of the child in stage II. At this stage, he is introduced to his family as a network of social interdependence. This introduction occurs at the point at which he begins to make claims and is able to honor certain claims by others. He knows little about the arrangements in the family that provide central control and coordination and does not try to use, modify, or subvert them. In stage III he challenges those arrangements.

Stage III: initiative vs. *guilt*

As Erikson pictures him, the child is now about four or five years of age. He has rights and confidence and skill and is encouraged to exercise his rights and to use his skill on behalf of others in the group. To put it another way, he is encouraged to become more of an independent enactor: to take initiatives and exercise discretion in sustaining and implementing the group's activities. The problem is that, in taking on the manner of his parents as independent enactors, he is certain to infringe on the status of one or both as heroes. When they resist this, he sees no justification for it and is frustrated and angry. He is also guilty. His initiatives were encouraged but he has somehow exceeded his rights and infringed those of someone else. He feels demeaned, frustrated, angry, fearful, uncertain, guilty. As we saw it in chapter 4, the person in a developing group that has generated a charismatic leader has similar experiences.

Stage IV: industry vs. *inferiority*

There seem good reasons to think that the stage of personal development that Erikson labels "industry *vs.* inferiority" involves a child, or other socializee, in specialized tasks within a division of labor. This specialization makes concrete and acceptable his growing contributions as an independent enactor.

If we focus on the child (now aged six to ten years), we find him being encouraged to advance in social participation while under the guidance of a hero or heroes. In the typical case, one parent, usually the father, has special responsibilities for task leadership; the other, usually the mother, for social-emotional leadership. The child is expected, and trained, to assume responsibility for specialized tasks within that division of labor; responsibilities in the care of the household and its resources, in the moderating of conflicts among its members, in the assembling and processing of materials (food, equipment, etc.), for collective undertakings, and so on. And he is pressed to assume similar responsibilities in informal groups of peers, in school, and in other organizations of the wider community (*e.g.*, religious, recreational, and other organizations). The performance of significant and sustaining roles in a division of labor requires systematic training and it promises benefits from the accomplishment of longer range objectives: pride and confidence from the performance of tasks which, given the division of labor, are important for all participants. And, as Erikson notes, systematic training means, in turn, that adults set goals for the child which they certify in advance as worthwhile. The child therefore is learning to accomplish things he would never have thought of himself; things which are not the product of his own play and fantasy and which provide a sense of growing competence as a participant in the real world of adults.

As we saw in chapter 4, having something specific to do that is personally and socially rewarding enables and motivates industriousness: serious, systematic effort. Doing it under the family's leaders and within a division of labor enables the child to be an independent enactor without his undermining the group. But, as in all stages of development, personal or collective, there are special dangers as well. In the beginning, a child, or other new socializee, is not competent in carrying sustained responsibilities. It takes time for him to gain the skill, understanding, and outlook that are required. While he is learning, he is inadequate by his own and others' standards. As Erikson suggests, he is likely to feel inferior and especially that he will never be any good at the activities which carry high prestige.

Stage V: identity vs. *identity diffusion*

Between the ages of 11 and 17, children typically seek an independence from, and within, their families, but an independence which will not destroy their integration with their parents or the continuity between their values and those of their parents or other adults whom they regard as important socializers. There are, of course, many sources of these developments when the child is reared in a contemporary family. He is moving in wider circles outside the family. He is being asked to assume larger responsibilities and to prepare himself to take primary responsibility for his decisions. He is approaching decisions about his career after he leaves home. He cannot carry his parents with him into this new world even if he wants to. In most cases, he wants something else. He wants the dignity of full adulthood. His parents, however understanding they may be, know him as a child. He wants the freedom and confidence that come from relating to objectives that can empower a responsible choice in a life of his own. These objectives may resemble those of his parents, but he has to determine that they have the power to open a life for him as well. He is likely, as Erikson reminds us, to display a ferocious sense of his independence and to offer a ferocious defense of his integrity in judgment. He is likely to challenge and overthrow the authority of his parents, as parents, but to accept them as persons – if they are able to join him as equals under a commitment to common values.

The perils of this transition are well-known. There may be a lasting alienation from the parents. The young person may not find a kind of life to which he can become committed. He may make the wrong decisions on subjects of major importance, suggesting a fatal incompetence. He may excel in criticism and a cruel overconscientiousness, aiming these at his heroes but feeling that he, too, falls short of his ideals.

As chapter 4 indicates, members of a developing group that is organized as a constitutional order face this same range of problems. They are obligated and empowered to assume diffuse responsibilities for the group as a whole. The clear separation in a constitutional order between the group's purposes and its personnel makes it possible for members to form an identity and a sense of personal independence based upon those purposes and upon contributing to social solidarity. It also opens new possibilities for failure and inferiority.

Unlike children, older people who become new members of existing groups can become "full adults" – *i.e.*, can exercise discretion on behalf of the group's broadest interests – without "leaving home." It is therefore significant for an understanding of the sources of identity formation and identity diffusion that these phenomena occur in such adults who are entering new groups – entering cloisters, for example, or voluntary associations – and not merely among children or adolescents in families.

Stage VI: intimacy and distantiation vs. *isolation and self-absorption*

The discussion of personal and collective development in chapter 4 took the story through the fifth of Erikson's psychosocial stages. Three of his stages remain to be associated with points in collective development and the whole analysis needs to be grounded in more fundamental considerations. I continue the analysis with Erikson's sixth stage.

A group that develops a constitutional order puts its members into a new relationship with one another. They continue to perform sustaining activities as members of a work group under officials, but they and their leaders are now equal under the group's values and under the basic principles of its organization. And they have equal responsibility for the application of those principles and for the actualization of those values in the daily round. They have come to make the group's problems and values their own; are committed to promote the group's interest as occasions permit. They are associated not simply as co-participants and members and specialists but as contributors.

As contributors, their association is the kind that Easton (1957, 1965; Swanson, 1967: 32–43, 51–60) terms a "political community." They need to become reacquainted in an intimate, personal way that is distinguished from their continuing positions as persons within a charismatic order or work group. Erikson writes of this as a period of intimacy and distantiation *vs.* isolation and self-absorption. The members meet this time as peers. Each accepts others, and seeks acceptance, as a fellow contributor and experiences the warmth and spontaneity, and the demands, of a shared comradeship: demands for judgment and skill as a contributor, for the development of a style of life consistent with his role as a contributor and the rejection of any forces, conduct, or values that conflict with that role; demands for confession and absolution, for reinforcement in his commitments, for a clarification and affirmation of shared values, and for a sympathetic tempering of unrealistic hopes.[3]

We need to remind ourselves again that these phenomena can be seen in self-developing groups if these collectivities are sufficiently complex and enduring. On the other hand, most individuals encounter these demands when they leave home to establish careers and families of their own. In this latter context, these demands are associated with courtship and a separate residence. Many of the specifics of Erikson's discussion of stage VI concern events in that particular setting.[4]

In any setting, there are inherent dangers. Erikson writes of "self-absorption": the temptation to lose oneself in the contemplation of values or in the pleasures of intimacy and not to move on to the actualization of the values which give purpose to one's new status.

[3] Bellah (1964: 366–8) catches the focus here on ultimate values in his discussion of a "transcendent" order and of a "church": a body of the committed gathered to celebrate whatever values are ultimate.

[4] If this interpretation is right, it gives a different cast to behaviors often found in late adolescence and young adulthood. The idealism and egalitarianism, the openness to community with peers, and the wanderings may be as much an affirmation of values and a demonstration of commitment to embody them in social relations as they are signs of other things: of immaturity, efforts to find a spouse, reluctance to settle into routines, or a continued search for one's self (Eisenstadt, 1956).

Stage VII: generativity vs. *stagnation*

The seventh stage in collective development is the establishment of a regime (Easton, 1957, 1965; Swanson, 1967: 32–43, 51–60, 226–62). With a constitutional order defined and a political community taking form, there remains the development of organizational machinery which makes it possible for that community to act collectively: which makes it capable of governance within the terms of the constitutional order. A regime is a specialized aspect of an organization for making authoritative choices, choices in which transcendent objectives are translated into specific policies and the resources of the group mobilized and committed. Among those resources is the loyalty of the members as contributors. As contributors, members can be mobilized only if they feel that policies are appropriate to objectives and if they understand the policies well enough to exercise discretion on their behalf.

When Erikson writes of generativity, he has in mind a sustained and self-directed pursuit of specific objectives. He has in mind the activities of a contributor who has found his vocation. When he writes of the danger of stagnation, he refers to the possibility that a dedicated person will not find his calling or will confuse methods of work with the values which give methods their importance. There is also the danger of the person's becoming so focused on values that he loses touch with the contingencies and particularities, the problems and opportunities, in daily life, all of which call for the renewal of groups and persons and of values as well.

One of those contingencies is the requirement in some groups that they recruit new members and prepare and incorporate them. This, says Erikson, is a special challenge to generativity in the life course of most individuals: their bearing of children and their making real, for children, the potency of values and of collective life in the solution of human problems.

Stage VIII: integrity vs. *despair and disgust*

A regime is like a charismatic center in that it requires a further refinement of the division of labor for the routinized conduct of its affairs. People with vocations must be organized for this purpose. They must become willing to accept a specific and limited understanding of what their vocations require; to accept constraints upon their discretion in the pursuit of those vocations. Without that understanding, and those constraints, the members' contributions cannot be brought together in a dependable and efficient collective effort.

These objectives are accomplished under a regime through the development of an administrative system. Continuing tasks are defined, limited, and coordinated and members are pressed to undertake one or a few of them as continuing responsibilities. Many of Erikson's points about integrity and about despair and disgust seem to apply to evaluations that people make of themselves in this situation. It is a matter of integrity under these circumstances to accept that one's contributions are meaningful, although highly specialized and, therefore, limited; to accept one's past as worthwhile in the light of this outcome; to be able comfortably to lead or to follow as the occasion requires; to feel comradeship with one's peers and one's successors as participants in a common life which continues.

There are also special dangers in this social situation. When functioning in a special role, and one subsidiary to a much larger enterprise, one can feel removed from the values that give one's own life, and the common life, their meaning. With the weakening of meaning, one can feel despair and disgust. The same feelings can be generated by the recognition that one has failed as well as achieved; that one's contributions are too often compromised by carelessness or by the pursuit of special interests.

Thinking of the life course of individuals, Erikson associates this period with ages 45 onward. This is the period in which people recognize that their occupational situation is unlikely to change, that their marriages and children will probably continue much as they are, and that they, personally, are much the sort of persons they are likely to be. They progressively anticipate the decline of their energies and health, their retirement, and their death. These facts give special qualities to his discussion of this eighth stage of development, but these qualities only supplement what are common features of a contributor's experiences as a specialist within an administrative system.

Piagetian stages

I want to consolidate my discussion of developmental stages by considering briefly the course of intellectual and moral development as described by Piaget.

We can see that Erikson's stages concern changes in the character of an individual's solidarity with others and himself: changes in the modes of interdependence through which people give and get and in the attachments that people have to themselves and others as a result of their roles and competence in these relationships. As I have shown elsewhere (Swanson, 1974), it is helpful to think of Piaget as interested primarily in the number of points of view that an individual takes into account in solving a problem and in the generality of the superordinate point of view from which he integrates other perspectives. Piaget himself associates advances in an individual's ability to solve complex problems with his first being trained to participate in social relations in which a larger number of points of view are differentiated and in which a more general basis is provided for the integration of diverse perspectives. In his own work, Piaget tries to specify different levels of abstractness in these integrating principles and to display the level of complexity in problems which greater abstractness enables a person to solve. (When his ideas are augmented by those of George Herbert Mead (1934), further connections with social experiences become possible.)

It is beyond the scope of this discussion to review Piaget's stages in detail, but I can indicate the essential points of connection between them and the stages of collective development. Piaget's cognitive stages return us to the newborn infant as he learns to act. The first stage in the child's behavior is called "sensory-motor" in being formulated by immediate stimuli and by the learned or unlearned motor patterns which such stimuli control. The second stage, termed "pre-operational," is occasioned by the child's acquisition of language and the role that symbols thereafter play in mediating between stimuli and motoric activity, especially in the child's symbolic manipulation of objects. In the third stage, that of concrete operations, the child can analyze wholes into parts and he understands that a change in one part of a system will modify relations among all of the other parts in an orderly way. In stage four, that of formal operations, the child acquires and uses abstract principles by which to analyze systems of relationships. The last stage, that of consolidated formal operations, is one in which the child learns the systematic relations among these principles.

We can turn now to column D of figure A3.1 where Piaget's stages of intellectual development are presented. Given Piaget's interests, social relations are important for infancy as part of a stable, orderly, nurturant environment in which a baby can learn to act and as the source of his learning to interact by means of gestures. Social relations are also the source of the symbols and symbolic usages which define pre-operational behavior. In the beginning, a child uses symbols to guide his own behavior as others have directed it, getting "outside" himself and controlling his action through role-taking – through anticipating his partners' responses and directing his acts accordingly. Mead and Piaget see this process as arising from experience in the reciprocal character of social interdependence.

Concrete operations, or, as Mead calls them, "reflective intelligence," involve self-direction by means of several perspectives and their interrelations. Mead thinks that this style of thought has its origins in a child's participation in a group having a division of labor: a work group. In the course of such participation, the child learns to pursue some master objectives (the group's goals) and to take into account several subsidiary objectives or perspectives (those associated with his own specialized role and with other, complementary, roles).

Extending Mead's proposals, one can argue that formal operations should be fostered by participation in a constitutional order because it is in that relationship that a sharp separation is made between, on the one hand, values, objectives, and general principles of action, and, on the other, concrete lines of action by means of which objectives can be implemented. That is consistent with the finding (Swanson, 1974) that children reared in families that are organized as constitutional orders are more likely than others to employ formal operations.

Consolidated formal operations involve sets of interrelated principles that are internally differentiated. Principles of that sort are embodied in complex constitutional orders and in political communities and the regimes built upon them. That is the basis for the suggested placement of these operations in figure A3.1[5]

Piaget (1932), Kohlberg (1969), and Kegan (1973, 1982) have proposed stages in the development of moral judgment which seem clearly associated with the stages of collective development as given in figure A3.1[6] Lacking the space to discuss all three, I will focus on Piaget's (figure A3.1, column E), his being the theory on which Kohlberg and Kegan have built. (I do, however, suggest placements for Kohlberg's stages in column F.)

As is well known, Piaget thinks of the young child as displaying a morality of constraint, a morality in which the child takes as given, and as right, the rules laid down by his parents. (More accurately, the child seems to treat those rules as immutable and as right in theory if not in practice.) Wrongdoing is judged according to the letter rather than the spirit of the law and the overt consequences of acts, rather than intentions, are the basis for judging degree of fault. This morality is gradually replaced by a morality of cooperation, a morality in which rules are seen as rational conventions which serve the interests of collective action and in which intentions as well as objective consequences are important in judging moral responsibility.

Piaget thinks a morality of constraint is produced by the young child's

[5] This placement is consistent with Piaget's suggestion that the social circumstances of Hellenic times were responsible for the first explicit definitions of formal operations and of consolidated formal operations. As Becker (1930) has shown, formal logic, mathematics, and other universalistic principles in philosophy arose among the Greeks when they were forced to examine and systematize constitutional principles and to ponder the nature of political community.

[6] For other sets of stages that seem associated with levels of collective development see Kegan (1973, 1982), Loevinger (1966), Hess and Torney (1967), and Harvey, Hunt, and Schroeder (1961).

position of subordination under his elders and that a morality of cooperation arises from social relations with peers outside the home. Both guesses may be correct, but the relations in figure A3.1 suggest additions and qualifications. The young child has rights as well as duties under social interdependence. He is encouraged to become an independent enactor even when subordinate to a charismatic center. In Piaget's own protocols, as well as in those of others, young children seem to be acquainted with notions of personal rights and of fairness and with notions of moral equality *vis-à-vis* parents and siblings. These data, and our conceptualization, indicate that "morality of constraint" catches only one facet of early moral judgment.

A morality of cooperation may be fostered by relations with peers, but it is also taught and encouraged by participation in a division of labor (hence the position of this entry in figure A3.1.) A relationship that fits Piaget's specifications will be one in which collective purposes have emerged and in which rules for their implementation have been devised. Such rules can then be judged by participants in the manner Piaget describes, that is, according to their fruitfulness in facilitating the common enterprise. And, as the discussion of collective development indicates, such cooperative relations, although requiring a kind of equality among participants, do not mean that authority and hierarchy are not also present and potent. By taking a wider view, we can see that Piaget gives us only a limited picture of the development of moral judgment.

Stages in development and in action

The stages and mechanisms in personal and collective development are not arbitrary. That much is already evident. But an argument of Parsons and Olds (Parsons, 1955; 1959a: 688–90; Parsons and Olds, 1955; Olds, 1956: 137–83, 248–50) suggests that these stages are grounded in more general phenomena than we have yet considered: that they are special instances of the stages of any act.

When Parsons and Olds write of acts or action, they have in mind goal-directed behavior and they treat as action all behaviors from "the single elemental habit of S-R psychology" (Olds, 1956: 138) to the largest collective undertakings of whole societies. They say that every act has the four main phases charted in figure A3.2. I find it helpful to think of these phrases as embedded in two dichotomous considerations: first, every act involves an actor's inner states (I shall call them "interests") and an environment; second, it involves an actor's relationship with an environment in the service of interests that are imminent (ready to be acted upon in the immediate situation)

Figure A3.2. Parsons' phases of action (adapted from Parsons, 1959b: 7)

Action relates	Action focused on	
	Imminent interests	All interests
Interests and environment	A *Adaptation* Adaptive function	G *Goal gratification* Goal-attainment function
Interests	L *Latency* Pattern maintenance and tension management function	I *Integration* Integrative function

as against the service of the whole of his interests, this system including those interests that are imminent.

The phases of action are familiar even if Parsons' and Olds' terms for them are not. An instance of problem-solving by a small, informal group can serve as an example (Parsons and Bales, 1953). In this case, "interests" will be held by individuals or by subgroups. If we begin with the lower left-hand cell in figure A3.2 and move clockwise, there exists a set of people who have interests (motives, needs, impulses, and the like), some of these interests having currently the highest priority as the joint goals of these people. The interests are called "latent" in being present and immanent but not involved, as yet, in overt activity. The first phase is the movement from cell L to cell A; from latency to overt instrumental activity aimed at modifying the environment in the pursuit of immanent interests (hence Parsons and Olds label cell A "adaptation"). The second phase moves from the activities designated by cell A to those of cell G; to the distribution of the proceeds – the costs and benefits – arising from adaptation among all interests in the system (these proceeds include the preservation of the system as a whole). In small groups, the process entails the allocating of the costs and benefits of adaptation to individual members and to subgroups, this being done in a way that makes likely their continuing willingness and ability to work together. Referring to the pay-off aspects of this phase, Parsons and Olds refer to the activities in cell G as "goal gratification."

The third phase follows from the second. As a result of the distribution of costs and benefits, members and interests are now in a different relationship than the one with which they began. Before joint action can proceed, they must go about a reintegration (cell I is labeled "integration"): mediating hostilities and taking account of feelings of deprivation that have arisen in the course of adaptation and goal gratification, celebrating their joint successes, acknowledging their interdependence, and either establishing new priorities for joint endeavors or reaffirming old ones. The last phase returns us to the situation in cell L. People are ready once more to act together in the service of immanent interests.

The clockwise cycle around figure A3.2 is that for performance or problem-solving. The counter-clockwise cycle is that for learning, hence for socialization. As Parsons and Olds see it, learning concerns the efforts of an actor, individual or collective, to change itself the better to adapt to an environment. Olds says that difficulties in attempting to adapt to an environment to interests lead an actor to try to determine more exactly the nature of that environment and of his activities and interests in their relevance for one another, "the aim is to engage an object system (*i.e.*, an environment), that is, to find out 'what sort of thing this is' " (Olds, 1956: 187).

The rationale for this interpretation appears in the references already cited. Its meaning for the phases of personal and collective development can be seen by applying it to stages like those of Erikson. Begin with a new socializee, an infant let us assume, and his socializers, all relating to one another as objects in the service of their personal interests. The first phase or stage involves the infant's discovery of the value and dependability of his socializers as objects: Erikson's trust *vs.* mistrust. In the framework of Parsons and Olds, this is a movement from cell A to cell L: a growing acquaintance, however unwitting, with the interests of others. The second stage, a movement from cell L to cell I, is occasioned by direct tuition and by the requirements of greater effectiveness in getting what one wants from others. It involves a more careful coordination of one's behaviors with theirs and, since there is more than one socializer and all of them interrelated, a growing acquaintance with contingencies in network or relations among those socializers. Questions of autonomy *vs.* shame and doubt come to the fore. This movement also involves the child, for the first time, in collective relations as well as in relations with individual socializers. In the third stage, from cell I to cell G, the socializee becomes progressively acquainted with arrangements for a centralized guidance and coordination which make collective relations possible and therefore becomes acquainted with the existence of the common interest and the agencies that represent it. This movement is attended by problems of initiative *vs.* guilt. The fourth stage is one in which the socializee is trained to act toward the environment in a sustained manner in the pursuit of common interests. This move from cell G to cell A involves him in considerations of industry *vs.* inferiority as an agent of the collective interest.

The cycle is repeated once more because, as we have seen, agents of groups find it hard to exercise the necessary degree of initiative and discretion until they gain a clearer picture of the general nature of the common interest. Whereas, in the first stage, they learned something of the value and dependability of their several socializers, they now learn comparable things, in a fifth stage, about the collectivity as a whole and its objectives (the movement is from cell A to cell L). This is the order of events that Erikson seems to have in mind as he described identity *vs.* identity diffusion. The sixth phase is one of the socializee's becoming integrated with other members of the collectivity as equally contributors in a political community, a movement from cell L to cell I in which questions of intimacy *vs.* isolation become salient: questions concerning the members' acceptance of one another as "brothers" and "sisters" or "comrades" in a new primary relationship based on consider-ations apart from kinship. This integration of collective life can result in collective action only if it is organized for that purpose. The movement from cell I to cell G in the seventh phase is an effort to relate to such an organization – a regime – or to create it and it makes salient issues of generativity *vs.* stagnation. The eighth phase, embodied in a movement from cell G to cell A, is one of growing acceptance of specific, sustaining activities as an agent of a regime: a focusing of the exercise of initiative and discretion upon those activities and a finding of rewards (or not finding them) in the steady pursuit of these responsibilities. As Erikson says, these circumstances make salient questions of integrity *vs.* disgust and despair.

Mechanisms of development

We have now surveyed a large part of the course of collective development, linking it to Erikson's sketch of personal development and, briefly, to Piaget's and have grounded development in more general concerns. This is the point to bring together the notes scattered throughout this survey concerning condi-tions that lead an individual to move from one stage to another.

A part of the answer is obvious. Most socializers find it profitable to have a socializee who is more than a dependent, who is able progressively to contribute to a collectivity's life and work. This is true in families and in all groups including the wider society. In all of them, wider powers and greater prestige are offered individuals at most higher stages and mounting costs are imposed upon those who lag behind the anticipated timetable of development.

Another part of the answer is less obvious. At any stage of development, personal or collective, people try to act on the basis of the kind of perspectives and solidarity that they have achieved. This gives their action a particular character, leading them to have experiences that are not available at other stages, experiences which, if they prove sufficiently problematic, must be faced, differentiated, and integrated. To recall an example already given, the collectivity which begins to act under a charismatic center will find that it now, inherently, makes a distinction between the conduct of relations with an environment from which resources and facilities must be drawn and the maintenance of solidary relations among members within the group. This distinction is inherent in such action because the very definition and institutionalization of a charismatic center consists in the identification of collective interests, of the organization committed to pursue them, and of the environment on which the consummation of those interests depends. These three components of action under a charismatic center must therefore be articulated. If there are difficulties in that articulation, and there usually are, the components must get special attention as must the conditions under which they can fruitfully be interrelated. The usual result is a division of labor as described in the rise of a work group.[7]

To recall an example of personal development, consider the child who is participating in a system of social interdependence and who is responding to encouragement to become an independent enactor. As we have seen, he discovers limitations on the kinds of independent enactments that are permissible; discovers that some of them are taken as threatening the solidarity of the group and his position in it. In particular, there are enactments that compete with those of the heroes. As indicated earlier in this appendix, such competition is inherent in the organization of the family under a charismatic center when it is taken in conjunction with the level of solidarity on which the child is basing his action.

In sum, action based upon a particular stage of development necessarily involves people in a new existential situation in relation to themselves and others. If that situation is sufficiently problematic so that action is impeded, its components must be differentiated and reordered in order for action to proceed. In this way, each stage contains the seeds of its own change.[8] When the change actually occurs depends upon further conditions.

[7] In these terms, collective development can be seen as the growth and shaping of a corporate organization through synchronized processes of collective learning and collective problem-solving (Swanson, 1971: 131–4).

[8] There seems to be a broad correspondence between the levels of collective organization and Max Weber's famous typology of authority: levels I through III with charismatic authority, level IV with traditional authority, and level V with rational-legal authority. For a suggestive discussion, see Collins (1975: 155, 292–302).

Collective and cognitive complexity: some implications

Some defenses are more complex than others. I have proposed that the complexity of the defenses which a person employs tends to correspond to the complexity of the social relations which, through defending, he seeks to preserve. In this appendix, I have tried to show that levels of cognitive or, more broadly, personal complexity can be associated with levels of collective complexity. This takes us a step beyond the views of Erikson and Piaget.

Both Erikson and Piaget are convinced that the phases of personal development are occasioned by the requirements set for an individual by his dependence upon other people. Rapaport (1959: 15) characterizes the essence of Erikson's position in this manner:

The crucial characteristic of this psychosocial theory of ego development . . . is that . . . it offers a conceptual explanation of the individual's social development by tracing the unfolding *of the genetically social character of the human individual* in the course of his encounters with the social environment at each phase of his epigenesis. Thus it is not assumed that societal norms are grafted upon the genetically asocial individual by "disciplines" and "socialization," but that the society into which the individual is born makes him its member by influencing the manner in which he solves the tasks posed by each phase of his epigenetic development.

Piaget's views are similar.

I propose, however, that the role of social relations is deeper still: that the principal "developmental tasks" associated with these and other major theories prove upon examination to be social in their contents, number, and ordering and that both the "solutions" to them and the "manner" in which individuals learn to solve them are socially specified (Brim, 1960; Brim and Wheeler, 1966).

This way of looking at the process has some advantages and provides a partial validation for conceiving of personal complexity as I have.

- It does account for the contents, number, and order of the stages commonly found in personal development.
- It does explain why stages found in the life course from infancy through adulthood are similar to the ones observed in adults who are "born" into a new social order.
- It does provide for differences in level of personal development that are found across groups, this by virtue of differences among groups in their level of collective development.
- It does provide for differences in the personal development of members within groups, this by virtue of differences in their capacity, training, and authorization for participation at given levels of collective life.

- It directs the search for explanations of individual differences in personal development to specific aspects of social experience, namely those associated with participation at particular levels of collective organization.
- More speculatively, it may provide a basis for understanding the nature and systematics of systems of age roles and for differences in these systems across societies (Eisenstadt, 1956; Elder, 1975). Perhaps age role distinctions are built upon the levels of social participation we have just examined.

Appendix 4. Interpretations of four more defenses

Turning against the self

1. Clinical descriptions

(Bibring and others, 1961: 71) the turning back upon the self of an impulse directed against an object. This usually refers to an aggressive impulse, but may also refer to turning of libidinal feelings toward the self rather than toward an object. Turning against the self is displacement onto one's self, but it is that singular displacement of using one's self as the object.

(Fenichel, 1945: 360–1) masochism represents a turning of sadism against one's own self... the typical beating fantasy... showed that the wish to be beaten was preceded by the wish that the hated rival might be beaten. (Fenichel, 1945: 392) Since depressions always start with an increase in narcissistic needs, that is, with the feeling "Nobody loves me," it might be expected that the patient will feel that everybody hates him. Actually, delusions of this kind do occur. However, the feeling of being universally hated occurs more frequently in cases representing transition states to delusions of persecution. The classic depressions tend rather to feel that they are not hated as much as they should be, that their depravity is not sufficiently apparent to others. The characteristic position is not so much "Everybody hates me" as "I hate myself.". . .

(Freud, 1915: 127) Reversal of an instinct into its opposite . . . affects only the *aims* of the instincts . . .
   The turning round of an instinct upon the subject's own self is made plausible by the reflection that masochism is actually sadism turned round upon the subject's own ego, and that exhibitionism includes looking at his own body . . . The essence of the process is thus the change of the *object*, while the aim remains unchanged. We cannot fail to notice, however, that in these examples the turning round upon the subject's self and the transformation from activity to passivity converge or coincide.

2. Interpretation

Turning against the self is self-blame, but self-blame for the sake of self-justification. As the clinical descriptions suggest, the circumstances for this defense may vary but they have in common the result that a person attacks himself for some misdeed in order to demonstrate his fundamental solidarity

200

with others. His hope is that, through suffering and remorse, he will set things right with himself and other people.

The use of this defense implies that the person has expressed an unacceptable desire, directly or indirectly. This suggests that turning against the self is likely to appear under the conditions identified in columns B, C, or D in figure 5.1. The defense also implies that other people should find the defendant convincing in his self-blame: that they will be blameworthy if they do not think he should be reinstated as a worthy member of the social order (Freud, 1917: 247–50). This suggests that a placement in column C may be most appropriate and that, in this family, there should be some reasonably clear sense of the extent of mutual rights and obligations such as begins to be found at, and above, level II (social interdependence) in figure 5.1. On the other hand, it is improbable that turning against the self would be a successful defense in relations at level IV (work group) or V (constitutional order) where acceptability depends more on the evidence of steady and positive contributions to a social order than on mere submission to its requirements. These considerations lead to the suggestion that conditions at levels II or III may be most appropriate.

Restriction of the ego (negativism)

1. Clinical descriptions

(Bibring and others, 1961: 70) the unconsciously determined limitation or renunciation of specific ego functions, singly or in combination, to avoid anxiety arising out of conflict with instinctual trends, with the superego, or with environmental forces or figures. Restrictions of ego function may be relatively benign, involving little interference with over-all ego effectiveness. Often, however, it becomes structuralized in the form of substantial inhibition of ego functioning.

(Freud, 1936: 101) A person suffering from neurotic inhibition is defending himself against the translation into action of some prohibited instinctual impulse . . . In ego restriction, on the other hand, disagreeable external impressions in the present are warded off, because they might result in the revival of similar impressions from the past.

2. Interpretation

Restriction of the ego suggests that the person has done something that is clearly unacceptable. That indicates placement in column D of figure 5.1.

The clinical literature describes two forms of restriction of the ego. In both of them, the person abandons a line of action that others encourage him to take and he does so because it leads to pain and failure. The difference between the two forms lies in the person's feelings about the action that other people encourage and in his rationale for doing what he does.

In the first form, negativism, he sees himself as pressured to meet collective standards that seem to him excessive and that prevent his doing things that he personally wants to do. At the same time, he wants to meet collective requirements that are legitimate. He handles this conflict by doing for others only the minimum service that he feels is clearly and legitimately required, resisting pressures to do more and freeing himself for activities that he personally prefers.

Negativism becomes an appropriate defense when there is sufficient clarity about the limits on a person's obligations. As we have just seen, this is the case at and above level II in figure 5.1. Negativism is not likely to be an appropriate defense at levels IV and V because, as with turning against the self, it expresses conformity to social regulations whereas relations at the higher levels in the figure require more positive contributions to the life of a social relationship.

Restriction of the ego (defensive independence)

1. Clinical descriptions (see negativism above)
2. Interpretation
Anna Freud (1936: 93–105) gives particular attention to a form of restriction of the ego that I will call "defensive independence." In this defense, the person refuses to do some things that he and others feel he should and he offers as his justification the fact that he is doing other things which should be as acceptable as the ones he does not do. As in negativism, his refusal to do some things is grounded in pain and failure. When he tried to do them, he failed or got into trouble in other ways. This suggests a placement in column D of figure 5.1. But defensive independence is unlike negativism in drawing upon the person's right and duty to choose the contribution he can best make to support collective interests. That suggests a placement at level V (constitutional order) in the figure. The person claims that which social relations at level V make possible: the right to exercise discretion concerning the course of action that is adequate to carry his share of a relationship; the right to prove that his choice was a good one by virtue of its positive contribution to the relationship. Having met these criteria, he rejects any claim by others that he owes them something else; something that they, not he, select as appropriate.

Undoing

1. Clinical descriptions

(Bibring and Others, 1961: 71) balancing or canceling out [of] an unacceptable action, affect, or thought by a subsequent action, affect, or thought in contradictory terms.

(Fenichel, 1945: 153) in undoing . . . something positive is done which, actually or magically, is the opposite of something which, again actually or in imagination, was done before.

(Symonds, 1946: 479) a special case . . . of isolation. Undoing refers to an act, feeling, or impulse which strives to annul or negate some earlier act not wholly completed. Reaction formations are akin to undoing. All attempts to expiate or atone for an act represent the mechanism of undoing.

2. Interpretation

As Symonds suggests, it is helpful to think of undoing as a variant of isolation. In isolation, the person claims that something he has thought, felt, said, or done should not be taken as representative of his real feelings about a social relationship. In undoing he goes a step further and takes some positive action to right any wrong he has committed, or might be thought to have committed, thus buttressing his claims about his real feelings. Undoing is thus more than a person's "putting things right" when he feels responsible for their having gone wrong. It works as a defense not simply because things are set right for others but because the person himself can feel that he has documented the state of his characteristic feelings and that these are acceptable. For these reasons, I would place this defense in the same cells of figure 5.1 as I have isolation.

There are, however, meanings of undoing that would lead to our placing it much lower in the figure. It can, for example, be treated almost as a feature of regression, the expiatory actions being more a gesture of good intentions than something likely in themselves to be helpful in reestablishing a relationship. It is overtones of this concepion that are caught in Fenichel's term "magical."

Appendix 5. Another categorization of defenses

A comparison with Haan's systematization

I have tried to systematize defenses according to the kind of threat with which they deal, the level of cognitive complexity they seem to present, and the sort of social relations which appear to embody each of these sets of considerations. Haan has employed a different approach. She sees each defense as a "nonoptimal" method of carrying out some general ego process. She believes, that, for each general ego process, there is an "optimal" method of implementation and this she calls a "coping process." Figure A5.1 (adapted from Haan, 1969: 16) presents these relationships. To take an example from that figure, Haan (1969: 14) sees empathy and projection as each being cases of a more general ego process, sensitivity. She defines sensitivity as "behavior that is attuned to formulating and understanding another's unexpressed or partially expressed thoughts and feelings." To take another example, Haan considers objectivity and isolation to be forms of the more general process of discrimination. Discrimination is defined (Haan, 1974: 149) as an ability "to separate idea from feeling, idea from idea, and feeling from feeling by the utilization of cognitive functioning and affective clues."

There is no doubt that Haan's method of arranging coping mechanisms and defenses has had heuristic power in communicating her ideas to others and in the training of clinicians to code interviews. The question at hand, however, is the status of this arrangement as a systematization.

A successful systematization should provide some principled rationale for the set of general ego processes that are divided into coping mechanisms and defenses. Haan seems not, as yet, to have provided such a rationale. In a satisfactory systematization, the coping or defense processes associated with a particular ego process should differ from coping processes or defenses associated with another ego process according to the differences in the two ego processes. It is not obvious that this is the case in Haan's scheme. Thus, for example, by her conceptions, projection as well as isolation would seem to entail a high degree of discrimination, and isolation as well as projection to

Figure A5.1. *Ego processes: coping and defensive*

Ego processes	Coping mechanisms	Defense mechanisms
1. Discrimination	Objectivity	Isolation
2. Detachment	Intellectuality	Intellectualization
3. Means-ends symbolization	Logical analysis	Rationalization
4. Delayed response	Tolerance of ambiguity	Doubt and indecision
5. Selective awareness	Concentration	Denial
6. Sensitivity	Empathy	Projection
7. Temporal reversals, affective and ideational	Regression in service of ego (playfulness)	Regression
8. Impulse diversion (expression)	Sublimation	Displacement
9. Impulse transformation (symbolization)	Substitution	Reaction formation
10. Impulse restraint	Suppression	Repression

involve a considerable sensitivity to relevant feelings or ideas of others. In a well-founded systematization using Haan's criteria, pairs of coping and defense mechanisms should be quite alike in all respects except for those features which distinguish any instance of coping from any instance of defense. This seems not to be so in her classifications. This can be illustrated by comparing objectivity with isolation. The key idea in objectivity is the purposeful use of criteria for reaching a conclusion, criteria that cannot be affected by the person's preferences concerning that conclusion. Isolation, however, is not objectivity gone astray. It is the rather direct expression of some unacceptable desires together with an effort to show that one's "real" desires are different from these and are acceptable and are the ones to be taken seriously.

Were Haan's general conceptualization correct, one might expect to find that individuals who tend more than others to use a given coping mechanism would also tend more than others to use the defense with which it is paired (this on the grounds that both mechanisms make exceptionally heavy use of the general ego process which the two have in common). Or one might expect such people to make less use of the paired defense than do other people (this on the grounds that these people are so involved with the use of this particular general ego process in coping that they have little time to employ it in defense). An examination of the data for parents and for children does show that people who are high on the coping process called intellectuality are also likely to be high on intellectualization as a defense. Apart from this, there are no significant tendencies for people high or low on a particular coping process to be especially high and/or low on any given defense.

All of these considerations suggest that Haan, although she has produced a fruitful array of processes of coping and defense (and of ego fragmentation), does not offer us a theoretical systematization of those processes. Nonetheless, anyone who seriously studies defenses will be greatly in her debt for what she does provide.

Appendix 6. Further analyses of two sets of factors

Four additional profile factors based upon unique scores for defenses

Profile factor III. High on isolation and doubt; low on denial

Isolation and doubt tend to be quite different in cognitive complexity and, as we saw in chapter 4, can involve some, or little, expression of deviant desires. They have in common that the person does not give up such desires but proceeds with caution in expressing them or in moving toward expressing them. The low score on denial reinforces this picture, denial involving fairly direct expressions of deviant desires. We have, then, suggestions of a person who sees strong grounds for thinking them unjustifiable; suggestions of a person hesitating between action and inaction.

Dr Haan immediately noted a similarity between this pattern and a well-known neurotic pattern (see also Pollak, 1979):

Almost a classical obsessive-compulsive picture; constantly compartmentalizing, can't get things together, very much a worrier; knows everything about himself in a way, but can't get it together; chronic tensions and unreferenced irritability. Ruminative.

The AID analyses in table A6.1 show that adolescents having high scores on factor III must deal with parents who are not easy-going or dependable. The mothers tend to be intelligent, active, and assertive but to be worriers and demanding. The fathers are likely to be open, sensitive, and thoughtful but rather inactive and cautious. The families are likely to have a secure socio-economic position with the opportunities and stability that that position implies, but the children tend not to receive much warmth or emotional support. There are, thus, the encouragements for the taking of initiatives and for an exercise of discretion associated with high social status but these same activities can be dangerous if they threaten parents who are insecure and unsupportive.

207

Table A6.1. *AID analysis of profile factor III*

Group to be dichotomized	Dichotimize on	To form groups	N	Mean	t	p<
Fathers' scores on the CPI and MMPI						
Total sample	Sense of well-being	3. High	55	−0.07	2.32	0.05
		2. Low	33	0.14		
3	Frequency	5. High	19	0.06	1.82	0.10
		4. Low	36	−0.14		
4	Hypochondriasis	7. High	16	−0.30	2.65	0.02
		6. Low	20	−0.01		
2	Hypomania	9. High	21	0.23	2.26	0.05
		8. Low	12	−0.03		
Mothers' scores on the CPI and MMPI						
Total sample	Self-acceptance	3. High	89	0.03	2.05	0.05
		2. Low	14	−0.18		
3	Psychasthenia	5. High	11	0.26	2.43	0.02
		4. Low	75	−0.01		
Other independent variables						
Total sample	SES	3. Class I	36	0.13	2.36	0.05
		2. Class II or lower	82	−0.04		
2	Fathers' undercontrol	5. High	39	−0.17	2.70	0.01
		4. Low	22	0.13		
3	Positive discipline	7. High	10	0.11	2.45	0.05
		6. Low	15	0.31		

Profile factor V. High on isolation and doubt; low on projection and regression

The picture here resembles that for factor III but is not filled with quite as formidable constraints against the expression of possibly deviant desires. The low scores on projection and regression suggest avoidance of assertive or aggressive or demanding justifications for the expression of these desires but not the broader hesitations suggested in factor III by the low score on denial. A cool and controlled approach may allow for at least some expressions of possibly deviant desires.

Dr Haan caught the same themes in her comments:

Like III except that here the person looks . . . less sensitive and interpersonally reactive, more remote and less aware . . . Looks to me like a type of adolescent boy: ascetic, excessively cool and rigid, interpersonally remote.

The AID analysis in table A6.2 indicates that the parents of high scorers have a greater personal stability than is the case for parents of adolescents who have high scores on factor III. The mothers tend to be intelligent, assertive, and confident, although restless and conflicted. The fathers tend to be active, agentic, outgoing, sociable people and to be well-balanced in their expression or control of impulses. There are suggestions of two rather different situations that are productive of high scores. Such scores are found among later-born children in families in which the breadwinner works in an entrepreneurial job, especially if the mother's marital bond is not strong. High scores are also found among children from families in which the breadwinner works in a bureaucratic setting and the mothers are not accepting in relations with the children. A possible interpretation is that "entrepreneurial families" stress high degrees of self-control and also the need to take initiatives in order to capitalize upon opportunities. Perhaps the emphasis on taking initiatives applies more to the first-born children in such families whereas emphasis on self-control is stressed for children who are born later. These children may have a further reason for caution in impulse expression if the marital ties between the parents are unstable. It may also be the case that "bureaucratic families" tend to be more permissive of impulse expression than are those of entrepreneurs but that this permissiveness is limited for a child if his mother is not accepting.

In any case, the findings indicate sources of encouragement or permissiveness for the child's pursuit of desires, even of somewhat deviant desires, and sources of danger from that kind of activity. The dangers, at least, seem less acute than those we found to attend high scores on profile factor III.

Profile factor IV. High on isolation, denial, reaction formation, and repression

Although none of the defenses in this profile is among the very simplest, they do range across the remaining levels of complexity. They also cut across the columns of figure 5.1. Three of these defenses – isolation, reaction formation, and repression – have been seen in previous studies (Miller and Swanson, 1960: 207–18, 235; Swanson, 1961) as representing a person's efforts to take responsibility for his own good behavior and carefully to control his expressions of deviant impulses. Three of the four defenses – isolation, denial, and reaction formation – allow for some expression of those impulses. The total profile seems therefore to represent a pattern of defense in which self-control is exercised to maintain and even enhance social relations and in which,

Table A6.2. *AID analysis of profile factor V*

Group to be dichotomized	Dichotomize on	To form groups	N	Mean	t	$p<$
		Fathers' scores on the CPI and MMPI				
Total sample	Hypomania	3. High	71	0.07	2.54	0.02
		2. Low	17	−0.14		
2	Hypomania	5. High	13	−0.14	2.66	0.01
		4. Low	58	0.11		
2	Femininity	7. High	41	0.04	2.76	0.01
		6. Low	17	0.28		
7	Social presence	9. High	12	0.18	2.04	0.05
		8. Low	29	−0.01		
		Mothers' scores on the CPI and MMPI				
Total sample	Self-acceptance	3. High	89	0.08	2.69	0.01
		2. Low	14	−0.18		
3	Flexibility	5. High	27	0.21	2.62	0.02
		4. Low	62	0.02		
4	Tolerance	7. High	19	−0.08	1.97	0.10
		6. Low	43	0.07		
5	Communality	9. High	16	0.09	2.39	0.05
		8. Low	11	0.38		
		Other independent variables				
Total sample	Entrepreneurial–bureaucratic	3. Entrepreneurial	48	0.18	3.38	0.01
		2. Bureaucratic	60	−0.06		
3	Birth rank	5. First-born or only child	20	−0.06	3.08	0.01
		4. Later-born	28	0.35		
2	Mother's acceptance of child	7. High	47	−0.02	2.60	0.02
		6. Low	13	0.37		
7	Parental acceptance of individuated interests	9. High	28	0.05	2.22	0.05
		8. Low	19	−0.12		
4	Strength of mothers' marital bond	11. High	11	−0.04	2.34	0.05
		10. Low	17	0.41		

within that context, some expression of desires, even deviant desires, is allowed. Earlier studies (*ibid.*) show that children tend to defend in this manner if their parents give them considerable freedom to determine their own lines of behavior but set, and enforce, standards that the children's choices should fulfill.

This is the only profile factor on which Dr Haan's interpretations and mine are widely different. Were this pattern to occur in a highly defensive person, it would not be unreasonable to conclude, as she does, that he is:

polymorphously defended in a tight, controlled, rigid way – no evidence of any provision for acting out, much less expressiveness, tenderness, or exposure of self or of relating to people in any differentiated way.

Clearly not able to see self as wrong-doing, goofing, making mistakes.

Globally evasive of self-involvement in unpleasantness; not integrative in thinking and affectivity; the ultra-good kid, proper kid, knowing what is correct.

. . . might do very well academically in lower grades, if school is highly routinized, but should experience difficulty later when more initiative is required and situations are not tightly structured.

Seems such a brittle constellation of self-protectiveness that I wonder whether it would be at all adaptive in later life – freer circumstances should force some kind of reorganization. Situations could arise that the child would not know how to handle or know what had caused a difficulty or how he felt about it.

Doesn't seem to be an "other-directed" person; . . . I mean directed by other adolescents – probably [is] by adults though.

The AID analyses (see table A6.3) associate high scores on this factor with the presence of parents who are highly capable and self-reliant. The mothers are also rather compulsive and tend to be excitable, impulsive, assertive, and aggressive. On the other hand, they tend not to be defensive. The fathers seem practical, balanced, cheerful, responsible, perceptive, and socially ascendant. These parents tend to give a child considerable freedom to exercise discretion but do not hesitate to intervene, and forcefully, if his conduct goes seriously astray. We have, then, many sources of encouragement for self-directed initiatives in behavior and for the exercise of discretion within wide boundaries. There are, at the same time, limits to the behaviors that are acceptable and these are enforced.

Profile factor VII. High on intellectualization; low on rationalization, denial, and projection

Intellectualization is always a complex defense and permits some expression of impulses. As found in adolescents, rationalization and projection can be associated with a style of child-rearing in which parents have low tolerance for

Table A6.3. *AID analysis of profile factor IV*

Group to be dichotomized	Dichotomize on	To form groups	N	Mean	t	p<
	Fathers' scores on the CPI and MMPI					
Total sample	Masculinity–femininity (MMPI)	3. High	15	−0.12	2.80	0.01
		2. Low	73	0.08		
2	Hypomania	5. High	10	−0.12	2.07	0.05
		4. Low	63	0.12		
4	Psychological mindedness	7. High	12	0.34	2.64	0.02
		6. Low	51	0.06		
6	Hypomania	9. High	26	−0.03	2.05	0.05
		8. Low	25	0.05		
	Mothers' scores on the CPI and MMPI					
Total sample	Correction	3. High	82	0.06	2.24	0.05
		2. Low	18	−0.15		
3	Self-control	5. High	67	0.01	2.96	0.01
		4. Low	15	0.29		
5	Tolerance	7. High	38	−0.05	1.81	0.10
		6. Low	29	0.10		
7	Depression	9. High	16	−0.20	2.34	0.05
		8. Low	22	0.06		
	Other independent variables					
Total sample	Parental acceptance of individuated interests	3. High	65	0.11	3.53	0.001
		2. Low	49	−0.11		
3	Mothers' total score on 3 defense factors	5. High	15	−0.12	2.98	0.01
		4. Low	50	0.17		
4	Discipline by power assertion	7. High	28	0.35	2.33	0.05
		6. Low	21	0.05		
2	Strength of mothers' marital bond	9. High	14	−0.20	3.49	0.01
		8. Low	35	0.05		
8	Mothers' total score on 3 defense factors	11. High	13	−0.03	2.86	0.01
		10. Low	22	−0.30		

deviant behaviors and use power assertion as a method of discipline. In these defenses, the person has expressed a deviant desire and he acts to justify it. In projection his action is assertive and in rationalization it can be.

This profile factor contrasts intellectualization with the other three defenses. This suggests that intellectualization represents a more cautious and socially acceptable style of acting on desires and a situation in which there is tolerance for that kind of behavior.

Dr Haan felt quite rightly that the pattern provides more grounds for an interpretation of its inverse than of its positive form. Considering, then, the meaning of high scores on rationalization, denial, and projection accompanied by low scores on intellectualization, she wrote:

A not very bright child. Interpersonally anxious. Very tenuous balance of defenses that shouldn't hold for long. Rationalization and denial, a drawing back from difficulties, is accompanied by projection which is an involvement with difficulty. Together, these defenses suggest an instability and perhaps a sequencing of defenses. In any case, the child can formulate his difficulties only at the intuitive or gut level.

Table A6.4 shows the AID analyses. Children with high scores tend to be older and to have parents who are tolerant of some degree of deviant behavior and who set a positive tone in discipline. These parents tend also to be capable, dependable, and confident. The child is thus encouraged or permitted to take initiatives and risk expression of possibly deviant desires and to do so within broad limits, especially if he has reached at least late adolescence.

The correlates of the inverse of this pattern (not shown) are consistent with Dr Haan's judgment and my own. The parents tend not to tolerate deviant behavior and not to use positive methods of discipline. The mothers are likely to be dependable, deliberate, moderate, conventional, quiet, passive, self-abasing; the fathers to be ambitious and capable but also cautious, fussy, sensitive, prone to worry, vacillating and uncertain in decisions, literal and unoriginal in thought and judgment.

Correlates of factors based upon raw scores

Factor II

There are associations, all negative, between the use of these simple defenses and certain of the parents' methods and orientations in rearing children: between such use and the closeness of interpersonal relations in the family ($r(114) = -0.20$, $p < 0.05$), the parents' approval of their children's having individuated interests ($r(114) = -0.19$, $p < 0.05$), and the parents' use of

Table A6.4. *AID analysis of profile factor VII*

Group to be dichotomized	Dichotomize on	To form groups	N	Mean	t	p<
		Fathers' scores on the CPI and MMPI				
Total sample	Masculinity–femininity (MMPI)	3. High	54	0.001	2.99	0.01
		2. Low	34	0.06		
3	Social presence	5. High	36	0.10	3.45	0.01
		4. Low	18	−0.19		
2	Schizophrenia	7. High	11	0.37	3.48	0.01
		6. Low	23	0.06		
5	Psychopathic deviate	9. High	14	−0.02	2.14	0.05
		8. Low	22	0.17		
8	Femininity	11. High	10	0.28	2.18	0.05
		10. Low	12	0.08		
		Mothers' scores on the CPI and MMPI				
Total sample	Self-acceptance	3. High	89	0.07	3.24	0.01
		2. Low	14	−0.22		
3	Psychasthenia	5. High	19	0.24	2.45	0.02
		4. Low	70	0.03		
4	Communality	7. High	51	0.09	2.98	0.01
		6. Low	19	−0.13		
7	Dominance	9. High	35	0.04	2.21	0.05
		8. Low	16	0.21		
		Other independent variables				
Total sample	Parental permission of direct expression of desires	3. High	39	0.08	2.53	0.02
		2. Low	55	−0.05		
2	Positive discipline	5. High	26	0.03	2.07	0.05
		4. Low	10	−0.22		
3	Age of child	7. 16 or older	22	0.19	2.81	0.01
		6. 15 or younger	17	−0.06		
5	Fathers' personal stability	9. High	15	−0.07	2.33	0.05
		8. Low	11	0.18		

positive appeals (parental disciplinary factor III) as a method of discipline ($r(74) = -0.25$, $p < 0.05$).

There likewise are negative relations between children's scores on factor II and certain indices of cognitive skill and complexity in the family: with the children's intelligence scores (-0.33, $p < 0.001$), the fathers' and mothers' scores on Haan's index of interpersonal moral reasoning (the respective correlations being -0.36 ($p < 0.05$) and -0.38 ($p < 0.05$)), the children's scores on Kohlberg's test of formal moral reasoning (-0.34, $p < 0.10$), and their scores on Haan's index of interpersonal moral reasoning (-0.32, $p < 0.10$).

We find several relations between the children's scores on factor II and indices of parental stress. Thus there are significant and positive correlations with four scales on the fathers' K-corrected MMPI protocols: hypochondriasis (0.23, $p < 0.05$), depression (0.22, $p < 0.05$), masculinity (0.20, $p < 0.05$), and psychasthenia (0.27, $p < 0.005$). In clinically normal populations like the one studied here, high scores on these scales have in common the respondents' tendency to worry and to be sensitive and emotional (Dahlstrom, Welsh, and Dahlstrom, 1972: 177–288).

By contrast, the children's scores on factor II correlate significantly and negatively with their fathers' scores on three of the scales of the CPI, a test designed to measure personal strengths in normal adults. The scales are those for sense of well-being (-0.24, $p < 0.05$), makes good impression (-0.22, $p < 0.05$), and communality (an indication of the degree to which an individual's responses are those modal for the CPI: low scores indicate a person who is impatient, changeable, complicated, imaginative, disorderly, nervous, restless, confused, and who has internal conflicts and problems: $r = -0.21$, $p < 0.05$.) Scores on factor II are also related to the number of the fathers' high scores on the three defense factors for fathers that I described in chapter 4 ($F(2,104) = 3.67$, $R = 0.27$, $p < 0.05$). Children's scores on this factor correlate positively with the fathers' scores on the second of the father's defense factors as described in chapter 4 (complex defenses against objective anxiety): $r = 0.30$, $p < 0.01$.

Scores on factor II are related to just one of the mothers' personality characteristics: responsibility ($r = -0.21$, $p < 0.05$).

Factor I

There are a number of significant relations between scores on factor I and the methods and orientations that parents use in rearing children. Scores on this factor are related negatively to a child's coming from an entrepreneurial home

($r(108) = -0.25$, $p < 0.01$), and, especially, one that is entrepreneurial and middle class (Hollingshead–Redlich classes I–III): $r(108) = -0.25$, $p < 0.01$). These scores also have a negative relation to parental approval of individuated interests ($r(114) = -0.23$, $p < 0.02$) or their permission of direct expressions of deviant desires in children ($F(2,91) = 5.51$, $R = -0.35$, $p < 0.005$).

Children with high scores on this factor tend slightly to have lower scores on intelligence (-0.16, $p < 0.10$). Their fathers tend to have low scores on Haan's index of interpersonal moral reasoning (-0.36, $p < 0.03$).

There are, however, suggestions that the fathers tend to have personal strengths. Thus, on the CPI, there are positive correlations with self-control (0.25, $p < 0.02$), tolerance (permissive, accepting, non-judgmental: 0.19, $p < 0.10$, achievement by means of independence (mature, strong, forceful, demanding, independent, self-reliant: 0.19, $p < 0.10$), and a negative correlation with Block's index of undercontrol (-0.19, $p < 0.10$). The single finding in the opposite direction is a negative relation with the fathers' CPI scores on self-acceptance (-0.20, $p < 0.10$). (There are no significant relations between the children's scores on factor I and indicators of their mothers' personalities.)

Factor III

Scores on this factor are related to only a few predictors. The children themselves tend to have low scores on Haan's index of interpersonal moral reasoning ($r(30) = -0.32$, $p < 0.10$) but also to have *low* scores on one of Block's indices of personal stress: undercontrol (-0.24, $p < 0.05$). On the other hand, the fathers tend to be undercontrolled according to Block's index (0.21, $p < 0.05$), to have high scores on many defense factors ($F(2,101) = 3.51$, $R = 0.26$, $p < 0.03$) and high scores on the second of their own defense factors (complex defenses against objective anxiety: $r = 0.22$, $p < 0.05$). Among the children whose fathers do *not* have high scores on *any* defense factors, children of fathers having entrepreneurial occupations are more likely than others to have high scores on factor III ($r(41) = 0.30$, $p < 0.05$).

Bibliography

Abend, Sander M., M. S. Porter and Martin S. Willick 1983 *Borderline Patients: Psychoanalytic Perspectives*. New York: International Universities Press

Abramson, Lyn Y., Martin E. P. Seligman, and John D. Teasdale 1978 Learned helplessness in humans: critique and reformulation. *Journal of Abnormal Psychology* **87** (February): 49–74

Aerts, Elaine 1979 Organizational and interpersonal patterns in whole families. Doctoral dissertation. Department of Sociology, University of California, Berkeley

Allport, Floyd H. 1924 *Social Psychology*. Boston: Houghton Mifflin

Arlow, Jacob A. and Charles Brenner 1964 *Psychoanalytic Concepts and the Structural Theory*. New York: International Universities Press

Aronfreed, Justin 1964 The origin of self-criticism. *Psychological Review* **71** (May): 193–218

  1968 *Conduct and Conscience, The Socialization of Internalized Control over Behavior*. New York: Academic

Aronson, Elliott 1972 *The Social Animal*. San Francisco: Freeman

Atkinson, John W. 1969 Change of activity, a new focus for the theory of motivation. Pp. 105–33 in Theodore Mischel (ed.), *Human Action, Conceptual and Empirical Issues*. New York: Academic

Baldwin, James Mark 1895 *Mental Development in the Child and the Race*. New York: Macmillan

Bales, Robert F. and Phillip E. Slater 1955 Role differentiation in small decision-making groups. Pp. 259–306 in Talcott Parsons and Robert F. Bales (eds.), *Family, Socialization and Interaction Process*. Glencoe: Free Press

Bandura, Albert and Richard H. Walters 1963 *Social Learning and Personality Development*. New York: Holt, Rinehart and Winston

Becker, Howard P. 1930 Ionia and Athens, studies in secularization. Unpublished doctoral dissertation. Department of Sociology, University of Chicago

Bellah, Robert N. 1964 Religious evolution. *American Sociological Review* **29** (June): 358–74

Bem, Daryl J. and Andrea Allen 1974 On predicting some of the people some of the time: the search for cross-situational consistencies in behavior. *Psychological Review* **81** (November): 506–20

Bennett, David H. and David S. Holmes 1975 Influence of denial (situation redefinition) and projection on anxiety associated with threat to self-esteem. *Journal of Personality and Social Psychology* **32** (November): 915–21

217

Berkowitz, Leonard 1973 Control of aggression. Pp. 95–140 in Bettye M. Caldwell and Henry N. Ricciuti (eds.), *Review of Child Development Research*, vol. 3. Chicago: University of Chicago Press

Berndt, Thomas J. and Emily G. 1975 Children's use of motives and intentionality in person perception and moral judgment. *Child Development* **46** (December): 904–12

Bertini, M. 1960 *Il tratto diffensivo dell' isolamento nella sua determinazione dinamica e strutturale*. Contributi dell' Instituto di Psicologica. Serie XXV. Milan: Catholic University

Bettleheim, Bruno and Morris Janowitz 1950 *The Dynamics of Prejudice*. New York: Harper

Bibring, Grete L., Thomas F. Dwyer, Dorothy S. Huntington and Arthur F. Valenstein 1961 A study of the psychological processes in pregnancy and of the earliest mother–child relationship. *The Psychoanalytic Study of the Child* **16**: 9–72

Blaney, Paul H. 1977 Contemporary theories of depression: critique and comparison. *Journal of Abnormal Psychology* **86** (June): 203–23

Block, Jack 1961 *The Q-sort Method in Personality Assessment and Psychiatric Research*. Springfield: Thomas
    1965 *The Challenge of Response Sets: Unconfounding Meaning, Acquiescence, and Social Desirability in the MMPI*. New York: Appleton-Century-Crofts

Block, Jack and Norma Haan 1971 *Lives through Time*. Berkeley: Bancroft Books

Blum, Alan F. and Peter McHugh 1971 The social ascription of motives. *American Sociological Review* **36** (February): 98–109

Blum, Gerald S. 1949 A study of the psychoanalytic theory of psychosexual development. *Genetic Psychology Monographs* **39**: 3–99
    1953 *Psychoanalytic Theories of Personality*. New York: McGraw-Hill
    1956 Defense preferences in four countries. *Journal of Projective Techniques* **20** (March): 33–41

Blum, Harold P. (ed.) 1983 *Defense and Resistance: Historical Perspectives and Current Concepts*. New York: International Universities Press

Bogo, Norman, Caroline Winget and Goldine C. Gleser 1970 Ego defenses and perceptual styles. *Perceptual and Motor Skills* **30** (April): 599–605

Brehm, Jack W. 1972 *Responses to Loss of Freedom: A Theory of Psychological Reactance*. Morristown: General Learning Press

Brenner, Charles 1981 Defense and defense mechanisms. *Psychoanalytic Quarterly* **50** (October): 557–69
    1982 *The Mind in Conflict*. New York: International Universities Press

Brim, Orville G., Jr. 1960 Personality development as role learning. Pp. 127–59 in Ira Iscoe and Harold Stevenson (eds.), *Personality Development in Children*. Austin: University of Texas Press

Brim, Orville G., Jr. and Stanton Wheeler 1966 *Socialization after Childhood: Two Essays*. New York: Wiley

Burt, Ronald L. 1982 *Toward a Structural Theory of Action: Network Models of Social Structure, Perception and Action*. New York: Academic Press

Campbell, Donald T., Norma Miller, Jacob Lubetsky and Edward J. O'Connell 1964 Varieties of projection in trait attribution. *Psychological Monographs* **78**, no. 15

Cantor, Nancy, Edward E. Smith, Rita D. French and Juan Mezzich 1980 Psychiatric diagnosis as prototype categorization. *Journal of Abnormal Psychology* **89** (April): 181–93

Chandler, Michael J., Katherine F. Paget and Diane A. Koch 1978 The child's demystification of psychological defense mechanisms: a structural and developmental analysis. *Developmental Psychology* **14** (May): 197–205

Collins, Randall 1975 *Conflict Sociology, Toward an Explanatory Science*. New York: Academic

Comte, Auguste 1830 *Cours de Philosophie Positive*, vol. 1. Paris: Baillière, 1877

Cronbach, Lee J. 1970 *Essentials of Psychological Testing*. New York: Harper and Row

Curle, Adam 1947 Transitional communities and social reconnection, a follow-up study of the civil resettlement of British prisoners of war, part I. *Human Relations* **1**: 34–86

Dahlstrom, W. Grant, George S. Welsh and Leona E. Dahlstrom 1972 *An MMPI Handbook*, vol. 1. Minneapolis: University of Minnesota Press

Dewey, John 1922 *Human Nature and Conduct, An Introduction to Social Psychology*. New York: The Modern Library, 1950

Dewey, John and James A. Tufts 1908 *Ethics*. New York: Holt.

Dohrenwend, Bruce P. and Barbara S. 1974 Psychiatric disorders in urban settings. Pp. 424–47 in Silvano Arieti (ed.), *American Handbook of Psychiatry*, vol. 2. New York: Basic Books

Dollard, John and Neil E. Miller 1950 *Personality and Psychotherapy: An Analysis in Terms of Learning, Thinking, and Culture*. New York: McGraw-Hill

Donovan, Dennis M., William H. Hague and Michael R. O'Leary 1975 Perceptual differentiation and defense mechanisms in alcoholics. *Journal of Clinical Psychology* **31** (April): 356–9

Dunphy, Dexter C. 1966 Social change in self-analytic groups. Pp. 287–340 in Philip J. Stone and others, *The General Inquirer: A Computer Approach to Content Analysis*. Cambridge: Massachusetts Institute of Technology Press

Earls, Felton 1976 The fathers (not the mothers): their importance and influence with infants and young children. *Psychiatry* **39** (August): 209–26

Easton, David 1957 An approach to the analysis of political systems. *World Politics* **9** (April): 383–400

1965 *A Systems Analysis of Political Life*. New York: Wiley

Eisenstadt, Schmuel N. 1956 *From Generation to Generation: Age Groups and Social Structure*. Glencoe: Free Press

Elder, Glen H., Jr. 1975 Age differentiation and the life course. *Annual Review of Sociology* **1**: 165–90

Elkind, David 1976 Cognitive development and psychopathology: observations on ego-centrism and ego defense. Pp. 167–83 in Eric Schopler and Robert J. Reichler (eds.), *Psychopathology and Child Development: Research and Treatment*. New York: Plenum

Engel, George L. 1962 *Psychological Development in Health and Disease*. Philadelphia: Saunders

English, Horace B. and Ava C. 1958 *A Comprehensive Dictionary of Psychological and Psychoanalytical Terms, A Guide to Usage*. New York: Longmans, Green

Eriksen, Charles W. and Jan Pierce 1968 Defense mechanisms. Pp. 1007–40 in Edgar F. Borgatta and William W. Lambert (eds.), *Handbook of Personality Theory and Research*. Chicago: Rand McNally

Erikson, Erik H. 1950 *Childhood and Society*. New York: Norton
1959 Identity and the life cycle. *Psychological Issues* **1**, no. 1
1968 *Identity: Youth and Crisis*. New York: Norton

Etzioni, Amitai 1975 *A Comparative Analysis of Complex Organizations*. New York: Free Press

Faris, Robert E. L. and H. Warren Dunham 1939 *Mental Disorders and Urban Areas*. Chicago: University of Chicago Press

Farrell, Michael P. 1976 Patterns in the development of self-analytic groups. *Journal of Applied Behavioral Science* **12** (October–December); 523–42

Fenichel, Otto 1945 *The Psychoanalytic Theory of Neurosis*. New York: W.W. Norton

Fingarette, Herbert 1963 *The Self in Transformation: Psychoanalysis, Philosophy and the Life of the Spirit*. New York: Harper, 1965

Fitz, Don 1976 A renewed look at Miller's conflict theory of aggression displacement. *Journal of Personality and Social Psychology* **33** (June): 725–32

Fouriezos, Nicolas, Max L. Hutt and Harold Guetzkow 1950 Measurement of self-oriented needs in discussion groups. *Journal of Abnormal and Social Psychology* **45** (October): 682–90

Freedman, Ronald 1950 *Recent Migration to Chicago*. Chicago: University of Chicago Press

Freud, Anna 1936 *The Ego and the Mechanisms of Defense*. Cecil Bains, translator. New York: International Universities Press, 1966

Freud, Sigmund 1909 Notes upon a case of obsessional neurosis. Pp. 155–249 in vol. 10 of *The Standard Edition of the Complete Psychological Works of Sigmund Freud*. James Strachey, editor and translator. London: Hogarth Press and Institute of Psycho-Analysis 1955
1915 Instincts and their vicissitudes. Pp. 117–40 in vol. 14 of *The Standard Edition of the Complete Psychological Works of Sigmund Freud*. James Strachey, editor and translator. London: Hogarth Press and Institute of Psycho-Analysis, 1957
1917 Mourning and melancholia. Pp. 243–58 in vol. 14 of *The Standard Edition of the Complete Psychological Works of Sigmund Freud*. James Strachey, editor and translator. London: Hogarth Press and Institute of Psycho-Analysis, 1957
1919 Psychoanalysis and war neuroses. Pp. 83–7 in vol. 5 of his *Collected Papers*. James Strachey, translator. New York: Basic Books, 1959
1924 Introductory lectures on psycho-analysis. Part III. Vol. 16 of *The Standard Edition of the Complete Psychological Works of Sigmund Freud*. James Strachey, editor and translator. London: Hogarth Press and Institute of Psycho-Analysis, 1963
1926 Inhibitions, symptoms, and anxiety. Pp. 87–174 in vol. 20 of *The Standard Edition of the Complete Psychological Works of Sigmund Freud*. James Strachey, editor and translator. London: Hogarth press and Institute of Psycho-Analysis, 1959
1930 Civilization and its discontents. Pp. 64–145 in vol. 21 of *The Standard Edition of the Complete Psychological Works of Sigmund Freud*. James Strachey, editor and

translator. London: Hogarth Press and Institute of Psycho-Analysis, 1961

1933 New introductory lectures on psycho-analysis. Pp. 5–182 in vol. 22 of *The Standard Edition of the Complete Psychological Works of Sigmund Freud*. James Strachey, editor and translator. London: Hogarth press and Institute of Psycho-Analysis, 1964

Friedman, S. C. 1967 Effects of intoxication upon cognitive control and defense functioning. Unpublished doctoral dissertation, Department of Psychology, Yeshiva University

Fromm, Erich 1947 *Man for Himself, An Inquiry into the Psychology of Ethics*. New York: Holt, Rinehart and Winston

Frosch, John 1983 *The Psychotic Process*. New York: International Universities Press

Garber, Judy and Martin E. P. Seligman (eds.) 1980 *Human Helplessness, Theory and Applications*. New York: Academic Press

Gardner, Riley, Philip S. Holzman, George Klein, Harriet Linton and Donald Spence 1959 Cognitive control, a study of individual consistencies in cognitive behavior. *Psychological Issues* **1**, no. 4

Garfinkel, Harold 1967 *Studies in Ethnomethodology*. Englewood Cliffs: Prentice-Hall

Gedo, John E. and Arnold Goldberg 1973 *Models of the Mind, A Psychoanalytic Theory*. Chicago: University of Chicago Press

Gerth, Hans and C. Wright Mills 1953 *Character and Social Structure, The Psychology of Social Institutions*. New York: Harcourt, Brace and World

Gibbard, Graham, S., John J. Hartman and Richard D. Mann (eds.)
1974 *Analysis of Groups*. San Francisco: Jossey-Bass

Gill, Merton 1963 Topography and systems in psychoanalytic theory. *Psychological Issues* **3**, no. 2

Gleser, Goldine C. and David Ihilevich 1969 An objective instrument for measuring defense mechanisms. *Journal of Consulting and Clinical Psychology* **33** (February): 51–60

Goffman, Erving 1962 *Asylums: Essays on the Social Situation of Mental Patients and Other Inmates*. Chicago: Aldine

1971 *Relations in Public: Microstudies of the Public Order*. New York: Basic Books

Goodenough, Donald R. 1976 The role of individual differences in field dependence as a factor in learning and memory. *Psychological Bulletin* **83** (July): 675–94

Gouin Decarie, Therese 1965 *Intelligence and Affectivity in Early Childhood, An Experimental Study of Jean Piaget's Object Concept and Object Relations*. Elizabeth P. and Lewis Brandt, translators. New York: International Universities Press

Greenacre, Phyllis 1952 *Trauma, Growth and Personality*. New York: Norton

Gur, Ruben C. and Harold A. Sackeim 1979 Self-deception: a concept in search of phenomenon. *Journal of Personality and Social Psychology* **37** (February): 147–69

Haan, Norma 1963 Proposed model of ego functioning: coping and defense mechanisms in relationship to IQ change. *Psychological Monographs* **77**, no. 8

1964 An investigation of the relationship of Rorschach scores, patterns, and behavior to coping and defense mechanisms. *Journal of Projective Techniques and Personality Assessment* **69** (December): 594–605

1969 A tripartite model of ego functioning values and clinical research applications.

Journal of Nervous and Mental Disease **148** (February): 14–30

1974 The implications of family ego patterns for adolescent members. Unpublished doctoral dissertation. San Francisco: California School of Professional Psychology

1977 *Coping and Defending, Processes of Self–Environment Organization.* New York: Academic

1978 Two moralities in action contexts: relationships to thought, ego regulation, and development. *Journal of Personality and Social Psychology* **36** (March): 286–305

Hall, Granville Stanley 1904 *Adolescence, Its Psychology and Its Relations to Physiology, Anthropology, Sociology, Sex, Crime, Religion, and Education.* 2 vols. New York: Appleton

Hartmann, Heinz 1939 *Ego Psychology and the Problem of Adaptation.* David Rapaport, translator. New York: International Universities Press, 1958

Harvey, O. J., David E. Hunt and Harold M. Schroeder 1961 *Conceptual Systems and Personality Organization.* New York: Wiley

Hedegard, Sheila A. 1968 A molecular analysis of psychological defense mechanisms. Unpublished doctoral dissertation. Department of Psychology, University of Michigan

Heilbrun, Alfred B. 1973 *Aversive Maternal Control: A Theory of Schizophrenic Development.* New York: Wiley

Hess, Robert D. and Judith V. Torney 1967 *The Development of Political Attitudes in Children.* Chicago: Aldine

Hoffman, Martin L. 1970 Moral development. Pp. 2613–59 in Paul H. Mussen (ed.), *Carmichael's Manual of Child Psychology.* New York: Wiley

Holland, Norman N. 1973 Defense, displacement and the ego's algebra. *International Journal of Psychoanalysis* **54**, part 2: 247–56

Hollingshead, August B. and Frederick C. Redlich 1958 *Social Class and Mental Illness, A Community Study.* New York: Wiley

Holmes, David S. 1978 Projection as a defense mechanism. *Psychological Bulletin* **85** (July): 677–88

Honzik, Marjorie P., Jean W. Macfarlane and Lucille Allen 1948 The stability of mental test performance between two and eighteen years. *Journal of Experimental Education* **17** (December): 309–24

Horowitz, Mardi S. 1972 Modes of representation of thought. *Journal of the American Psychoanalytic Association* **20** (October): 793–819

Inhelder, Bärbel and Jean Piaget 1958 *The Growth of Logical Thinking from Childhood to Adolescence.* Anne Parsons and Stanley Milgram, translators. New York: Basic books

Kaplan, Seymour R. and Melvin Roman 1963 Phases of development in an adult therapy group. *International Journal of Group Psychotherapy* **14** (January): 10–26

Keasey, Charles B. 1977 Young children's attribution of intentionality to themselves and others. *Child Development* **48** (March): 261–4

Kegan, Robert G. 1973 Constructions of community: new theory and research in human development. Paper presented at the meetings of the Society for the Scientific Study of Religion

1982 *The Evolving Self, Problem and Process in Human Development.* Cambridge: Harvard University Press

Kohlberg, Lawrence 1969 Stage and sequence: the cognitive-developmental approach to socialization. Pp. 347–480 in David A. Goslin (ed.), *Handbook of Socialization Theory and Research.* Chicago: Rand-McNally

Kohlberg, Lawrence and Cheryl Armon 1984 Three types of stage models used in the study of adult development. Pp. 383–94 in Michael L. Commons, Francis A. Richards and Cheryl Armon (eds.), *Beyond Formal Operations: Late Adolescent and Adult Cognitive Development.* New York: Praeger

Kohn, Melvin 1971 Bureaucratic man. *American Sociological Review* **36** (June): 461–74

Kris, Ernst 1952 *Psychoanalytic Explorations in Art.* New York: International Universities Press

Kroeber, Theodore C. 1964 The coping functions of the ego mechanisms. Pp. 178–98 in Robert W. White (ed.), *The Study of Lives,* New York: Atherton

Krohn, Alan 1978 *Hysteria: The Elusive Neurosis.* New York: International Universities Press

Lamb, Michael E. (ed.) 1976 *The Role of the Father in Child Development.* New York: Wiley

Lampl-de Groot, Jeanne 1957 On defense and development: normal and pathological *The Psychoanalytic Study of the Child* **12**: 114–26

Laplanche, Jean and J.-B. Pontalis 1973 *The Language of Psychoanalysis.* Donald Nicholson-Smith, translator. New York: Norton

Lasswell, Harold D. 1930 *Psychopathology and Politics,* Chicago: University of Chicago Press

1935 *World Politics and Personal Insecurity.* New York: McGraw-Hill

1948 *Power and Personality,* New York: Norton

Lazarus, Richard S. 1966 *Psychological stress and the Coping Process.* New York: McGraw-Hill

1968 Stress. Pp. 337–48 in David L. Sills (ed.), *International Encyclopedia of the Social Sciences,* vol. 15. New York: Macmillan and Free Press

Levinson, Daniel J., Charlotte N. Darrow, Edward B. Klein, Maria H. Levinson and Braxton McKee

1978 *The Seasons of a Man's Life.* New York: Knopf

Lewin, Bertram D. 1950 *The Psychoanalysis of Elation.* New York: Norton

Lichtenberg, Joseph D. and Joseph W. Slap 1972 On the defense mechanism: a survey and synthesis. *Journal of the American Psychoanalytic Association* **20** (October): 776–92

Lienhardt, Godfrey 1961 *Divinity and Experience: The Religion of the Dinka.* Oxford: Clarendon

Loevinger, Jane 1966 The meaning and measurement of ego development. *American Psychologist* **21** (March): 195–206

Loewald, Hans W. 1952 The problem of defense and the neurotic interpretation of reality. *International Journal of Psychoanalysis* **33**, part 4: 444–9

Luborsky, Lester, Barton Blinder and Jean Schimek 1965 Looking, recalling, and GSR as a function of defense. *Journal of Abnormal Psychology* **70** (August): 270–80

Lukes, Steven 1973 *Individualism*. Oxford: Blackwell

Lynn, David B. 1974 *The Father: His Role in Child Development*. Monterey: Brooks-Cole

Maccoby, Eleanor E. and John A. Martin 1983 Socialization in the context of the family: parent-child interaction. Pp. 1–101 in Paul H. Mussen (ed.), *Handbook of Child Psychology*, vol. 4. New York: Wiley

Macfarlane, Jean W. 1971 Objectives, samples, and procedures. Pp. 10–22 in Mary C. Jones, Nancy Bayley, Jean W. Macfarlane and Marjorie P. Honzik (eds.), *The Course of Human Development*. Waltham: Xerox College Publishing

Mahl, George F. 1971 *Psychological Conflict and Defense*. New York: Harcourt Brace

Mann, Richard D., Graham S. Gibbard and John J. Hunt 1967 *Interpersonal Styles and Group Development*. New York: Wiley

McNemar, Quinn 1969 *Psychological Statistics*. New York: Wiley

Mead, George H. 1934 *Mind, Self and Society from the Standpoint of a Social Behaviorist*. Chicago: University of Chicago Press

Megargee, Edwin I. 1972 *The California Psychological Inventory Handbook*. San Francisco: Jossey-Bass

Menninger, Karl 1963 *The Vital Balance, The Life Process in Mental Health and Illness*. New York: Viking

Miller, Daniel R. 1963 The study of social relationships: situation, identity, and social interaction. Pp. 639–737 in Sigmund Koch (ed.), *Psychology: A Study of a Science*, vol. 4. New York: McGraw-Hill

Miller, Daniel R. and Guy E. Swanson 1958 *The Changing American Parent, A Study in the Detroit Area*. New York: Wiley
 1960 *Inner Conflict and Defense*. New York: Holt

Miller, Neil E. 1944 Experimental studies of conflict. Pp. 431–65 in J. McVicker Hunt (ed.), *Personality and the Behavior Disorders*, vol. 1. New York: Ronald
 1948 Theory and experiment relating psychoanalytic displacement to stimulus response generalization. *Journal of Abnormal and Social Psychology* **43** (April): 155–79

Mills, Theodore M. 1964 *Group Transformation, An Analysis of a Learning Group*. Englewood Cliffs: Prentice-Hall

Minard, James G. and William Mooney 1969 Psychological differentiation and perceptual defense: studies of the separation of perception from emotion. *Journal of Abnormal Psychology* **74** (April): 131–9

Moser, U., Ilka von Zeppelin and W. Schneider 1969 Computer simulation of a model of neurotic defense processes. *International Journal of Psychoanalysis* **50**, part 1: 53–64

Mowrer, O. Hobart 1940 An experimental analogue of 'repression' with incidental observations on 'reactive-formation'. *Journal of Abnormal and Social Psychology* **35** (January): 56–87

Olds, James 1956 *The Growth and Structure of Motives, Psychological Studies in the Theory of Action*. Glencoe: Free Press

Ornston, Darius 1978 On projection, a study of Freud's usage. *The Psychoanalytic Study of the Child* **33**: 117–66

Oshman, Harvey P. and Martin Manosevitz 1976 Father absence: effects of stepfathers upon psychological development in males. *Developmental Psychology* **12** (September): 479–80

Palmer, Stephen E. 1978 Fundamental aspects of cognitive representation. Pp. 259–303 in Eleanor Rosch and Barbara B. Lloyd (eds.), *Cognition and Categorization.* Hillsdale: Erlbaum

Parke, Ross D. and Ronald G. Slaby 1983 The development of aggression. Pp. 548–641 in Paul H. Mussen (ed.), *Handbook of Child Psychology*, vol. 4. New York: Wiley

Parsons, Talcott 1951 *The Social System.* Glencoe: Free Press

  1954 The father symbol: an appraisal in the light of psychoanalytic and sociological theory. Pp. 34–56 in his *Social Structure and Personality.* New York: Free Press, 1964

  1955 Family structure and the socialization of the child. Pp. 35–131 in Talcott Parsons and Robert F. Bales (eds.), *Family, Socialization and Interaction Process.* Glencoe: Free Press

  1959a An approach to psychological theory in terms of the theory of action. Pp. 612–711 in Sigmund Koch (ed.), *Psychology: A Study of Science*, vol. 3. New York: McGraw-Hill

  1959b General theory in sociology. Pp. 3–38 in Robert K. Merton, Leonard Broom and Leonard S. Cottrell, Jr. (eds.), *Sociology Today: Problems and Prospects.* New York: Basic Books

Parsons, Talcott and Robert F. Bales 1953 The dimensions of action-space. Pp. 63–109 in Talcott Parsons, Robert F. Bales and Edward A. Shils, *Working Papers in the Theory of Action.* Glencoe: Free Press

Parsons, Talcott and James Olds 1955 The mechanisms of personality functioning with special reference to socialization. Pp. 187–257 in Talcott Parsons and Robert F. Bales (eds.), *Family, Socialization and Interaction Process.* Glencoe: Free Press

Peck, Robert F. and Robert J. Havighurst 1960 *The Psychology of Character Development.* New York: Wiley

Peterson, Christopher 1979 Uncontrollability and self-blame in depression: investigation of the paradox in a college population. *Journal of Abnormal Psychology* **88** (December): 620–4

Piaget, Jean 1932 *The Moral Judgment of the Child.* M. Gabain, translator. New York: Free Press, 1965

Pollak, Jerrold M. 1979 Obsessive-compulsive personality: a review. *Psychological Bulletin* **86** (March): 225–41

Prelinger, Ernst and Carl N. Zimet 1964 *An Ego-Psychological Approach to Character Assessment.* New York: Free Press

Rapaport, David 1951 The anatomy of the ego. *Bulletin of the Menninger Clinic* **15**: 113–23

  1959 Introduction: a historical survey of psychoanalytic ego psychology. *Psychological Issues* **1**, no. 1: 5–17

  1967 *The Collected Papers of David Rapaport*, Merton M. Gill (ed.), New York: Basic Books

Rodgers, David A. 1966 Estimation of MMPI profiles from CPI data. *Journal of Consulting Psychology* **30** (February): 89

  n.d. Estimation of MMPI profiles from CPI data. Unpublished report. Scripps

Clinic and Research Foundation, University of California, San Diego

Rosch, Eleanor 1978 Principles of categorization. Pp. 27–48 in Eleanor Rosch and Barbara B. Lloyd (eds.), *Cognition and Categorization*. Hillsdale: Erlbaum

Sackeim, Harold A. and Ruben C. Gur 1979 Self-deception, other-deception, and self-reported psychopathology. *Journal of Consulting and Clinical Psychology* **47** (February): 213–15

Sandler, Joseph 1962 Research in psycho-analysis: the Hampstead Index as an instrument of psycho-analytic research. *International Journal of Psycho-Analysis* **43**: 287–92

Sandler, Joseph and Anna Freud 1983 Discussions in the Hampstead Index of *The Ego and the Mechanisms of Defense. Journal of the American Psychoanalytic Association* **31** (Supplement): 19–146

Sartori, Giovanni 1968 Democracy. Pp. 112–21 in *International Encyclopaedia of the Social Sciences*, vol. 4. New York: Macmillan and Free Press

Schafer, Roy 1968 The mechanisms of defense. *International Journal of Psycho-Analysis* **49**, part 1: 49–61

1976 *A New Language for Psychoanalysis*. New Haven: Yale University Press

Schimek, J. G. 1968 Cognitive style and defenses: a longitudinal study of intellectualization and field independence. *Journal of Abnormal Psychology* **73** (December): 575–80

Scott, Marvin B. and Stanford M. Lyman 1968 Accounts. *American Sociological Review* **33** (February): 46–62

Sears, Robert R., Eleanor E. Maccoby and Harry Levin 1957 *Patterns of Child Rearing*. Evanston: Row, Peterson

Seligman, Martin E.P. 1975 *Helplessness: On Depression, Development, and Death*. San Francisco: Freeman

Selman, Robert L. 1980 *The Growth of Interpersonal Understanding, Developmental and Clinical Analyses*. New York: Academic Press

Selznick, Gertrude J. 1960 Functionalism, the Freudian theory, and philosophy of value. Doctoral dissertation, Department of Philosophy, University of California, Los Angeles

Semin, G. R. and A. S. R. Manstead 1983 *The Accountability of Conduct: A Social Psychological Analysis*. New York: Academic Press

Shapiro, David 1965 *Neurotic Styles*. New York: Basic Books

Sjöbäck, Hans 1973 *The Psychoanalytic Theory of Defensive Processes*. New York: Wiley

Slater, Philip 1966 *Microcosm: Structural, Psychological and Religious Evolution in Groups*. New York: Wiley

Smelser, Neil J. 1967 Mechanisms of defense and their contextual relations. Unpublished seminar paper. San Francisco: San Francisco Psychoanalytic Institute

1984 Depth psychology and the social order. Paper presented to a conference, "Relating Micro and Macro Levels in Sociological Theory", American and German Sociological Associations, Giesen, West Germany

Smith, Gudmund J. and Anna Danielsson 1982 *Anxiety and Defensive Strategies in*

Childhood and Adolescence. New York: International Universities Press
Sonquist, John A., Elizabeth L. Baker and James N. Morgan
1974 *Searching for Structure.* Ann Arbor. Survey Research Center, University of Michigan
Spiro, Melford 1982 *Oedipus in the Trobriands.* Chicago: University of Chicago Press
Suppes, Patrick and Hermine Warren 1975 On the generation and classification of defense mechanisms. *International Journal of Psychoanalysis* **56**, part 4: 405–14
Swanson, Guy E. 1959 The effectiveness of decision-making groups: a study of the effects of institutional arrangements on group efficiency. *Adult Leadership* **8** (June): 48–52
1961 Determinants of the individual's defenses against inner conflict: review and reformulation. Pp. 5–41 in John C. Glidewell (ed.), *Parental Attitudes and Child Behavior.* Springfield: Thomas
1965a On explanations of social interaction. *Sociometry* **28** (June): 101–23
1965b The routinization of love: structure and process in primary relations. Pp. 160–209 in Samuel Z. Klausner (ed.), *The Quest for Self-Control: Classical Philosophies and Scientific Research.* New York: Free Press
1967 *Religion and Regime, A Sociological Account of the Reformation.* Ann Arbor: University of Michigan Press
1970 Toward corporate action: a reconstruction of elementary collective processes. Pp. 124–44 in Tamotsu Shibutani (ed.), *Human Nature and Collective Behavior, Papers in Honor of Herbert Blumer.* Englewood Cliffs: Prentice-Hall
1971 An organizational analysis of collectivities. *American Sociological Review* **36** (August): 607–24
1973 The quest for a guardian spirit: a process of empowerment in simpler societies. *Ethnology* **12** (July): 359–78
1974 Family structure and the reflective intelligence of children. *Sociometry* **37**: 459–90
1980 A basis of authority and identity in post-industrial society. Pp. 190–217 in Burkhart Holzner and Roland Robertson (eds.), *Authority and Identity.* Oxford: Blackwell
1985 The powers and capabilities of selves: social and collective approaches. *Journal for the Theory of Social Behaviour* **15** (October): 331–54
1986a Phobias and related symptoms: some social sources. *Sociological Forum* **1** (Winter): 103–30
1986b Schizotypic and other profiles in college students: some social correlates. *Social Psychology Quarterly.* Forthcoming
1987 Tricksters in myths and families: studies on the meaning and sources of "pregenital" relations. In Leland Donald and Joseph G. Jorgensen (eds.), *Themes in Ethnology and Culture History.* Berkeley: The Folklore Institute. Forthcoming
Symonds, Percival M. 1946 *The Dynamics of Human Adjustment.* New York: Appleton-Century-Crofts
Toulmin, Stephen E. 1958 *The Uses of Argument.* Cambridge: Cambridge University Press

Tyron, Robert C. and Daniel E. Bailey 1970 *Cluster Analysis*. New York: McGraw Hill

Tuckman, Bruce W. 1965 Developmental sequence in small groups. *Psychological Bulletin* **63** (June): 384–99

Vaillant, George E. 1971 Theoretical hierarchy of adaptive ego mechanisms, a 30-year follow-up of 30 men selected for psychological health. *Archives of General Psychiatry* **24** (February): 107–18

    1977 *Adaptation of Life*. Boston: Little, Brown

Van Maanen, John 1976 Breaking in: socialization to work. Pp. 67–130 in Robert Dublin (ed.), *Handbook of Work, Organization and Society*. Chicago: Rand McNally

Wallerstein, Robert S. 1967 Development and the metapsychology of the defense organization of the ego. *Journal of the American Psychoanalytic Association* **15** (January): 130–49

    1983 Defenses, defense mechanisms, and the structure of the mind. *Journal of the American Psychoanalytic Association* **31** (Supplement): 201–26

Wanous, John P. 1977 Organizational entry: newcomers moving from outside to inside. *Psychological Bulletin* **84** (July): 601–18

Weinstock, Allan R. 1967a Family environment and the development of defense and coping mechanisms. *Journal of Personality and Social Psychology* **5** (January): 67–75

    1967b Longitudinal study of social class and defense preferences. *Journal of Consulting Psychology* **31** (October: 539–41

Whiteman, Martin 1967 Children's conceptions of psychological causality. *Child Development* **38** (March): 143–55

    1970 The development of conceptions of psychological causality. Pp. 339–60 in Jerome Hellmuth (ed.), *Cognitive Studies*, vol. 1, New York: Brunner/Mazel

Willick, Martin S. 1983 On the concept of primitive defenses. *Journal of the American Psychoanalytic Association* **31** (Supplement): 175–200

Witkin, Herman A. and Donald R. Goodenough 1976 *Field Dependence Revisited*. Research Bulletin. Education Testing Service. Princeton, NJ

Wolff, Peter H. 1960 The developmental psychologies of Jean Piaget and psychoanalysis. *Psychological Issues* **2**, no. 1

Yarrow, Marian R., Carolyn J. Waxler and Michael Chapman

    1983 Children's prosocial dispositions and behavior. Pp. 469–545 in Paul H. Mussen (ed.), *Handbook of Child Psychology*, vol. 4. New York: Wiley

Zajonc, Robert B. and Gregory B. Markus 1976 Birth order and intellectual development. *Psychological Review* **82** (January): 74–88

Zelditch, Morris 1955 Role differentiation in the nuclear family: a comparative study. Pp. 307–51 in Talcott Parsons and Robert F. Bales (eds.), *Family, Socialization and Interaction Process*. Glencoe: Free Press

Index

229

Other books in the series

J. Milton Yinger, Kiyoshi Ikeda, Frank Laycock, and Stephen J. Cutler: *Middle Start: An Experiment in the Educational Enrichment of Young Adolescents*

James A. Geschwender: *Class, Race, and Worker Insurgency: The League of Revolutionary Black Workers*

Paul Ritterband: *Education, Employment, and Migration: Israel in Comparative Perspective*

John Low-Beer: *Protest and Participation: The New Working Class in Italy*

Orrin E. Klapp: *Opening and Closing: Strategies of Information Adaptation in Society*

Rita James Simon: *Continuity and Change: A Study of Two Ethnic Communities in Israel*

Marshall B. Clinard: *Cities with Little Crime: The Case of Switzerland**

Steven T. Bossert: *Tasks and Social Relationships in Classrooms: A Study of Instructional Organization and Its Consequences**

Richard E. Johnson: *Juvenile Delinquency and Its Origins: An Integrated Theoretical Approach**

David R. Heise: *Understanding Events: Affect and the Construction of Social Action*

Ida Harper Simpson: *From Student to Nurse: A Longitudinal Study of Socialization*

Stephen P. Turner: *Sociological Explanation as Translation*

Janet W. Salaff: *Working Daughters of Hong Kong: Filial Piety or Power in the Family?*

Joseph Chamie: *Religion and Fertility: Arab Christian–Muslim Differentials*

William Friedland, Amy Barton, Robert Thomas: *Manufacturing Green Gold: Capital, Labor, and Technology in the Lettuce Industry*

Richard N. Adams: *Paradoxical Harvest: Energy and Explanation in British History, 1870–1914*

*Available from the American Sociological Association, 1722 N Street, N.W., Washington, DC 20036

231

Mary F. Rogers: *Sociology, Ethnomethodology, and Experience: A Phenomenological Critique*

James R. Beniger: *Trafficking in Drug Users: Professional Exchange Networks in the Control of Deviance*

Andrew J. Weigert, J. Smith Teitge, and Dennis W. Teitge: *Society and Identity: Toward a Sociological Psychology*

Jon Miller: *Pathways in the Workplace: The Effects of Race and Gender on Access to Organizational Resources*

Michael A. Faia: *Dynamic functionalism: Strategy and Tactics*

Joyce Rothschild and J. Allen Whitt: *The Co-operative Workplace: Potentials and Dilemmas of Organizational Democracy*

Russell Thornton: *We Shall Live Again: The 1870 and 1890 Ghost Dance Movements as Demographic Revitalization*

Severyn T. Bruyn: *The Field of Social Investment*